More Praise for *Everyday Revolutions*

'*Everyday Revolutions* provides a richly detailed, insightful, and inspiring account of the full array of social movements that emerged out of the Argentine economic meltdown of late 2001 – a key, though oft-neglected, antecedent to the Occupy movements and other waves of mobilization currently sweeping the globe.'

Sonia E. Alvarez, author of *Engendering Democracy in Brazil*

'Without arrogance, in a direct and simple way, Marina dares to challenge the prevailing categories and theories. She can do that well-rooted in the reality she observes and because she is involved in movements that are not only generating theory, but are themselves a theory, a new theory expressing a new reality. This is the book we need to begin to understand the new era of revolutionary change inaugurated by the Zapatistas in 1994 and now exploding everywhere.'

Gustavo Esteva, author of *The Commune of Oaxaca*

'*Everyday Revolutions* is a book that speaks about us: of those who seek to explain the world from the inside; of those who intend to challenge and change it; in our struggles to produce autonomous spaces and collective ability to recapture political space. Looking at the recent history of some of the most interesting recent social movements, *Everyday Revolutions* speaks of things that are happening here and now.'

Ana Méndez de Andés, architect and urbanist, part of the research project Observatorio Metropolitano de Madrid and Traficantes de Sueños

'Marina Sitrin delves deeply into the questions most books about movements avoid or simplify far too much, such as the question of production or the complex relation with the state. *Everyday Revolutions* could only have been written by a long-time activist and researcher such as Marina Sitrin, who knows about the challenges we face.'

Dario Azzellini, author of *Partizipation,* Arbeiter

'Essential reading for those trying to un movement for horizontal democracy.'
Michael Schwartz

'*Everyday Revolutions* truly conveys not only what an affective politics is, but what this affective politics can do. Moving with the movements it both describes and analyses, this is not just a book, it is a companion on the journey through the worlds worth fighting for in the streets, squares, factories, fields, chat rooms and classrooms of our everyday lives.'

Emma Dowling, Queen Mary, University of London

'A living history of a living revolution ... Reading *Everyday Revolutions* we read of the emergence, the collective self-making, of new people. Beautiful!'

David Harvie, author, with The Free Association,
of *Moments of Excess*

'Marina Sitrin has long been pioneering the kind of intellectual practice that is now becoming more and more crucial, with its cherished sensitivity toward the struggling/questioning/thinking in common from which all revolutionary thoughts arise. With both passionate and rigorous analyses of Argentinean processes, *Everyday Revolutions* embodies what theory can and should do today in the age of global insurgency.'

Sabu Kohso, writer and translator

'Sitrin's smart and incisive analysis of horizontalism and autonomy in Argentina as an alternative form of not-power is a critical, timely, and lively contribution to understanding both why and how. Crackling with acuity, bits of history, and keen insights of a participant observer and social scientist, Sitrin joins those making an activist social science indispensable for those of us both committed to close, careful scholarship and passionate about social justice.'

Eric Selbin, author of *Revolution, Rebellion, and Resistance*

'In *Everyday Revolutions* radical transformation of life is as affective as running a factory, as concrete as raising children, and as utopian as struggling for dignity. Marina Sitrin has managed to bring to life various strands of contemporary social theory to understand the power of horizontal relations among commoners in struggle.'

Massimo De Angelis, author of *The Beginning of History*

About the Author

Marina Sitrin holds a PhD in Global Sociology and a JD in International Women's Human Rights. Her work focuses on social movements and justice, specifically looking at new forms of social organization, such as *autogestión*, *horizontalidad*, prefigurative politics, and new affective social relationships. Her first book, *Horizontalism: Voices of Popular Power in Argentina* (AK Press 2006), is an oral history based on the then emergent autonomous movements in Argentina, published in Spanish (Chilavert 2005) and English. She has published in a range of journals and books, from the *International Journal of Contemporary Sociology* to *Znet*, *LeftTurn*, and *Yes! Magazine*. While much of her most recent published work has been on contemporary social movements in Argentina, she has worked throughout the Americas, the Caribbean, and Japan. Her current research includes global mass assembly movements, specifically in Greece, Spain, and Egypt.

EVERYDAY REVOLUTIONS

Horizontalism and Autonomy in Argentina

Marina A. Sitrin

Zed Books
London & New York

Everyday Revolutions: Horizontalism and Autonomy in Argentina was first published in 2012 by Zed Books Ltd, 7 Cynthia Street, London N1 9JF, UK and Room 400, 175 Fifth Avenue, New York, NY 10010, USA

www.zedbooks.co.uk

Typeset in Sabon by Swales & Willis Ltd, Exeter, Devon
Index: rohan.indexing@gmail.com
Cover photo: *Interbarrial* © Ignacio Smith
Cover design: www.alice-marwick.co.uk
Printed and bound in the United States of America

Distributed in the USA exclusively by Palgrave Macmillan, a division of St Martin's Press, LLC, 175 Fifth Avenue, New York, NY 10010, USA

A catalogue record for this book is available from the British Library
Library of Congress Cataloging in Publication Data available

ISBN 978 1 78032 050 2 hb
ISBN 978 1 78032 049 6 pb

Dedicated to those creating everyday revolutions – and especially the *compañer@s* of Argentina.

Contents

Acknowledgements

How to begin to acknowledge, thank, and give respect and love to everyone who was a part of this project? This section has taken me the longest to write, perhaps in part because I know in some ways that it is an impossible task to thank everyone.

Within this book are my attempts to reflect movements that encompass hundreds of thousands of people. How does one thank a movement? Then there are the many dozens of people who helped me think through the various ideas and meanings that I was encountering – and then there are those who helped me as I struggled with my role as a movement participant, someone who is not an Argentine, and someone writing but not through an academic lens. Then there is all the personal support I received from friends and loved ones, those who have accompanied me along this journey. So, where to begin?

This is not a traditional acknowledgement where I will list the people who supported me or helped me in editing – if that were the case I would be writing a never-ending list. This has been a many-year project of revolutionary transformation, one that I hope will be a tool that will help us, together, to reflect better on its meanings and lessons. This necessarily means thousands of people. No thought is original, and no movement is born from nothing. So, first and foremost, I acknowledge and give respect to all of those who have come before us, fighting and organizing to make possible where we are today. Of course, most importantly, I would like to thank the social movement actors in Argentina and around the world who are creating new worlds on a daily basis.

Now, I fear, I have resolved to make a few lists. What this list should be is multiple pages in which I reflect on the role of the dozens, the hundreds of people, collectives, assemblies, and workplaces that affected my thinking. Followed by a list of all my friends, *compañeras*, and family who have supported and aided me in my thinking. Since that is not possible, I want to apologize to any reader who may be reading it to find themselves and who perhaps does not – I do hope you feel the respect, love, and solidarity that I feel. If for some reason you feel you have not been mentioned, I am sure I am mistaken and I apologize.

In Argentina: Alberto, Candido, Carina B, Claudia A, Diego, El Vasco, Emilio, Leandro, Maba, Martín K, Neka, Paula H, Sergio, Soledad, and Toty.

My family as a whole, all of you, powerful grandmothers and little nieces and nephews, you all give me strength and love. In particular my parents, Sherman Sitrin and Carolina Cositore, who have supported me and made me the person I am, from your intellectual and political influence to a total love that grounds me daily. You both helped and supported this project in so many ways, from traveling, writing, and editing to helping me as I agonized over sections of the book. Thank you.

To those who are and have been like family to me: Claudia Acuña, Alex Fradkin, Sabu Kohso, Sibyl Perkins, Amanda Rouse, David Solnit, and Rebecca Solnit.

To those friends and *compañeras* who have provided political and intellectual guidance, many of you having read versions of the book or chapters in their many permutations over the past few years: Claudia Acuña, Dario Azzellini, Diego Benegas, Carolina Cositore, John Cox, Alex Fradkin, John Holloway, Sabu Kohso, Tim Moran, Naomi Rosenthal, Michael Schwartz, Samantha Sitrin, and Sherman Sitrin.

And a special thanks to the participants in the Committee on Globalization and Social Change at the CUNY Graduate Center, for feedback on sections of this book, and especially to Susan Buck-Morss, Kandice Chuh, and Gary Wilder.

I also want to thank the fabulous team at Zed Books, in particular Ken Barlow, who was immediately and continuously supportive, and Kika Sroka-Miller, an editor extraordinaire, who was both thorough and meticulous with ideas as well as always grounding that support and critique in affect – thank you.

Preface

In late 2001 the Argentine economy collapsed. People's bank accounts were frozen and the state offered nothing by way of a solution; the people went out into the streets, banging pots and pans, singing '*Que se vayan todos*' ('They all must go'), and with popular power forced out five consecutive governments. While the governments were being forced out, and as a product of being in the streets together, they began to look to one another and organize in horizontal assemblies – on street corners, in workplaces and unemployed neighborhoods. Hundreds of thousands became engaged in autonomous self-organized projects (*autogestión*), finding ways to support one another and solve their problems, both together and horizontally. Land and workplaces were recuperated, a barter network of millions of people developed, and the movements linked with one another. The state and forms of representation were the problem; *autogestión*, autonomy, and horizontalism were the tools for creating new subjectivities and dignity.

I never would have imagined, strong as my imagination is, that ten years after the popular rebellion in Argentina, millions of people around the world would be organizing in such similar ways. Much in the same way as in Argentina, people around the globe are rejecting representational politics while simultaneously experimenting with forms of direct democracy, autonomy, and direct action, from Cairo and Athens to Madrid, New York, London, Frankfurt, Lisbon, Reykjavik, and so many other thousands of cities, towns, and villages around the world. In these thousands of locations people are using public space to assemble and create new relationships, to create alternative forms of power – not by looking to the state or institutional powers as their point of reference, but instead by looking to one another. Often these people are using the language of *horizontalidad*: horizontalism or horizontality. This myriad of occurrences makes reflections on the lessons and challenges of the autonomous movements in Argentina all the more important and urgent. For example, what happened to the massive neighborhood assemblies, recuperated workplaces, and unemployed movements there? Do they still practice *horizontalidad*? What sorts of structures have evolved? What about the question of autonomy and the relationship to the state? Have people begun to create a path that is 'with, against, and beyond the state', as many claim they desire? The goal of this book is to help answer these questions, and simultaneously open up more questions, based on current global practices, with the desire to go further and get closer toward freedom.

The global emergency break

'Marx says that revolutions are the locomotive of world history. But perhaps it is quite otherwise. Perhaps revolutions are an attempt by the passengers on the train – namely, the human race – to activate the emergency break.' Walter Benjamin's words, written decades ago, resonate perfectly with what has been going on across the globe, from the 2001 popular rebellion in Argentina to the 2010–2012 and ongoing uprisings and movements.

The Zapatistas emerged in Chiapas, Mexico in 1994, declaring a resounding 'Ya Basta!' ('Enough!'); in Argentina in 2001 the popular rebellion sang 'Que Se Vayan Todos!'; in Spain and Moscow the slogan was 'You do not represent us!'; in Egypt they declared 'Kefaya!' ('Enough!'). In that moment, the scream of 'No!', these people pulled the emergency brake. In the USA we are the 99 per cent, in Spain *Democracia Real Ya!* (Real Democracy!), and in Argentina it was or is *horizontalidad* and *autogestión*. It is not about asking for power, it is about creating a different power. It is not about asking liberal democracy to be democratic, but rather about creating real democracy.

The how and why of this book

The reasons for writing *Everyday Revolutions* have become increasingly apparent and important to me. The how is a longer story. I moved to Argentina soon after the popular rebellion, hoping to help facilitate the many voices of participants in the movements with others around the world. The result was first a Spanish compilation, *Horizontalidad: Voces de Poder Popular en Argentina*, and then its English translation, *Horizontalism: Voices* of *Popular Power in Argentina*. In the years since completing the books in 2005 and 2006, I have continued to spend time in Argentina and relate with the many movements. As things changed, challenges grew, and new paths to surpass them were experimented with, I continued to do interviews, again imagining another oral history. However, after many conversations with *compañeros* about what might be most useful, I made the difficult decision to write more of a reflective and analytical book instead, relying on what people had said and what I had observed, but using my voice as the motor and refractor. This book is a result of that process. It is also a product of what was my dissertation, although from the beginning my relationship to Argentina has been one of militancy and that of another movement actor from another place, not as an academic doing fieldwork or research on an 'other'.

I have struggled a great deal in writing this book, and I can still honestly say that I am not totally comfortable with having written it. Not that I think the ideas are not important, or the lessons not central – I do, otherwise you would not be reading these words. My struggle is that of place and location, of being a movement participant based in the USA, or anywhere 'outside' a struggle to which one is not an active participant, which is a complicated position. I see this, acknowledge it, and struggle with it all the time. This position also means that I may have made many mistakes. If this has resulted in any misrepresentation of a person, action, or event, I apologize. Over the years in Argentina I became much closer to some movements and movement participants than others. This will be apparent in the reading of these pages. That I became closer to certain movements does not mean that those movements are responsible in any way for the conclusions I have reached: again, these words and conclusions are mine alone. I have been influenced and inspired by the many *compañeros* throughout Argentina, but I remain ultimately responsible for what is written here.

Photo 1 Workers in support of the recuperated Hotel Bauen

Introduction

On the night of the 19th, while the news was on television
and the middle class was at home watching, seeing people
from the most humble sectors crying, women crying in front
of supermarkets, begging for or taking food, and the State
of Siege was declared, then and there began the sound of the
cacerola (the banging of pots and pans.) In one window, and
then another window, in one house and then another house,
and soon, there was the noise of the *cacerola* ... The first person
began to bang a pot and saw her neighbor across the street
banging a pot, and the one downstairs too, and soon there were
four, five, fifteen, twenty, and people moved to their doorways
and saw other people banging pots in their doorways and saw
on television that this was happening in another neighborhood,
and another neighborhood ... and hundreds of people gathered
banging pots until at a certain moment the people banging pots
began to walk.

(Sitrin 2006: 22)

Argentina: a crack in history – 19 and 20 December 2001

Hundreds of thousands joined the *cacerolazo* on 19 and 20
December 2001 in Argentina, and continued in the streets for
the days and weeks that followed. Within two weeks five governments had resigned: the Minister of the Economy being the first
to flee on 19 December, with the president rapidly following on
the 20th.[1] The institutions of power did not know what to do. On
the evening of 19 December a state of siege was declared, revert-
ing back to well-established patterns of state power and violence.
The people were breaking with the past, with what had always
been done: they no longer stayed at home in fear, they came
onto the streets with even more bodies and sounds – and then
the sound of the *cacerolazo* found a voice, a song. It was a shout

Photo 2 Neighborhood assembly

of rejection and a song of affirmation. Que Se Vayan Todos! ('They All Must Go!') was sung, and sung together with one's neighbor. It was not just a shout against what was, but it was a song of affirmation sung together by the thousands and hundreds of thousands. 'Ohhh Que Se Vayan Todos, que no quede ni uno solo' ('They all must go, and not even one should remain'). People sang, banged pots, and greeted one another, kissing the cheeks of neighbors whose names had been discovered only recently. People were seeing one another for the first time. It was a rupture with the past. It was a rupture with obedience. It was a rupture with not being together. It was the beginning of finding one another, oneself, and of meeting again. The 19th and 20th was a crack in history upon which vast political landscapes unfolded. Revolutions were created – revolutions of everyday life.

Throughout history, in numerous places and various eras, there are moments like 19 and 20 December 2001 in Argentina, when the ways in which we see things drastically change: something occurs that allows our imagination to open up to alternative ways of seeing and being, opening cracks in history (Zapatistas). These openings can come from any number of places, from natural disasters to rebellions, strikes, and uprisings. This book addresses what happens in the wake of this rupture, and how the often-inspiring moments that emerge in that space can become lasting, transforming rupture into revolution. When formal institutions of power are laid bare, as often takes place in the moments of a crisis, people frequently come together, look to one another, and create new supportive relationships (Solnit 2005, 2009). These can be some of the most beautiful moments, and moments of the greatest solidarity, that we ever experience. However, what happens repeatedly is that after a period of time, these new relationships are co-opted by institutional power and our previous ways of relating return. How can we prevent this? Under what circumstances is this less likely to occur? How can we bring about moments where history breaks open, where our imaginations are freed and we are able to envision and create new landscapes towards new horizons?

Around the world communities and movements are successfully creating everyday revolutions in social relationships. The autonomous social movements in Argentina are one of these many movements. This book examines what has been taking place in Argentina over the past ten years so as to help us glimpse what alternatives are possible. In particular it looks at the question of rupture as an opening for new social relationships, and asks how we can not only open up a space for new ways of being in a crisis, but continue to develop these relationships. This book shows what has worked in the Argentine experience, what has continued to transform people and communities, and what some of the obstacles have been to an even deeper, longer lasting, and more transformative revolution. The overarching question of what success means is at the heart of what is addressed within these pages.

This book will examine concrete experiences, and I will argue that what allows rupture to continue as revolution of the everyday is a combination of the following:

- *horizontalidad* – a form of direct decision making that rejects hierarchy and works as an ongoing process;
- *autogestión* – a form of self-management with an implied form of *horizontalidad*;
- concrete projects related to sustenance and survival;
- territory – the use and occupation of physical and metaphorical space;

- changing social relationships – including changing identity with regard to the personal and collective;
- *politica afectiva* – a politics and social relationship based on love and trust;
- self-reflection – individual and collective, as to the radical changes taking place and how they break from past ways of organizing; and
- autonomy, challenging 'power over' and creating 'power with' – sometimes using the state, but at the same time, against and beyond the state.

Taken together, these new social relationships, grounded in concrete experiences and social creation, form a new way of being, a new way of relating and surviving, and do so in a way that is successful – as defined by those in the movement, measuring this success by dignity and the creation of new subjectivities.

Many autonomous movements and communities around the globe are prefiguring the world that they wish to create, that is, creating the world that they desire in their day-to-day relationships. Many use the language of prefigurative politics to describe this relationship.[2] Prefigurative politics, as it sounds, is behaving day-to-day as much as possible in the way that you envision new social and economic relationships: the way you would want to be. Worldwide these are not small 'experiments', but are communities that include hundreds of thousands, if not millions of people – people and communities who are opening up cracks in history and creating something new and beautiful in the opening.

These new social relationships have existed, sometimes for many years: enough time to have children born of the new experience who speak as new people. The specific example I use is Argentina, in part because of the diversity of backgrounds of the movement and its participants, from class and social diversity, to political and experiential.

From cracks to creation: the emergence of horizontal formations

In the days of the popular rebellion people who had been out in the streets *cacerolando* (banging pots) describe finding themselves, finding each other, looking around at one another, introducing themselves, wondering what was next and beginning to ask questions together. They also spoke of this new place where they were meeting, one without the forms of institutional powers that previously existed. Five governments had resigned and the legitimacy of the state was a question. The *Que Se Vayan Todos* occurred, many of those in power left, and now the question was what to do in this opening. There is no documentation or exact memory recorded by those participating in the neighborhood assemblies as to how they began; but what is remembered is looking to one another, finally seeing each another, gathering in the open, and forming neighborhood assemblies. The feeling of *no te metas* ('don't get involved') was melting away, and a new meeting was emerging (this will be addressed in detail in Chapter 2).

The social movements that arose in Argentina are socially, economically, and geographically diverse. They comprise working-class people taking over factories and running them collectively; middle-class urban dwellers, many recently declassed, working to meet their needs while in solidarity with those around them; the unemployed, like so many unemployed around the globe, facing the prospect of never encountering regular work, finding ways to survive and become self-sufficient, using mutual-aid and love; and autonomous indigenous communities struggling to liberate stolen land. All of these active movements have been relating to one another, and constructing new types of networks that reject the hierarchical template bequeathed to them by established politics. Part of this rejection includes a break with the concept of 'power over': people are attempting to organize on a flatter plane, with the goal of creating 'power with' one another (Colectivo Situaciones 2001; Holloway 2002). Embedded in these efforts is a commitment to value both the individual and the collective. Simultaneously, separately and together these groups are organizing in the direction of a more meaningful and deeper freedom, using the tools of direct democracy, *horizontalidad*, and direct action. Together, what is created is a revolution of the everyday. Even with the changes, challenges, and decrease in numbers in many movements, this revolution continues, quietly perhaps, slowly perhaps, but it is walking.

The movements in Argentina, and the new relationships and articulations of the process of creation there, have become a point of reference for many others around the world: from a network of Greek assemblies collectively translating the oral history of the Argentine movements and organizing dozens of conversations about the experience in 2011, to the US Occupy movements using horizontal language, whether it be horizontalism or another derivation, to describe what they are creating; and in the movements that emerged in Egypt, Greece, Spain, and other parts of Europe and from 2010 onwards, speaking of the forms of democracy that they are constructing as horizontal.

Revolution with a small 'r'

In discussing revolution, I am using a concept that has been expressed by many in the movements and further articulated by the sociologist and militant scholar John Holloway (2002; Holloway and Pelaez 1998). His writings on the concept of power and revolution reflect what has been taking place in the autonomous movements in Argentina, both in action and expression:

> The whole conception of revolution becomes turned outwards: revolution becomes a question rather than an answer. 'Preguntando caminamos: asking we walk' becomes a central principle of the revolutionary movement, the radically democratic concept at the centre of the Zapatista call for 'freedom, democracy and justice'. The revolution advances by asking, not by telling; or perhaps even, revolution is asking instead of telling, the dissolution of power relations ... A revolution that listens, a revolution that takes as its starting point the dignity of those in revolt, is inevitably an undefined revolution ... The open-ended nature of the Zapatista movement is summed up in the idea that it is a revolution, not a Revolution ('with small letters, to avoid polemics with the many vanguards and safeguards of THE REVOLUTION') ... Revolution refers to present existence, not to future instrumentality.
> (Holloway and Pelaez 1998: 167)

Here, Holloway is talking about the specific example of the Zapatistas in Mexico, but this conception of revolution is one that works for so many around the world in contemporary autonomous social movements. These movements define themselves as autonomous precisely because they do not want to take over the state, and see themselves in a position different and separate from the state, therefore autonomous. They do not desire state power, as many left-wing groups and political parties have in the past, but rather want to try to create other forms of horizontal power with one another, in their communities and workplaces. This concept of power and revolution is about a total transformation of society, but one that takes place and continues to expand from below. As the Zapatistas in Mexico say: 'From below and to the left.' In Argentina the movements prefiguring the change that they desire are revolutionary in this same sense. They are creating horizontal relationships, transforming their ways of being and organizing, with a focus on that relationship deepening and expanding. This conceptualization of revolution as an everyday transformation, not a storming of the Bastille, is an important distinction put forth at the outset of the book.

Martín, from the Buenos Aires neighborhood assembly of Colegiales, explains how the vision of social change and revolution is a break from these past conceptions and forms:

> A lot of things have happened that show that suddenly this other world is possible … of course the difference is that it is not a revolution in the sense that there could have been a revolution in the 1970s, where what they saw was the future. This is a revolution that is seen in flashes, and one where worlds come together. Something along the lines of: 'It isn't necessary to wait for the revolution, we can begin now.'
>
> (Conversation in Colegiales, Buenos Aires, 2003)

One of the central arguments implicit throughout the book, and within the movements in Argentina, is a rethinking of the meaning of revolution.

New social relationships

As of 2011, people and movements have continued to take over buildings, land, and factories. Part of what is so unique about the movements in Argentina is the ways in which people are doing this, how they are organizing as they transform their day-to-day realities, not just that they are doing it. Not only are communities finding creative ways to sustain themselves, they are recreating themselves in the process, creating more loving and trusting spaces, and different, more confident people. The language of subjectivity and protagonism is used repeatedly to explain what is happening to people and within people. They feel like agents in their lives: not just because they are running their workplace now, but because they are doing it together, with one another, basing their actions in love and trust. As a *compañera*[3] in the unemployed workers' movements so eloquently described:

> Everything depends on how far one wishes to go in creating a new society. If you begin with loving yourself first and if you can love those in your immediate surroundings, you have the greatest potential for transformation. A life previously devoted to a single leader now assumes a radical stance that is much more profound, it assumes a devotion that is much more profound. We have seen this in our day-to-day lives and in our day-to-day relationships. As we come together to work, or as we come together to carry out a joint project, we generate affective ties that strengthen common support for a project, the things that are fought for by the other person are the same things that I feel I must fight for. And so, it's as if things take on a different meaning, it's a completely different horizon, and that is something very new, very of the now.
>
> (quoted in Sitrin 2006: 234)

Horizontalidad

Horizontalidad is a word that encapsulates most directly the ideas upon which the new social relationships in the movements in Argentina are grounded. It is a word that previously did not have political meaning, and emerged from a new practice and way of interacting which has become a hallmark of autonomous movements. People speak of the newness of the relationship as it relates to the movements, and as a break with previous ways of relating and being.

Horizontalidad is a social relationship that implies, as its name suggests, a flat plane upon which to communicate, but it is not only this. *Horizontalidad* implies the use of direct democracy and striving for consensus: processes in which attempts are made so that everyone is heard and new relationships are created. *Horizontalidad* is a new way of relating based in affective politics and against all the implications of 'isms'. It is a dynamic social relationship. It is not an ideology or set of principles that must be met so as to create a new society or new idea. It is a break with these sorts of vertical ways of organizing and relating, and a break that is an opening.

One of the most significant things about the social movements that emerged in Argentina after 19 and 20 December 2001 is how generalized the experience of *horizontalidad* was and is (Zibechi 2003; Lavaca 2005). This new social relationship is used by those in the middle class in assemblies, with the unemployed in neighborhoods, workers taking back their workplaces, and all sorts of art and media collectives that emerged in the wake of the crisis. *Horizontalidad*, and a rejection of hierarchy and political parties, was the general experience.

Horizontalidad is a living word reflecting an ever-changing experience. Months after the popular rebellion, many participants in the movement began to speak of their relationships as horizontal as a way of describing the new forms of decision making. Years after the rebellion, those continuing to build new movements speak of *horizontalidad* as a goal as well as a tool: a means and an end. Our relationships remain deeply affected by capitalism and hierarchy, and thus by the sort of power dynamics that these promote in all of our collective and creative spaces, especially how we relate to one another in terms of economic resources, gender, 'race', access to information, and experience. As a result, until these fundamental social dynamics are overcome, the goal of *horizontalidad* cannot be achieved. Time has taught that in the face of this, simply desiring a relationship does not make it so, but the process of *horizontalidad* is a tool for achieving this goal. (*Horizontalidad* and new forms of democracy, as well as the challenges, are explored in Chapter 3).

Power and autonomy

I use the term 'autonomous' to describe the social movements in Argentina because this is the way that these movements self-identify. Autonomy is a way of distinguishing oneself and the movement from the state and other hierarchical groups and institutions. Autonomy is used also to reflect a politics of self-organization, *autogestión*, direct participation and a rejection of power as a thing, something that is used over someone else. In its essence, the concept of autonomy as used by the people in the movements is a 'do it yourself' approach to politics and social organization. This includes an increasingly complex relationship to the state (recently explained by someone in one of the unemployed workers' movements of the south as a 'Take what you can and run' sort of relationship; Patricia, Erwin and El Vasco, MTD Cipolletti, Patagonia). Movements want to maintain their own agenda and, at the same time, see what the state has as rightfully theirs; so the dilemma arises, as addressed throughout this book, as to how to be autonomous and yet still relate to the state while transforming society and eventually eliminating (and replacing) the institutional power that exists with something altogether different.

Autogestión

Autogestión is a word that has no exact English translation. Many have used the term 'self-management', which it is in part, but it also implies the concepts of *horizontalidad* and autonomy. Projects in autonomous spaces, for example, are '*autogestiónados*': they are self-created and self-managed. In the unemployed movement, bakeries, organic farms, popular schools, and clinics are all *autogestiónados*. They are run collectively, directly democratically and horizontally, often using decision-making processes based on consensus.

Furthermore, *autogestión* is a practice based not only in 'the what', but in 'the how'. It is the relationships among people who are creating a particular project, not simply the project itself. For example, a neighborhood assembly that decides to organize a neighborhood medical clinic or communal kitchen and how to do it, coordinating things such as schedules, location, gathering materials, etc. – these spaces are *autogestiónados*. This is a different situation from a community kitchen that is organized by the government. In the government organized kitchens neighbors sometimes volunteer to cook or pass out food, but they do not participate in any decision making. So, the difference lies not in the act of food being distributed by the community, but in who organizes it and how the community directly participates in the entire process.

The longest and most detailed chapter in this book, Chapter 6, is on *autogestión*, territory and alternative value. Within this chapter I delve into what is being produced, how, and how the relationships to production (as well as the question of work and production itself) are being conceived of in a new way, grounded in the new social relationships created in and by the movements.

New subjectivity and protagonism

A friend from Chilavert, an occupied printing press, once corrected me in a conversation by explaining that he is not 'political', but rather 'an actor and protagonist' in his life. Chilavert, like hundreds of other recuperated workplaces, uses *horizontalidad* as a tool and goal for making decisions collectively. Decisions that range from whether or not all workers, should be paid the same despite different hours and tasks, to questions about what to produce and how much. Many in the autonomous movements do not call themselves activists, but rather 'protagonists and subjects'. Politics is interpreted as something political that parties engage in, or that the state imposes on them. When people say that they are not political but are actors in their lives, they are describing a new sort of politics that is against the hierarchy of the state, political parties, and decisions being made for them.

The new subject is the new person formed as a part of these new relationships; a subject grounded in *politica afectiva* – a politics of affection, love and trust. Along with this new individual protagonism, a new collective protagonism arises with a need for new ways of speaking of *nosotros* ('we/us') and *nuestro* ('our') as these relate to *yo* ('I/me'). This aspiration is a genuinely new conception of the individual self through new conceptions of the collective. These new relationships, compelled by the notion of dignity, are the measure of success for these revolutions. (Chapter 4 explores the question of new subjectivity and *politica afectiva*, and Chapter 8 considers the measures and meanings of success.)

Collective reflection

A few months after the rebellion, participants from numerous autonomous movements, assemblies, unemployed workers' movements (Movimiento de Trabajadores Desocupados, MTDs), recuperated workplaces and various art, media and culture collectives began to gather on Saturdays to reflect on what they were creating, what they were breaking from, and the obstacles that they faced. In all of my years of militancy I have never experienced such high-level theoretical discussions, all based in the day-to-day experiences of the social movements. For example, one Saturday the entire day was dedicated to a discussion of the meaning of autonomy, based in each group's experience. Since there were close to 100 people there, we broke into small groups, with people from the media collective of Argentina Arde, for example, discussing with unemployed workers from Solano, Guernica and Allen, and *asembleístas* from Plaza Rodriguez, Cid Campeador, Colegiales, Pompeya, and workers from Ceramica Zanon and Chilavert. This collective reflection, as well as the weekly reflection that took place in each movement, has been fundamental to the continuation of the autonomous movements, regardless of the new forms that they are taking.

The state

Early on in this book I discuss the various forms of solidarity and mutual aid that emerge arising in the spaces created in these situations by the liberating of the collective imagination. Often in these spaces forms of institutional power are removed from the foreground of everyday interaction. People relate to one another without mediation from the state or other forms of hierarchical power. In the later sections of this book I discuss what happens when the state becomes cognizant of a society moving ahead without it. It is in these moments that those creating these vast new landscapes face some of the most serious challenges. It is most often, in this time of reaction to and from institutional power, that autonomous communities are defeated. Inherent in the role of the state is its resistance to people organizing outside of it, much in the same way as corporations resist parallel economies; it is here that often these institutions apply direct repression and cooptation, or a combination of the two.

In this sense there are many instances where the state has been successful: the movements it intended to demobilize stopped organizing in an autonomous way – or worse still, ceased existing altogether. The methods used by the state have ranged from co-opting movements through direct payment and invitations to participate in state agencies, as well as more direct means such as physical eviction of occupation of land and buildings, through to repression, sometimes even resulting in the murder of activists. However, throughout Argentina, there was successful resistance to this: 'successful' meaning that the movements or groups involved did not get sidetracked in their agendas by the state's attempts at demobilization. Many groups shrunk numerically, but as of 2009, many began to regroup and become more public in their activities, taking over land again and creating new micro-enterprises and parallel economies. Many of those I interviewed in 2009 believe that they are even stronger for the experience, explaining that they now have a much deeper understanding of the meaning of autonomy. (These questions and challenges are addressed in greater detail in Chapter 8.)

Challenging the contentious framework

Contentious politics is a framework generally used by US sociologists studying social movements to understand movement dynamics and goals. A contentious relationship to the state and authoritative powers is always an explicit or implicit part of the theory. A crucial aspect of this argument is that all social movements are in a contentious relationship to the state, or another form or institution with formal 'power over', whether demanding reforms from or desiring another state or institution.

While useful in many spheres, I will argue that the politics of contention is not sufficient in explaining these contemporary, autonomous social movements, because of these movements' choice not to focus on dominant institutional powers (such as the state), but rather to develop alternative relationships and forms of power. This reconceptualization of power is linked to the nonhierarchical and directly democratic vision of their organizing.

Walking – and slowly

The Zapatistas say, 'Walking we ask questions'; they also say, 'We walk slowly since we are going far'. The walk towards autonomous creation continues in Argentina despite the massive challenges posed by the state and political parties. This creation in the years since 2004, when the state began a full legitimization campaign, has been uneven and moving more slowly. Lessons are being learned in many movements, while in some the state's attempts at demobilization have been much more successful and lessons have yet to be internalized.

Sometimes, the challenges that have arisen were foreseen by movement participants, and in these situations the groups were more prepared for them. In some cases it was predicted that some of the structures of organization might disappear or be challenged, but it was believed that this could be withstood: the argument being that the movements would continue as long as people's subjectivities had changed. Today, more than ten years into the popular rebellion, this appears to be true. Participants speak of the success of the movements, and of a success that is not measurable by traditional social science, but rather one that is measured by the formation and continuation of new social relationships, new subjectivities, and a new-found dignity.

ONE

A brief history of movements and repression in Argentina

Historical events are not points, but extend to before and after in time, only gradually revealing themselves.
(Jameson 2008: 1, cited in Zibechi 2008b)

Appeals to the past are among the commonest of strategies in interpretations of the present. What animates such appeals is not only disagreement about what happened in the past and what the past was, but uncertainty about whether the past really is past, over and concluded, or whether it continues, albeit in different forms, perhaps.
(Said 1994: 3)

From what are new movements born? Are they ever entirely new? What role does the past play? Must it be a conscious past? What is the role of myth and stories in the historical and collective imagination? Must the stories be real? How, or indeed, are we motivated by historical events? Do the events of previous generations, events perhaps that we never learned about, live in our collective memories? Can history be carried forward in a collective unconscious? Can history and memory perhaps be, as Walter Benjamin so eloquently put it, a 'secret rendezvous between past generations and our own' (1973: 179)?

An action

It is growing dark. A group of young people begin to gather in front of a hospital. It is an old hospital, which now serves the general population and was formerly a military hospital. It is a hospital with a memory. It is a hospital that was not used to heal. This hospital was used by the military for torture during the brutal dictatorship that lasted from 1976 until 1983.

More young people arrive. There is a small stage erected. People grow quiet. Clearly something has been planned. Many

Photo 3 One of the weekly marches of the Madres de la Plaza de Mayo
(the banner reads 'No to the payment of the external debt')

people have masks and wear costumes. The mood is somber.
No, it is not so much somber as chilling and quiet ... we are
waiting ... the feeling is that you do not really want to be there,
but you don't want to leave either. It is a strange and powerful
sensation. Like the pull of watching a suspenseful film, your
heart begins to beat faster as you know something bad will take
place, but yet you cannot turn away.

A performance begins. A woman is alone. She is in a cell.
Three men in military uniforms enter the cell. She begins to
whimper ... the crowd begins to shift a little uncomfortably ... I
shiver, dreading what they are going to act out. As the men get
closer to her, her whimpers begin to get louder – it becomes a
scream as the two men hold her down and the third rapes her.
She screams again, they change places, and again ... and then
there is silence.

The stage goes dark.

The stage begins to lighten, brighter and brighter until
there is a harshly lit bed, surrounded by white lights. We are
no longer in a prison cell but a small hospital room. The same

woman is there. She is pregnant. She is chained to the bed. Her legs are in stirrups. She cries out again, this time in labor. Two men and a woman enter the room: they deliver the baby. A military man smiles widely to the crowd and takes the infant. He holds it up in the air for all to see, like a proud father. The woman screams – she is injected – her screams fade …

The infant is gone.

A speaker with a mask tells us that this was done at the military hospital that we have all assembled in front of – we are told that some of the doctors from the time of the dictatorship still work there. Ones like we just saw deliver the baby before the woman, the mother, was murdered.

The crowd erupts – things are thrown at the hospital walls that explode on impact, creating huge red splatters. It looks like blood is dripping down the walls. It moves down the wall, and the chill remains in the air.

This is an *escrache*.

In 2006, in an action against the dictatorship, Victoria, a daughter and one of hundreds stolen by the military as described in the above theater production, spoke:

'A sector of society continues to respect beasts like Jorge Rafael Videla, who led this massacre. And that is why we are going to do the *escrache* at Videla's house – because we don't forget and we don't forgive.' Victoria Donde Perez is the daughter of a 'disappeared' woman. Thanks to the work of HIJOS and the Abuelas they have recuperated the identity of 82 sons and daughters.

Victoria continued, 'We want to tell our dear disappeared *compañeros* and parents not to worry because we are here and we will find your children. Today we are 82 but soon we will find all of them. Along with your children we are recovering the dreams of the disappeared, their dreams of life, their dreams of freedom, because that's who our parents were, they were builders of courageous dreams.'

(Trigona 2006b)

HIJOS: an introduction to the movements

Where to begin with the history and context of the contemporary revolutionary movements in Argentina? Is it based in the anarcho-syndicalism of the 1930s? Is it grounded in the guerilla movements of the 1960s, in part a reaction to hierarchy but inspired by militancy? Is it a part of the complicated history of Peronism, both a rejection of gift politics and hierarchy, but also inspired by the mass popularity that affected day-to-day life? Is it not related to any of this, or is it related to all of it? What is the role of history and previous generations' experiences on contemporary actions? What about the movements that took place only a decade or two ago: do they still somehow inspire contemporary action? The latter question is one that is argued by many in Argentina, particularly those who were a part of these movements. I am referring here to the MTDs that emerged in the 1990s as well as HIJOS (Hijas y HIJOS por Identidad y Justicia y contra el Olvido y Silencio; Daughters and Sons for Identity and Justice and Against Silence and Forgetting) and the Mesa de Escrache (the 'table' of organizing the *escrache*). The latter two, discussed in this chapter, organized in ways that are quite similar to current ideas of *horizontalidad*.

History can deeply affect the ways in which people relate and organize, but this does not necessarily mean that history is repeated or imitated. Often historical experiences are rejected, as can be witnessed in frequent, drastic governmental shifts from Left to Right. Indeed, this has been seen in contemporary Argentina, where conscious rejections of previous ways of organizing within the Left have occurred. However, rejecting the type of hierarchical organizing that took place in previous decades does not necessarily equate with embracing the anarcho-syndicalism of the early 1900s. My argument here is that history is important, but one should be careful not to overemphasize or, worse, prescribe activities and organizations based on the past.

While the late 1800s and early 1900s have many similarities to the social movements in Argentina today, and will be addressed, the main focus of this chapter will be the more recent past. It is this recent past that most adults in Argentina either lived through themselves, or through which their parents lived. It is to these pasts and stories of the past that most movement participants refer and use as a point of conscious reference. There is no longer an active conscious memory of the movements of the early 1900s, but these stories still loom large in the current imagination. Interestingly, there is little direct research and information on exactly what took place during these early years of revolutionary foment, thus making it that much more mythical, and perhaps allowing it to loom that much larger in the collective imagination.

The beginning: the 1990s

Beginning with the most recent past, and the one which has had the most direct influence on autonomous movements today in their affirmative action (rather than rejection) are HIJOS, Mesa de Escrache and the Grupo de Arte Callejero (GAC, Street Artists Group). All three of these groups comprise to varying extents the children of those who disappeared during the dictatorship; their contemporaries as well as the relatives of the children of the disappeared. With 30,000 disappeared, the number of children, grandchildren, nieces, nephews, cousins, etc., the number of family members who could be a part of HIJOS could easily reach many hundreds of thousands – all touched directly by the dictatorship.

HIJOS is significantly different from the Madres de la Plaza de Mayo (Mothers of the Disappeared), who continue to demand that the government return their children and that those responsible are punished; or even the Abuelas, the grandmothers, who continue to look for those children stolen and 'adopted' from the prisons and torture chambers during the dictatorship. HIJOS is not placing demands upon the government, but rather speaks to society as a whole. Its members address society as a way of consciously breaking with the silence around what took place, what it calls a 'social silence' (Benegas forthcoming).

Most of the HIJOS generation were in their twenties during the 1990s. They were born of a rupture – not the sort of rupture that I discuss, from which new movements are created, but rupture in a much more literal sense. Most of the HIJOS grew up without a parent, aunt, cousin, or other close relative, that person having been literally taken from their home and family, tortured, and perhaps dropped into the river to die. Murdered – and murdered because of their ideas of social change, or their identification with those who wanted and sought change. These children grew up with other relatives caring for them, sometimes in Argentina, Brazil (as with Paula, who is quoted at length in this book), and Cuba (as with Diego from Colectivo Situaciones, a militant research and writing group in Buenos Aires, also interviewed for this book). HIJOS is a group of young people who grew up with an ever-present rupture: the mother who never came home, or the father who was tortured so badly that despite surviving, seemed only the shell of a human being. Perhaps worst of all, these children grew up in a society that did not blame or punish the people who tortured and killed their parents. They grew up in an atmosphere of silence and forgetting.

The Madres de la Plaza de Mayo, who have won respect from people all over the world for their struggle to win back their children, are demanding justice – and demanding punishment. Now their children, the children of the disappeared – HIJOS – are demanding justice. HIJOS is a central social movement actor in Argentina. HIJOS formed as an organization in 1995, but began meeting much earlier. It began in the time of 'democracy', in 1983, when people were taken much less frequently from their homes, never to be seen again. Repression and kidnapping did not stop but were reduced greatly. It was less a time of terror and more a time of repression. What it was not was a time of remembering or punishing those responsible for the dictatorship – quite the opposite.

Most members of the military were left untouched by the transition to 'democracy'. This protection was legislated with Law No. 23492 – the Ley de Punto Final of 1986 (the 'Full Stop' Law), which was passed at the end of the dictatorship. This law prohibited not only the prosecution but also the investigation of people accused of political violence during the dictatorship. New 'democratic' rule took place on 10 December 1983, and the Ley de Punto Final was passed three years later on 24 December 1986. As a complement to the law, Law No. 23521, the Ley de Obedencia Debida of 1987 (Law of Due Obedience) was passed, which included the exemption of subordinates from prosecution if they were carrying out orders. These laws were not repealed until 2003, and not removed from the Argentine Statute Book until the end of 2005.

One of the most emblematic of these pardons, although they are numerous, was Alfredo Ignacio Astiz, known as the 'blond angel of death'. Astiz was the director of ESMA, one of the most famous torture and death centers during the dictatorship. Many Argentines refer to these places as concentration camps. It is believed that more than 5,000 people were tortured and murdered there under his command (Trigona 2010). It is unclear for which act he is most famous. He is responsible for infiltrating the Madres de la Plaza de Mayo, kidnapping one of the founders, Azucena Villafor, on International Human Rights Day – the day that the Mothers published a list of the disappeared in the newspaper. Villaflor was never seen again, not after entering ESMA. Astiz' actions resulted directly in the murder of two French nuns, a seventeen-year-old Swiss-Argentine citizen, and the journalist Rodolfo Walsh. Astiz was not only excused from standing trial, based on the Ley de Punto Final of 1986, but was promoted in the navy twice after the transition to 'democracy', holding an important military position as Argentina's naval attaché in South Africa.[1] In 1988 he was made a full captain and decorated for valor in the 'fight against subversion'. This was five full years into 'democracy'.

There was no public outcry at the Ley de Punto Final, neither at the fact that military officials and torturers from the dictatorship were living, seemingly happily enough, among everyone else in society. People were afraid. People were silent. HIJOS organized to speak specifically to this silence. Many in HIJOS have, and had, little confidence in the government, whether 'democratic' or otherwise. When HIJOS formed in 1995 there were hundreds to thousands of known *genocidas* (those who committed genocide) living in society,[2] unpunished, free – and not only unpunished by the state, but living in peace in society as a whole. The term *genocidas* was chosen by HIJOS, as well as other human rights groups, to describe those who participated in the torture and killing under the dictatorship, and it since has become quite commonplace among those who opposed the dictatorship. HIJOS' goal is not to speak to the *genocidas*, but their neighbors and society in general: those who were letting people who committed such atrocities live in peace and silence (Benegas forthcoming). The form that their protest took was more of a public outing than a protest, and part of a serious and long campaign which became known as the *escrache*. An *escrache* is this process of outing – a tactic for social awareness using direct action, theater and education against silence and forgetting.

Another important aspect of speaking to neighbors and community goes back to the time of the dictatorship itself, as according to reports in the Comisión Nacional sobre la

Desaparición de Personas (National Commission on the Disappearance of Persons), the majority of the kidnappings occurred in the person's home and in front of witnesses, usually neighbors.

Un escrache: an action

As mentioned previously, an *escrache*, or *escrachar* in slang, means 'to put into evidence, disclose to the public, or reveal what is hidden' (Colectivo Situaciones et al. 2009). *Escraches* begin with research. The person who is 'outed' has been researched in great depth. There are often people who can testify directly that they tortured them, or that they witnessed this person carrying out torture. There are oral or actual records of the person's participation in or with the military. Once the person's actions have been confirmed, education in the neighborhood begins. Maps are made, based on the city maps used by tourism or the subway system, and a location is pinpointed which says '*AQUI*' ('here') – as many maps can indicate where one lives – then it says, '*Aqui vive un genocida*' ('Here lives a person who has committed genocide'). The map contains footnotes which go into detail as to who the person is, what atrocities they have committed, and so forth. These maps are pasted over local maps, on street lamps, newspaper stands, store fronts, walls, and throughout the neighborhood.

HIJOS and its supporters distribute information leaflets to the people who live in the neighborhood, asking if they know that a *genocida* lives there. The flyer campaign continues for a few weeks and then action is scheduled.[3] Action takes on different forms. There is the one described above, outside of a hospital, but most often they are in front of a person's home. The police are always there, in large numbers, protecting the house. However, HIJOS' intention is not to attack the house; instead, it does street theater, sometimes acting out what the person did, the horrors they committed. Sometimes it is more informational: HIJOS states what the person has done, then throws red paint bombs at the door of the house or apartment at the end. Sometimes it creates songs, and goes through the neighborhood singing about what happened – as is the case with the *escrache* against a priest and church that collaborated with the military in the neighborhood of Paternal, Buenos Aires.[4] One of the main chants at an *escrache* is '*Si no hay Justicia, Hay escrache!*' ('If there is no justice, then there is an *escrache!*'). Justice here signifies both definitions of the word, as in social justice and making a situation equal or fair, and justice referring to the legal process in which one is accused by the state and judicial system (in Spanish the word is the same).

However, the point of this action is not for justice in either definition. The point is that there is no justice by the very nature of the person living freely in society, without any social outcry. HIJOS makes that outcry. HIJOS takes the silence and breaks it. HIJOS speaks to neighbors, to society, and makes people uncomfortable. HIJOS makes noise in the silence. The point is that there cannot be silence. HIJOS began making noise in this silence in the mid-1990s and continues through 2012, at the time of writing.

HIJOS works with a number of other groups, from human rights groups, such as the Madres de la Plaza de Mayo and the Abuelas, to having relationships with most of the new social movements after the rebellion, from recuperated factories to neighborhood assemblies and MTDs. In the 1990s, when it first began to organize, the groups that HIJOS was closest to were the Mesa de Escrache and GAC. Both groups played a pivotal role in the tactics used by HIJOS. Mesa de Escrache is literally translated as the 'table of the Escraches', which discusses which action to organize next, against which *genocida*, when, how, and so forth. It then brings these proposals to HIJOS, and from there, works with the GAC. GAC is a group of artists that use public space to make political interventions. This can range from 'public art' or graffiti to making the maps that are used by HIJOS to publicize an *escrache* or the location of a *genocida*, including signs that look like road detours, but instead say things like, 'Beware, a *genocida* lives 500 meters ahead.'

Organization

The ways in which HIJOS, GAC, and Mesa de Escrache work is in network formations, without hierarchy or central power structures. In fact, many in the groups refer to the ways in which they organize as horizontal. They were not using the language of *horizontalidad* before the rebellion, but the ways in which they organized were much the same. It is not that HIJOS or GAC stake any sort of ideological claim on nonhierarchy or horizontal ways of relating; the way that many of the participants described it to me was just that it made more sense for organizing and was the only way that they could all feel like full participants and create the affective relationships that they desired. Since the popular rebellion and widespread use of *horizontalidad* as a social relationship and word, HIJOS and GAC both use it to describe their ways of functioning:

> *Horizontalidad* and consensus: this expresses a form of construction without bosses or hierarchy, that democratizes political practices and brings forward the role of the individual with the collective. Respect for the opinion of the other person and diversity of thought is all part of what we bring together to create a synthesis.
>
> (HIJOSriocuarto.blogspot.com)

As Diego Benegas writes, based on his personal experience in HIJOS as well as his research into the group:

> H.I.J.O.S. emerged as a network, a loose collective that evolved into a union of groups, thus it rather looks like a federation. The different local chapters, called 'the *regionals*', do not respond to a central authority. The principle of group autonomy was present from the start and H.I.J.O.S. members defended it consistently throughout the years (Mendoza interview 2002c), but they remain one national organization rather than an articulation of local chapters. Local groups are autonomous and all their members meet weekly in an *assembly* that makes all the decisions for the regional (group). The *commissions* are smaller subgroups that perform the actual work. They are for example: Legal Matters, Siblings, Direct Action, Anthropological Investigation, Schools, Reception, Archive, and Radio. Recently, individuals outside of the organization have begun to participate in the commissions without becoming full (*organic*) members.
>
> (Benegas forthcoming; emphasis in original)

The politics of HIJOS, GAC and Mesa de Escrache, together with their horizontal form of organizing, created a bit of a precursor to the ways in which people organized after 19 and 20 December 2001. This is not linear, as history never is, but there is more than coincidence in the fact that these groups rejected hierarchical methods of organization, chose not to focus on demands of the state, but instead spoke to, and speak to, society as a whole. Breaking with silence, cultures of silence, and looking to one another and the community generally to rethink history, the future and *justicia*. (More about the forms of organization and political interventions of HIJOS, GAC and Mesa de Escrache will be discussed in future chapters, which describe the movements in detail along with their horizontal and affective forms of organization.)

The dictatorship

As this chapter is working in reverse chronological order, after the 1990s, the next significant period for discussion is that of the dictatorship. The time of the early 1970s through to 1983, reaching a high point of terror in 1976, was the most brutal and terrifying in Argentine history:

> There were many victims, but the true objective was to reach the living, the whole of society that, before undertaking a total transformation, had to be controlled and dominated by terror and by language ... Only the voice of the state remained, addressing itself to an atomized collection of inhabitants.
> (Romero 2002[1994]: 219)

Juan Corradi called this a 'culture of fear' (Corradi et al. 1992). Some who were able, fled abroad, mainly for political reasons but for professional ones as well. Every level of society was monitored and censored. Artists, psychologists and architects were under particular attack, but no one was exempt. However, many others that did not leave lived in what the Argentine historian Luis Alberto Romero has called 'internal exile'. With this term he refers to people who hid out within Argentina, sometimes just by keeping a low profile, and others who literally were hidden in basements and attics, as with the Jews in Nazi-occupied Europe. He also refers to something much more profound affecting society at the time and future generations: those people who saw what was taking place and had the opinion of *no te metas* or, when the brutality was impossible to ignore, with the opinion that 'they must have done something' (Romero 2002[1994]). Between 1976 and 1978 the vast majority of people were 'disappeared'.

One-third were women, hundreds of whom gave birth in captivity. The vast majority of all people were between fifteen and thirty-five.

What role did and does the dictatorship play in the social movements that emerged out of 19 and 20 December 2001? In this case, a great deal. As HIJOS intended, and so many participants in the movements explain, the rebellion was a break with the past. It was a break with fear and a massive break with not being together. *No te metas* no longer held. People were together, and were no longer afraid – not of one another anyway, but perhaps still afraid of the state. However, no longer was there to be the silence of the past. (The experience of breaking with this past is dealt with more in Chapter 2.)

HIJOS has recorded the difference in the participation and reception of the *escrache*s, particularly looking at the changes after the popular rebellion in 2001. In the mid-1990s they were met with hesitation, sometimes fear, and the *escrache*s themselves were never very large. They were almost always repressed by the police, and participants were often followed, filmed and harassed by phone by government agents.

In the months following 19 and 20 December 2001 the *escrache*s became increasingly larger, often reaching the thousands and even tens of thousands (Benegas forthcoming). HIJOS, GAC and Mesa de Escrache have all been a part of the new social movements, in the organizations mentioned as well as often in their neighborhood assembly, local MTD or other art and media groups.

The role that the dictatorship plays on memory and the new movements is as a break and a memory. It is a break with the past, but not just the past of horror and repression. As HIJOS says, it is for remembering, and against forgetting.

Revolutionary armed struggle: the 1960s–1970s

Of those captured and murdered by the dictatorship, some did belong to revolutionary armed groups, mainly the Ejercito Revolucionario del Pueblo (ERP, People's Revolutionary Army) and the Montoneros. The ERP was completely destroyed by the state's campaign of repression and murder. The Montoneros continued, but shifted its tactics mainly to terrorism, including high-profile kidnappings and assassinations, including killing the chief of police of Buenos Aires. However, before the dictatorship, armed struggle in Latin America was spreading like wildfire. 'Be like Che Guevara', the leader of the Cuban Revolution, was a popular slogan, and movements throughout the Americas fought to create anti-capitalist and anti-imperialist revolutions; this was also the growing desire of poor and working people throughout the continent and the world. The forms that this revolutionary struggle took varied. In many parts of Latin America, armed struggle was a component of the fight for a better world – for the future and in the present, with armed groups sometimes supporting local infrastructural projects. In Colombia for example, the slogan of the Ejercito de Liberación Nacional (ELN, National Liberation Army) was 'El poder no se toma se construya' ('Power is not taken, it is constructed'), and the ELN worked consistently in the countryside as well as taking up arms. In Argentina, the armed struggle was the largest recorded in all of Latin America. Social and political revolution, in the sense of taking over the state, was becoming a very a real question and possibility.

What effect did the past mass guerilla army and revolutionary armed forces have on the social movements that emerged after 19 and 20 December 2001? From the interviews I conducted it does not seem that it has had the effect that one might have imagined – or at least I would have imagined that people would have been more inspired by the revolutionaries and want to walk in their footsteps by picking up a gun and taking out the repressive state, for example. However, the agenda is a different one: it is not about taking up arms (although very few people I spoke with would call themselves pacifists or even disregard the need for some sort of armed defense at some point). The point is not to take over the state, but to recreate society, individually, socially, and grounded in neighborhoods and workplaces. Person after person would explain to me that on 19 and 20 December there was a real possibility of taking over the Casa Rosada (the Pink House, the official executive mansion of Argentina), but they did not want to do that. Some said that power is not located there, while others just said that they were going back to their neighborhood – not to go home and watch television, but to organize. To create an assembly and begin to recreate what was broken during the dictatorship. The rupture that people spoke of was a rupture with ways of *being*, with not being together, with *no te metas*.

The effect of the Ejercito Revolucionario del Pueblo (ERP) and Montoneros is not exactly clear. There is no disrespect for them or their memory – quite the opposite, in fact – but their tactics of armed struggle and hierarchical forms of organization are things that are not being borrowed from that particular history. If anything, learning from the period of armed struggle (that went hand-in-hand with the military dictatorship) has brought into question the notion of defense. Neka, from MTD Solano, describes the group's approach to social change, and it includes rejecting the idea of taking power from the state with weapons:

> The issue isn't just the physical confrontation with the system. Every day we're forced to confront a system that is completely repressive. The system tries to impose on us how and when we struggle. The question for us is how to think outside this framework. How to manage our own time and space. It's easier for them to overthrow us when we buy into concepts of power, based on looking at the most powerful, based on something like weapons or the need to arm the people. We're going to build according to our own reality, and not let them invade it. I think this idea of power as a capability and a potential, not a control, is a very radical change from previous struggles.
>
> (Sitrin 2006: 163)

There is no question that the memory of the revolutionaries of the 1960s and 1970s remains, but it does so without the desire to replicate their methods. There is no need to 'be like the ERP', as once people wanted to 'Be like Che' or create more Vietnams, more Cubas. Instead, the movements today speak of creating new social relationships – asking while questioning, and doing so horizontally. The revolution is in the day-to-day practice.

Peronism: the 1950s–1960s

My friends in Argentina, especially in my first year there, would regularly ask me how I was dealing with Peronism in my work. I would reply with the same regularity, 'No tengo ni idea' ('I have no idea') – and then we would all laugh. Peronism is an ideology, a person, a politic, a relationship, and an identity. It can be negative, implying centralized rule or even dictatorship, or it can mean democracy and workers' power (Auyero 1999). This plurality creates a situation which for some has very little meaning, while for others it can be heavily weighted. It all depends on who is speaking and why.

Based in the person, Peronism, now represented by the Justicialista Party, began with Juan Domingo Perón, a military general and politician. He was elected president three times after serving in several government positions, including Secretary of Labor and the vice-presidency. Juan Perón was overthrown in a military coup in 1955, but there was such an outpouring of support, particularly from working people, and pressure that continued that eventually he returned to power in 1973. He was only president at that time for nine months, when he died and was succeeded by his third wife, Isabel Martinez.

Perón and his second wife, Eva, were immensely popular among many Argentines, and to this day play an incredibly iconic role. One cannot walk down a street in the city of Buenos Aires without passing posters from the Justicialista Party, and since the election of Néstor Kirchner and then his wife Cristina, posters with the faces of Néstor and Cristina have papered the city. Their popularity, as with Perón's, was with working people, the unemployed and sectors of the middle class: the middle class believing that they will keep the poor under control, the workers believing they will continue working, the poor believing that they will give them gifts, and the unemployed believing that they will get work. Any or none of this can be true. The rhetoric remains, but it is the same Peronist government that crushed labor unions and gave gifts of basic necessities to the poor at the same time.

Overall, what the Peróns and the Justicialista Party have in common, and what many in the new movements are breaking from, is a paternalistic relationship to the population. Some see this relationship as good, when the government is giving out food and unemployment subsidies, while many see this as negative, that the government is forcing people into a dependent relationship. Regardless of opinion, Peronism is something with which any political person must engage.[5] The Peronist governments are fighting hard to win back their patrons in the unemployed, including giving people money to leave autonomous movements, or evicting them outright from occupied land and housing. In fact, in some neighborhoods of the unemployed one can see an increase in clientalistic relationships again – relationships of brokerage with political party representatives (Auyero et al. 2009).

Why the historical context is important here is that people have begun to rebel against clientalism in large numbers and consciously; they are breaking with *punteros* (political party brokers) and creating their own dignity. As Neka from MTD Solano describes, their politics are not measured by poverty, but by the 'politics of dignity'.[6] It is an ongoing and active struggle, but the fact that it is being actively engaged in for the first time in history (and often rejected), opens up many possibilities.

Radical labor movements: 19th–early 20th centuries

Argentina has a long and powerful labor history. Some of the strongest labor organizations in the Americas were in Argentina, particularly in the very early 1900s (James 1988). In 1905 La Federación Obrera Regional Argentina (FORA, Argentine Regional Workers' Federation) and other syndicalist movements had many dozens of groupings, and multiple newspapers published simultaneously (Yerrill and Rosser 1987). Not only was the membership diverse and militant, but the tactics used were often those of strikes and general strike. Influenced by anarchism and anarcho-syndicalism, the level of worker consciousness was high, with workers organizing against management, the bosses and often capitalism itself.

From the mid-1800s until almost 1920, Argentina's economy grew exponentially, making it one of the world's strongest economies (Romero 2002[1994]). The majority of investment in this growth was from European capital, as were the workers, comprising 84 per cent of the workforce. Workers began organizing as early as the 1870s and formed the first trade union in 1886, with the first national labor association established in 1879 (Romero 2002[1994]). It was during this time that the first formal anarchist group was organized: the International Socialist Circle. By the late 1800s there were dozens of labor organizations, with thirty in the city of Buenos Aires alone. Militancy was a part of the new labor movements, with strikes and occupation beginning at the same time as the formation of the groups. The exact extent of the influence of anarchist ideas on the labor movement has been contested, but what is clear is that it was substantial. Most of the immigrants who migrated to Argentina in the late 1800s were from Italy and Spain: two countries where anarchist ideas held a great deal of sway over working people.

In 1901 the Federación Obrero Argentina (FOA, Argentine Workers' Federation) was founded. Influenced by anarchism, this federation rejected political parties, including the Socialist Party, and unified around the concept of general strike and working-class solidarity against capitalism. The federation rapidly grew in membership, and by 1904 had close to 11,000 members. In that time it led a number of significant strikes, including twelve general strikes, of which the FOA led the most (Bayer 2002). In 1903 the Union General Trabajador (General Workers' Union) was founded, in part to counter the militancy of the FOA.

In 1905 the FOA re-founded itself as FORA, adding 'Regional' to its name. It also became more explicitly anarchist, adding in its foundation documents: 'it advises and recommends the widest possible study and propaganda to all its adherents with the object of teaching the workers the economic and philosophical principles of anarchist communism' (Thompson 1999: 169).

By 1906 FORA comprised more than 30,000 members. Over the course of the next ten years there were a number of splits within the federation, leading to the formation of other groups based on the same ideas, as well as those who split off and either joined the Union General Trabajador or other socialist groups. The new FORA (V and IX) claimed between 100,000 and 120,000 members in 1919. From 1917–1920 there were a large number of militant strikes, as well as a heightened level of repression. The government called the police on strikers, killing dozens of people and then, once the government was forced to stop direct repression due to tremendous pressure, business owners formed a vigilante group who then carried out massive repression against striking workers, killing dozens in one strike. Workers responded in self-defense and in the course of what has become known as the *Semana Tragica* (the Tragic Week), hundreds of workers were killed (Bayer 2002). By the early 1920s there were many divisions in the labor movement, particularly with a newly-formed Bolshevik-inspired union. These inner debates and fights led to a decrease in labor militancy.

However, what remains is the memory of a very high level of militancy, where workers by the hundreds of thousands were on the streets and striking in national unified action. Were all the unions anarchist, and did they really mobilize by the hundreds of thousands? Possibly, but how true is not the main point here. The larger question is how the imaginary, or real, role of anarcho-syndicalism plays into the imaginations of those organizing in movements today. People refer to the history of militancy and action without hierarchy, and perhaps this is one of the many places from which *horizontalidad* has developed. Miguel Mazzeo (2007) has written about the importance of myth and tradition in Latin American popular movements, and this is one of those occasions where the role of the story is as important as the historical event.

Conclusion

This chapter has served as a very brief overview into the history of movements and repression in Argentina. Perhaps most directly relevant is the relationship to the dictatorship and the movements that responded to deal with its consequences in society, from the Madres de la Plaza de Mayo and the Abuelas to HIJOS. In many ways HIJOS has paved the way for the sorts of organizing taking place in today's more autonomous movements in Argentina.

TWO

From rupture to creation: new movements emerge

The 19th and 20th was an uprising – or an insurrection – that marked the entire decade, up 'till today ... It is an event that profoundly changed the politics, cultural, society and economy of Argentina. There is a before and an after. As the Mexicans say, is a parting of the waters.

(Zibechi 2010)

Families sat at home, many before their television sets, in a night that began as so many others: what to watch, what to make for dinner, the regular nightly questions. Then a TV newscaster appeared on every channel and announced that from this moment on all bank accounts were frozen. Silence in the house. The economic crisis was here. People sat in silence, stared at the TV ... they waited, they watched and they waited. And then it was heard, outside one window and then another, outside one balcony and another, neighborhood by neighborhood ... tac! tac tac! tac tac tac! ... People went to their windows, went out onto their balconies and heard the sound. The sound was people banging spoons on pans, spatulas on pots, the sound of the *cacerolazo*. The sound became a wave, and the wave began to flood the streets. We heard it, and then on the television sets accompanying our solitude, we saw it: newscasters, dumbfounded, captured the first *cacerolazos*; people in slippers, shorts, robes and tank tops, with children on their shoulders, entire families, out in the streets, tac! tac tac! tac tac tac! hitting their pots and pans. What they were saying was not expressed in words, it was done, bodies spoke, and spoke by the thousands and hundreds of thousands. Tac! tac tac! in slippers, tac tac!, old people, tac tac!, children, tac tac tac! The *cacerolazo* had begun.

The institutions of power did not know what to do, they declared a state of emergency in the morning, falling back on what had always been done: law and order. But the people broke with the past, with what had been done, and no longer stayed at home in fear. They came out onto the streets with even more bodies and sounds – and then the sounds, the tac tac tac! turned into a song. It was a shout of rejection, and a song of affirmation. Que se vayan todos! ('They all must go!') was sung, and sung together with their neighbors. It was not just a shout against what was, it was a song sung together, by the thousands and hundreds of thousands. People sang and banged pots, and greeted one another, kissing the cheeks of neighbors who in the past had only been seen, but now, for the first time, were truly being seen. It was a rupture with the past. It was a rupture with obedience, and a rupture with not being together, with not knowing one another. It was a rupture that cracked open history, upon which vast new histories were created.

(From author's notes based on interviews)

'One no, many yesses'

'The 19th and 20th' is how many in the movements refer to both the moment and process of what took place in Argentina. They are the days when everything broke open. People's imaginations broke open and new possibilities and imaginaries were created. To speak of 'the 19th and 20th' is to speak of the social creation and all that it implies breaking from; it is not to speak of a fixed time or stagnant date. 'Ya Basta!' ('Enough!') was shouted on that infamous day of 1 January 1994 when the Zapatistas appeared to the world and took over seven cities, declaring that they would not disappear, that they were rejecting 500 years of domination. They took back their land as they shouted 'No'. The Zapatistas speak of 'One no and many yesses'.[1] In Argentina they shouted and sang, 'Que se vayan todos!', and from the 19th and 20th millions of 'yesses' have emerged, their singing resonated around the world.

Throughout Latin America over the past ten years, people and communities have been breaking with past ways of organizing themselves and their communities, and with their relationship to institutional power and authority. Decisions are being made in the hands of the people, and being done so collectively and democratically. New and various forms of nonrepresentative democracy are being created as people organize. In Argentina this is called *horizontalidad*; in Chiapas, Mexico, people are creating new 'good government councils'; in Oaxaca, Mexico, in the Asamblea Popular de los Pueblos de Oaxaca (Popular Assembly of the Peoples of Oaxaca); in the regions around Cochabamba, Bolivia in the *Regantes*, the self-governed and self-policed autonomous communities; and in the highlands of La Paz, in El Alto, in neighborhood councils. Each of these examples of new forms of decision making comes from a break with previous forms of organizing. Not that they are entirely new; in many cases these 'new' forms of direct democratic decision making are in part a revival of segments of old practices, such as '*usos y custumbres*' ('customs and uses', as with some indigenous communities), or forms of council decision making that are linked, at least in practice, to older anarchist traditions.

From these new democratic processes people are speaking of new relationships, new selves, new collective selves, new subjects, protagonists, and social subjects. These new relationships form a break from relationships of domination and oppression, a break with silence and from the state, a break with alienation and capitalist modes of production relations and value production.

People have come together, have taken over workplaces to run them in common; they have taken over land to grow crops on so as to feed their communities; they have created alternative forms of education and healthcare. In some places the barter networks that were organized have involved millions of people, bartering services as well as goods. This production of alternative ways of surviving coupled with alternative forms of being and relating is what has created new subjects, new people. This is a new value relationship and a rejection of capitalist mode of relations, as explained by Raul Zibechi when interviewed by the alternative media group, Lavaca in 2010:

I believe that the world of those from below is growing, not only numerically, but also it is becoming stronger, gaining in self-esteem, while also getting more profound and complicated. It is also not just the poor, as they have been, but rather a new generation of poor, from the former middle class. And there are new knowledge and new skills. For example, the ability to self-organize. Before the organization was the union. They had not learned to organize in territory. First they learned to follow leaders, or *punteros*. Then they learned to self-organize autonomously from the *punteros*. For example, with time they learned to produce, recuperate workplaces, create gardens and bakeries, all sorts of micro-enterprises for production. From the production for survival, like the communal kitchens, to the production of material. And they learned to organize their own health care, with clinics autonomously constructed by those from below. And spaces of formation of many diverse types, including often the use of popular education.

(Lavaca 2010)

The break that took place was also with how to think about and organize for change. Linked with *horizontalidad* and autonomy, and the desire for the creation of new subjectivities, there was a break with political parties telling people what to do and how. As the Argentine sociologist Norma Giarracca, also in conversation with Lavaca, reflecting on ten years since the popular rebellion, explained, 'The message was: we do not want political representation any more. We want to take our own history into our own hands' (Lavaca 2010). This was not just a break with parties from formal institutions of power, but also with radical and revolutionary Left parties, from the Peronists to the Trotskyist. Many people broke with the concept of power as a thing, to take or to build for, and rejected that vision within the radical Left. Instead, people are creating a new power, a power with, a power to, power as *potencia*[2] – power as a verb.

What is rupture?

Rupture can come from many places. Sometimes it comes upon us, surprisingly or seemingly surprisingly, as is the case in Argentina, or the *Caracazo*[3] in Venezuela, and sometimes we the people create the rupture, as with the Zapatistas in Chiapas, or the Occupy Wall Street movement in the USA.

Rupture can be a break that occurs because of outside circumstances, circumstances that are that are not of our creation, even if their ramifications are within our power to prevent: events such as earthquakes, flood, fire, or economic collapse. These ruptures often inspire thousands, even hundreds of thousands, to come together and help one another. When massive collapse happens, often formal institutions of power collapse with them, or go into crisis. People then look to one another, begin to try to find solutions together, and often do so in such ways that are more 'effective' and definitely more empowering – 'affective'. Rebecca Solnit (2009) has done a great deal of work on this question, grounding much of it in disaster sociology and anarchist theory. Her work focuses on a number of global historical examples, from earthquakes in Mexico and Nicaragua to 9/11. She highlights how people find numerous ways to take care of themselves and each another, and how they do it even better than institutional organization of the crisis, when this is the case. Most people who have lived through any moment where formal institutions of power go away, or are forced away, agree with this point. When left alone, when left with one another, people turn to one another and use forms of mutual aid and support. The wake of the break is a beautiful opening up of possibility. This is what was seen in Argentina: the crisis caused the break, the rupture.

However, what is different with the Argentine example is that this creation did not stop: people continued to organize, and did so self-consciously. As Emilio, a movement participant, reflected in an interview in 2009:

> The people began to discuss politics when they went into the streets, to say enough of this unsustainable situation that we will not tolerate anymore, and from there began to develop new politics. It is when one questions the existing structures that another way always emerges, it liberates a creative force to do things in another way.

The rupture caused people to go out onto the streets and meet one another, but the new politics of *horizontalidad*, *autogestión*, other power, and *politica afectiva*, combined with creative new ways of meeting their needs and creating new values, kept people on the streets organizing and did not allow the opening that emerged with the crisis to close.

Without these 'new' forms of organization helping to facilitate an analysis of power, and doing so together, recognizing one another, and creating changes in subjectivity, the movements in Argentina could have easily gone in the same direction as those in so many other parts of the world when there is a rupture. These short-term experiences range from France in May 1968 to what is now referred to as the *Comuna de Oaxaca*, referring to the ninety days in 2006 when the people occupied the *zócalo* (central park), setting up alternative forms of decision making and survival (Esteva 2008); both of these experiences being the sort of rupture that the Zapatistas refer to, the creation of a break in a politically unsustainable situation. Similar sorts of assemblies and mass democracies have been seen throughout 2011 in Egypt, Greece and Spain. The outcomes of these mass gatherings and prefigurative political formations has yet to be determined, but what is certain is that new relationships are being created. Ruptures that have come from 'natural' events – or at least some moment of spark, such as an earthquake or terrorist attack – have witnessed short-term versions of the same. This was seen in New York during and immediately after 9/11.

In addition, rupture can be an intentional break, opening, crack, or as Holloway (2003a) discusses, a fissure. This is more the case with the Zapatistas in Chiapas. The space of creation and mutual aid was desired, and they knew that a rupture might help to facilitate this opening, so they prepared ahead of time the various components necessary to keep open a momentary opening, such as radical forms of horizontal decision making, new values and anti-capitalism, territory and time, a conscious grounding of collective memory in the present, as well as a profound and complicated analysis of power so as to not allow the opening to become co-opted. This is what the Zapatistas were preparing for, for more a decade before they 'came out' to the world with their insurrection. The insurrection was not so much a declaration of war as an invitation to new social creation. The Zapatistas announced on the radio day after day after arriving in San Cristobal de las Casas an invitation to do the same in every area. Not a declaration to join them, more an invitation to rebellion.

'To Open a Crack in History' (Marcos 2001) is one of the many ways that the Zapatistas refer to what they are doing. Opening this crack in history is to make it a part of a process, to open up possibilities that are changing, and come from as well as going to a place. It is also a conscious opening that they discuss, distinct from the Argentine economic crisis. The Zapatistas carefully chose a time and place to open this crack.

Holloway explains this concept in a piece that he wrote discussing anti-capitalist movements:

Fissures: these are the thousand answers to the question of
revolution. Everywhere there are fissures. The struggles of
dignity tear open the fabric of capitalist domination. When
people stand up against the construction of the airport in
Atenco, when they oppose the construction of the highway in
Tepeaca, when they stand up against the Plan Puebla Panama,
when the students of the UNAM [National Autonomous
University of Mexico] oppose the introduction of fees, when
workers go on strike to resist the introduction of faster rhythms
of work, they are saying 'NO, here no, here capital does not
rule!' Each No is a flame of dignity, a crack in the rule of
capital. Each No is a running away, a flight from the rule of
capital. No is the starting point of all hope. But it is not enough.
We say No to capital in one area, but it keeps on attacking us,
separating us from the wealth we create, denying our dignity as
active subjects. Yet our dignity is not so easily denied. The No
has a momentum that carries us forward.

(Holloway 2003a)

In each case there was a break and an opening. Something
happened such that there are now massive and deep forms of
direct democracy and *horizontalidad* when previously there was
not. What is this? Why this shift in forms of decision making?
Where did it come from, and why? From what are people breaking such that there is an opening that seems almost to necessitate
direct participation?

As rupture is a break, what I am arguing here is that this
break necessitates an opening. I am helping to bring to light what
comes out of the fissure, at the same time, as a rejection and a
creation. Too often social scientists and scholars of revolution
focus on the moment of rupture, and use this to explain the
historical event. In Russia the focus on revolution is the October
Revolution, not the Soviet workers. What would have happened
if the focus were on the Soviets and people running society,
rather than the state and the concept of the revolution as the
rupture? Scholars of Mexican history speak of the earthquake
in 1985 as a moment when things changed, but do not look to
what was opened up with popular and collective organization
in neighborhoods. Rupture in these cases was not the moment
of the revolution, or the earthquake, just as with Argentina and

Chiapas, the rupture is not just the *cacerolazo* or the taking of San Cristobal de las Casas. It is the creation of new social relations and communities.

Rupture needs to be understood as a break in ways of doing things, as a shift in people's imaginations from which new social relationships emerge, relationships that can be, and in the examples I use, that are autonomous from forms of institutional power. (This new way of perceiving and experiencing revolution is based in different conceptions and practices of power and autonomy that will be addressed in the following chapters.)

Rupturing 'No te metas' and fear

I believe what detonated the explosion of the 19th and 20th was seeing the lootings, followed by the declaration of the state of siege. It was like something in our collective memory said, 'No, I am not going to put up with it, I'm not going to take it.' It began with some *cacerolazo*s, and I remember … boom! People lost their fear, the fear we had from the military era … and well, this is like waking up.

(Conversation with Paloma in Paternal, Buenos Aires, 2003)

The break that Paloma refers to, the declaration of 'No', is massive, but that this took place within the context of a state of siege is that much more powerful. After a day of hundreds of thousands *cacerolando* (banging pots and pans), the state of siege was declared yet people continued to fill the streets, and in even greater numbers. Expelling five governments was also part of the long moment of rupture, but the most important change happened in the space 'beneath' the government. Beneath, people went outside and broke a history of silence: the history of *'no te metas'* – an often-used phrase during the decades of the dictatorship and for years after when 'democracy' had returned. Paloma, a small, frail, yet amazingly strong woman in her seventies, explained to me for hours all of what had changed in the aftermath of the 19th and 20th. She spoke of losing fear, of a shift in memory – that an alternative memory was being recovered and something was beginning to grow in that recovery. She says: 'And now we are advancing. Our advances although small, go … little by little, but they go.' This rupture with a past and a shift in collective memory went further still. What happened in the streets during those days of rebellion was not only a struggle against something, but simultaneously a creation of something. People began to meet one another on the street and form neighborhood assemblies. They met and began to talk face-to-face about what was going on, and what they were going to do about it. As Ezequiel, someone who was not previously political but who later took on a very active role in the Cid Campeador assembly, described:

> What began angrily, with people coming out on the street
> in a rage, quickly turned joyful. People smiled and mutually
> recognized that something had changed ... It was a very intense
> feeling that I will never forget.
> (Conversation in Porto Alegre, Brazil, 2002)

The years of the dictatorship were a time of absolute terror. To this day, even with the rupture and changes in society in Argentina, people are slow to speak in detail of the horrors that took place. During my time in Argentina it was only people that I got to know well who shared their experiences and reflections from the time of the dictatorship with me. The dictatorship was a brutal and intentional ripping apart of society through the conducting of mass murders, tortures of every imaginable type, deeply psychological torture combined with physical torture, the creation of fear (in everyone) of everything and everyone else. Trust was broken and replaced with danger, fear, pain, stolen memories and stolen loved ones. Society was ripped open and left to bleed, and people were forced to watch the bleeding.

In 1976 a military coup took power in Argentina, and until 1983 it terrorized the entire country. More than 30,000 people were 'disappeared': meaning that they were not to be found again, they no longer existed in society, no bodies, graves, or physical traces. This was a part of the terror campaign on behalf of the government. It was a conscious attempt to take people's memories, to erase people. This was done during the dictatorship, and repeatedly by government after government with their refusal to punish those responsible for the *genocidio* (genocide). Government after government refused to aid in any serious way the search for the disappeared bodies, the disappeared mothers, fathers and children. Many explanations are given for this inaction, but I would argue that it was not inaction, but in fact *action*. By not prosecuting and refusing to find the bodies of those murdered by the state and military, the government continues to keep a significant amount of fear in society. That *no te metas* was an expression up until 2001 reflects this. That the government declared a state of siege on the night of 19 December, reflects this. The state wanted to keep people in fear, and to a large extent it was successful.

In particular, and perhaps most of all, people continued to fear the police and military. Here Paula explains what the 19th and 20th meant for her in the context of this fear:

> For me the 20th was very strange, it was as if something took a hold of me. I'm not a person who is very … I don't know, really I don't have much courage, I'm not very brave. I see the police and I run away, terrified. Repression is something I've always been very afraid of. I see a policeman and I split, the police scare me very much. Nevertheless, on the 20th I was at home watching television very early with my sister, and we saw how the police were repressing the Madres de la Plaza de Mayo, using horses and everything, and I was seized with such a powerful indignation that I said, 'Come on, we're going!' It was crazy, because we knew they could kill us – they had killed someone the night before. We headed first to the area of Congreso, in the center of the city, but very close by police were using tear gas so, with another friend as well, we took a different street to get to the Plaza de Mayo. We could see what was happening. We saw the police kill someone right in front of us. I cannot tell you how horrible that was, but it still didn't deter us – it was something unconscious, you know? We needed to be there.
>
> (Conversation in Paternal, Buenos Aires, 2003)

For some, coming out onto the street was a break with the state telling them what to do and not do. For some it was anger at not having access to their money, and not trusting that the government would give them access to it ever again. And for some it was a break that can be more directly connected to the past.

Clientalism and punteros

From the *cacerolazo* people met one another, explored ways to meet their needs, and did so in horizontal ways. Nonhierarchical social relationships were formed. Argentina has a long history of clientalistic relationships: relationships which have been described by those who study them as 'domination networks' (Auyero 2000a). A clientalistic relationship is one 'based on political subordination in exchange for material rewards' (Fox 1994: 153). Javier Ayuero (2000b), one of the foremost scholars of clientalism in Argentina, states that political clientalism is a form of social and political control as well as a form of cultural domination. People in unemployed neighborhoods in particular would explain to me repeatedly how they were unable to get anything done without having to go through their local *puntero*, the political party broker in the clientalistic relationship. This *puntero* works for the local Peronist Party and their job is to turn out votes at election time, and bodies at the time of political rallies. In exchange for this participation the *puntero* might be able to get things for people. Because so many of these neighborhoods are completely devastated by poverty, people are often willing – or at least feel forced, so they agree – to function in these relationships. They receive light bulbs in exchange for participation in a rally, shouting some politician's name or other; hammer and nails in exchange for a vote. This was how most things were done, and to some extent still are in unemployed neighborhoods – but there was a break. There was a rupture in this relationship. The unemployed workers' movements were born, and consciously broke with these forms of delegation and hierarchy. As a participant in the unemployed workers' movement of Allen, in the far south of Argentina, explains:

> The movement in Allen is surging forth, and from it all the freshness and naturalness of the movement. From the moment that it is born with all that fresh spontaneity, it bursts forth rupturing the social controls that political parties and *punteros* (party brokers) exercise over the unemployed. The first rupture is the casual dismissal of the *punteros*, the setting aside of political parties, and seeking one's own path. Imagine that. And this is done without a previously elaborated theory about this practice, surging as a spontaneous expression of social practice

that seeks to carve out a different path, like some sort of quest. Don't you think?

(Sitrin 2006: 108)

From a dignified worker to dignity

As discussed previously, Peronism is a deeply complicated term and movement in Argentina. There are left-wing and right-wing Peronists, there are those who have supported Perón but not the celebration of workers, there are Peronists who do not feel that Perón empowered workers, but did love them. There are Peronists who do not believe that workers should have power, but should be given the things that they need to survive. There have been guerilla groups that are Peronist and believe in taking power for a workers' government, and then there are guerilla groups that only wanted to take power so that Perón could come back and do for the working class. The Montoneros who kidnapped and killed a former president of Argentina, Pedro Eugenio Aramburu, in the 1970s are Peronists, as is the current president of Argentina, Cristina Kirchner.

In this conversation on rupture and creation, what is interesting to examine in relationship to Peronism is the concept of 'dignity under Peronism', and how that concept has been consciously retaken and redefined by those in the unemployed and working class movements.

Daniel James is one of the preeminent writers and scholars of Peronism in Argentina. In his article, 'Rationalisation and Working Class Response: the Context and Limits of Factory Floor Activity in Argentina', he discusses some of the challenges to workers' self-activity under Perón. He quotes from a conference of employers that took place to discuss their concerns about low production levels, something for which of course they blamed the workers. The document asserts: 'while the worker has a right to receive a minimum salary compatible with his needs and his dignity he also has a dignity to achieve a minimum level of output for his day of work' (1981: 378). The report then concludes that if a worker does not do this, he should be fired without compensation. The point that this passage demonstrates is not that employers might fire workers – of course they would, and consistently do – but the use of the term 'dignity'.

The dignified worker under Perón is one who works hard and produces. Workers were to feel proud of their work and country: a good worker, a dignified worker was the person who went to work, arrived early, worked hard, maybe even doing overtime, and then went home and was able to buy things for their family due to this hard work. This work and the ability to buy back one's value with the wages from that work was dignified. In this sense, dignity comes from the relationship of exploitation and subjugation. This is not to belittle the fact that workers did earn higher wages overall under Perón; there was an economic boom, but this did not necessarily mean that workers received higher wages. Sometimes they did, sometimes things were given in the form of infrastructure in neighborhoods such as clinics and schools, although often the funding to create this infrastructure came from a fund controlled by Eva Perón to which workers were obliged to donate (James 1988: 38). Other times, again, particularly under Eva Perón, gifts were given to some workers – not many or often, but in highly symbolic ways – making it look as though she loved the workers and took care of them. Even if this idea of taking care were entirely true – which it was not – it is not the concept of dignity that comes from the workers themselves, and is hardly an emancipatory conception. 'The Peróns extended dignity to the workers, making work an honorable occupation and creating a powerful group identity' (Berho 2000: 38). Daniel James speaks of the construction of the dignified working class by Perón as follows: 'In an important sense the working class was constituted by Peron: its self-identification as a social and political force within national society was, in part at least, constructed by Peronist political discourse' 1988: 38). This is a really important point: an identity constructed by those who have power over you.

The Peróns did raise workers' wages and made it possible for workers to buy things that they could not have done before. A possibility of another way of living, a sort of 'Argentine Dream' emerged with Perón, as long as one was dignified in the way defined by the government. If you behaved in this dignified way, then you were given dignity.

Dignity cannot be given. This is the cry of the *piqueteros* (the unemployed) and recuperated workplace movements. Among the slogans of the autonomous MTDs is 'Dignity, Autonomy and *Horizontalidad*'. Here, dignity is about creating your own relationship to work and your community. In the MTDs a conscious choice has been made to break with the employer–employee relationship, and they are constructing other ways of surviving, based on micro-enterprises autonomously run within the movement, with gardens and raising animals, by taking over land upon which to build housing and more gardens.[4] People who were left on the margins of society have decided to take that margin and make it the center. They are creating dignity in where and who they are. They consciously choose not to sell their labor power to the highest bidder, but instead to create and work together in the neighborhoods. To create a new conception of work and dignity. As two *compañeras* from MTD Solano explained:

Maba: We started getting some money from the state with these protests, but in the assemblies we discussed fighting for more than the tiny amount of subsidies they threw at us. Together we decided that we had to fight for something much larger, and that's where the whole idea of fighting for dignity emerged. Fighting for freedom. Fighting with *horizontalidad*.

Claudia: So, our perspective is grounded in the need for a new construction, no? A new society. I believe that many experiences have appeared which, despite having an objective that attempted to achieve a common good, their way of relating was that of ordering and obeying. I think that many of them fell apart precisely due to the shortcomings of this sort of relationship. This is true because the most important thing is affect, or rather, not something superficial or spectacular, but something that is born from human need – the need to recognize others, to feel like I am recognized, and to recover our self-esteem. That is to say, to recover our dignity.

(Conversation in Lanus, outside Buenos Aires, 2003)

While participants in the recuperated workplace movement do not use the language of dignity in the same way as the unemployed workers' movement, consciously reclaiming the term from the past, their practices are the same. The basic premise for the occupation and recuperation of a workplace is that the boss and owners have either abandoned the workplace or refused to pay or respect the workers. The rupture here is that workers say 'Enough is enough', and over time take the workplace back. There is no engagement with the previous owner or management; it is now between the workers, who rebuild and recreate their work environment without the hierarchy of the past. Workplace after workplace, person after person spoke of no longer tolerating the bad treatment and exploitation of the past. They were rejecting the precarity decided by others, the lack of respect, the lack of dignity, and took over the means of production so as to create better conditions together. As Liliana, an older worker from the Brukman garment factory explained to me, simply and clearly:

> We are all older women here, almost all of us are over forty, and our only source of employment is this factory. What we know how to do is work with the machines that are inside. Because of this whole experience I have now begun to think, why does the worker always have to keep quiet? The boss doesn't pay you, the boss owes you money, and you're the one that has to leave, to hang your head and go. Well, we made the decision that we weren't going to be quiet any longer. They've done a lot of things to us and I believe that, well, enough already with staying quiet. No? All our lives we kept quiet, in the past we would have left and looked for another job. That's no longer my way of thinking. I want that to be clear. I want all this corruption that is carried out against us workers to stop. We, as workers, have stopped being stupid, and that's it. We are steadfast.
>
> (Conversation in Once, Buenos Aires, 2003)[5]

The formation of new solidarities: 'El otro soy yo'[6]

One of the manifestations of the often right-wing nature of the middle class before the rebellion was its rejection of the poor and unemployed. Middle-class neighborhoods would regularly complain about the unemployed shutting down streets and bridges, sitting in front of cafés asking for money, or even riding the trains. These complaints were made to the police: a complaint that was not insignificant within the context of military dictatorship. Worse even than the unemployed, to the middle class, were the *cartoneros*. *Cartoneros* are people who collect cardboard by night and sell it to local recycling places by day to collect whatever change it might produce so as to subsist; they are similar to those people in the USA who collect bottles and plastic containers for recycling, and travel from block to block with overflowing supermarket carts. In Argentina this is done by going through the trash in various neighborhoods and collecting the cardboard, sometimes using carts to hold it, and sometimes sharing mule-drawn carts when the quantity warrants it. Poor neighborhoods generally reuse their cardboard or recycle it themselves, so it is the middle-class neighborhoods that the *cartoneros* go to at night in search of cardboard.

Throughout the late 1990s there were media campaigns led by the middle class attempting to ban the *cartoneros* from neighborhoods. This was never linked to violence, but other more masked arguments were made, including that some *cartoneros* use mules to pull their carts and that this is abusive to animals: thus the *cartoneros* should be banned, since they sometimes arrived with maltreated mules. Often the language used was crass, and as with the unemployed, *cartoneros* were referred to as 'dirty and brown' (they are in fact often darker-skinned, more likely tracing their roots to a mix of Guarani and other indigenous backgrounds).

With the rise of neighborhood assemblies, all of this changed. A new slogan emerged with regard to the *piqueteros* (the unemployed): '*Cacerola, Piquetero, una Sola Lucha*' ('The pot bangers and the unemployed are in one struggle'). As for the *cartoneros*, they became almost a campaign for the neighborhood assemblies. Some of this was reflected in concrete support, with food being cooked and provided along with places to rest throughout the many neighborhood assemblies that occupied spaces such as banks and cafés, which stayed open at night and served warm milk and food, as well as allowing them to use the bathroom and get warm. In addition – both formally and, from what I could observe, informally – people began to separate their trash.

During my first months living in Argentina I was in the neighborhood of Paternal, a working-class area with the neighborhood assembly of Cid Campeador, located in an occupied Banco de Mayo. This neighborhood separated the trash from cardboard from the first time I arrived. When I moved in 2003 to the more middle-class neighborhood of Palermo Viejo, I found that some people separated the trash and some did not. The more expensive buildings still had their trash in one container at night, but in the more modest dwellings, like my apartment building, people separated the cardboard from the trash. This may not seem that significant, but the meaning was deep. While once the *cartoneros* were equated with trash, worse even, now these same people who tried to prevent them from even coming into their neighborhoods were going through their own trash so that the *cartoneros* would not have to do it. This did not happen in all places or with all assemblies, and in fact there were occasions of assembly members not wanting the *cartoneros* to use the neighborhood space:

> One of the central relationships that the neighborhood assemblies made was to the *cartoneros*. These relationships were 'uneven' ranging from direct assistance and cooperation to direct confrontations in the spaces occupied by the assemblies.
> (Svampa 2002a: 3)

New movements, groupings and solidarities formed throughout the country. Those groups which had previously existed changed: some drastically, such as the fairly new MTDs; and some only slightly, such as the political parties. Some groups took longer to internalize the changes taking place around them, such as the trade unions, but they were affected and continue to shift and change in the new context.

Neighborhood assemblies

The first, most visible and rapid to organize out of the rebellion were the neighborhood assemblies. Hundreds of thousands of people took to the street, began *cacerolando*, and then soon after, sometimes within hours or days, began to look to one another and ask what was next. Then, days and weeks later, together they sought ways to meet their needs: from the concrete, such as food and medical attention, to the affective, such as the need for support and the creation of community and *companerismo*. This new organization took place neighborhood by neighborhood, in predominantly urban areas. Sometimes, in the larger neighborhoods there would be two or even three neighborhood assemblies, such as in the neighborhood of Palermo, a medium-size neighborhood in Buenos Aires that divided into three: Palermo, Palermo Viejo and Palermo Soho. The names of the assemblies were simply taken from the names of the neighborhoods. As far as how the assemblies began meeting, many participants describe chalking on the street or writing on walls, 'Neighbors meet here, Wednesday 9pm' and the meeting times and places spread by word of mouth and graffiti.

One assembly, described by an artist and writer who moved to Argentina from the UK soon after learning of the rebellion, wrote:

> The local assemblies meet weekly, are particularly popular
> in middle-class areas and are open to anyone, so long as they
> don't represent a political party. The first one I attended
> involved some 40 people: a breastfeeding mother, a lawyer, a
> hippy in batik flares, a taxi driver, a nursing student ... a slice
> of Argentinian society standing on a street corner, passing
> around a megaphone and discussing how to take back control
> of their lives. It seemed so normal, yet this was perhaps the most
> extraordinary radical political event I'd ever witnessed: ordinary
> people discussing self-management, understanding direct
> democracy and putting it into practice.
>
> (Jordan 2003)

The Argentine social scientist, Maristella Svampa, has written a great deal on the phenomenon of the neighborhood assemblies and *piquetero* movements. She refers to the assemblies as both new and 'a multidimensional space':

> No one can negate that the fact that the neighborhood
> assemblies constitute one of the newest expressions of the
> social mobilizations that live and have been developed sine
> the 19th and 20th of December of 2001. In the middle of the
> heterogeneity that characterizes this movement, we believe that
> the assembly process has created a space where many different
> dimensions can come together and intersect.
>
> (Svampa 2002b)

Hundreds of neighborhood assemblies emerged in the first year after the rebellion, each comprising anything from one to 300 participants. One of the neighborhood assemblies that still continues, and remains an important organizing center, is the assembly of Cid Campeador, which occupies a bankrupt Banco de Mayo. The neighborhood of Cid Campeador is lower-middle class, located outside the downtown of Buenos Aires. There are events most nights in the assembly and have been since the first months of the rebellion, ranging from tango and salsa classes to book readings, political discussions, assemblies and cultural events. Throughout the day the assembly is open as a library, community and study space, as well as a popular kitchen for people in need of food. A number of participants reflected to me that the reason that Cid Campeador continues while other assemblies have stopped is that they organize regular events and activities, try to maintain their own agenda in relation to the state, are not dominated by political parties, and continue to maintain their horizontal weekly assemblies.[7]

Interbarrial

Within a few weeks of the neighborhood assemblies taking off there was a call for an *interbarrial* (inter-neighborhood assembly). This *interbarrial* was to be, and was for a year, an assembly of assemblies. It was an incredible display of mass participatory democracy, the likes of which have rarely been seen in history. It has been recorded that at times upwards of 10,000 people participated in the assemblies, each participating as a part of their local assembly. As Svampa describes in the section of an article entitled '*Interbarrial* and the Centenario Park':

> This stage of the '*cacerolazo*' appeared as key in identifying the emerging movement. It was the most dynamic period. General plenaries had the participation of 100–150 people per assembly [with hundreds of assemblies participating in the plenaries]. From February to March the various commissions began to fully function (health, politics, press, unemployed, among others) and there was support at this stage for the discussion process and action.
>
> (Svampa and Pereyra 2003a: 2)

The level of organization of the assemblies in Argentina in the *interbarrial* was profound. At first anyone from an assembly could come along, and when decisions were made, every person had a vote in that decision. Represented at the *interbarrial* were many hundreds of assemblies and groups, with thousands of people attending, representing many thousands more. The votes were unwieldy, as were the discussions, although most found them incredibly inspiring.

One of the many challenges (as will be discussed in greater detail in Chapter 3), was political party disruption. Here I am speaking of Left political parties, for the most part the Trotskyist *Partido Obrero* (Workers' Party) (Svampa 2002b). Individuals in political parties came to the *interbarrial* and claimed to be part of an assembly, and often that grouping of people would form an *ad hoc* assembly for this purpose; they then were able to speak in the *interbarrial* as well as vote. This shifted the discussion away from the neighborhoods' desires as well as made for an imbalanced vote. Due to this disruption many thousands stopped going to the *interbarrial*. After only a year the *interbarrial* no longer met.[8]

Barter networks

Along with many developing and poor nations, Argentina has a long history of barter and exchange of goods outside the formal market economy. Unique in Argentina, especially after the economic crisis of 2001, the barter network that existed grew exponentially and the forms of exchange expanded beyond any preceding network. The absolute numbers are not known, and estimates range from 2 to 7 million (Alcorta 2007). Throughout this book the reference to barter could mean an exchange of goods for goods, but also might refer to the exchange of various forms of services, such as computer repair for childcare, or psychoanalysis for electrical work.

Unemployed workers' movements

The unemployed workers' movement in Argentina arose in the north and south of the country in the 1990s when, in the context of a growing economic crisis, unemployed workers as well as broader-based popular movements organized against local governments and corporations. Generally led by women, unemployed workers in the provinces of Salta, Jujuy, and Neuquén took to the streets by the thousands, blocking major transportation arteries in order to demand subsidies from the government. In a decisive break with the past, this organizing was not done by or through elected leaders, but directly by those in the streets, deciding day-by-day and moment-to-moment what to do next. In some places neighbors came together first, trying to discover what needs existed in the neighborhood, and from there decided to use the tactic of blockading roads (*piquetes*). It is from this tactic, the *piquete*, that the name for the unemployed workers' movements emerged: *piqueteros*, those who create the *piquete*. Before the popular rebellion the middle class referred to the *piqueteros* with disgust, anger and outright hostility. However, for the *piqueteros* it was something to be proud of and use with dignity and power. On a blockade people would sing and chant, often incorporating the word *piquetero*. For example, even children sing '*Piqueteeerrroooo Carajo!*', meaning literally, '*Piquetero*, damn it!' Or in a positive and proud way, 'I am a fucking *piquetero!*'[9]

Many of the neighborhoods in which the MTDs are now located are on the outskirts of cities, in areas that some might refer to as slums. These are neighborhoods that often do not have paved roads, sometimes no electricity or water, and have a level of unemployment that it is not so much an occurrence as a state of being. One is unemployed, likely to be regularly unemployed, and one's children face similar prospects (Davis 2006). Not having a location of work – the traditional means of protest for a worker – strike or job action was unavailable, thus the *piquete* was created. Many talk about the *piquete* as not only being a space for protest, but for what opens up when the road is shut down. Movement participants sometimes refer to this as free territory, and it is in this freed space that forms of *horizontalidad* and new subjectivities emerged.

From the *piquete*, which forced the government to give the first (small) unemployment subsidies in the history of Latin America, many groups became movements, expanding their strategies and tactics beyond, creating autonomous areas upon which they have built housing and gardens, raise livestock, create alternative education and healthcare along with many other subsistence projects. These autonomous projects are organized geographically,

MTDs emerging with neighbors in different neighborhoods, many of whom work together in network formations. Whereas once it was the local *puntero* who decided what the neighborhood participants would have to do to receive subsidies or any sort of relief from the state, now, in the autonomous movements, people are deciding together, without hierarchy, what to do next and where to go.

In other neighborhoods, for example in Solano, outside of Buenos Aires, some of the projects beyond the bakeries and kitchens are things such as fish hatcheries and acupuncture. In the MTD La Matanza, also outside Buenos Aires, the movement has come together with the others in the neighborhood to create a school run by the movement and the neighbors; and in La Plata they are taking over land and building housing. In the MTD Allen there is an autonomous clothing production micro-enterprise that is called 'Discover'. As a *compañera*, Patricia, explains:

> They named it 'Discover' because through the MTD they
> discovered the value of *compañerismo* – the value of solidarity.
> Through the MTD, they discovered experiences that enable one
> to express oneself beyond words.
> (Conversations in Allen and Cipolletti, in Patagonia, 2003)

There are a few dozen MTDs and similar organizations of the unemployed throughout Argentina. Most have emerged in similar way, although not all of the groups emerged using *horizontalidad* and forms of direct decision making, and some have ambitions either to become political parties or to have direct representation in the government. These sorts of groups are not new in Argentina; they are also some of the many *piquetero* groups that are now referred to as Piqueteros K ('K' standing for Kirchner), meaning that these groups are generally on the side of the government and the wing of the Peronist Party to which the Kirchners belong. For the most part Piqueteros K no longer blocks roads or bridges; instead, it mobilizes outside the congressional building, both demonstrating to receive more subsidies for its members while holding up banners in support of the Kirchners: first Néstor, and then Cristina. This kind of politics is reminiscent of the sorts of mobilization under the rule of the Peróns.

It is important to clarify that the movements to which I refer in this book and with whom I have spent so much time over the past eight years are in no way related to Piqueteros K, and in fact are in opposition to it. That is, not in the confrontational sense, but politically and with regard to a vision of social and political change. The groups I discuss in this book are: MTD Solano, MTD Guernica, MTD La Matanza, MTD Allen, MTD Cipolletti, MTD San Telmo, MTD Almirante Brown and Union de Trabajadores Desocupados (UTD, Union of Unemployed Workers) Mosconi. Of these groups, a few have shifted their positions with regard to their relationship to political parties and state power. MTDs Solano, Cipolletti and Guernica are all struggling to remain autonomous, and most recently how to take what they can from the state while maintaining their own agenda. MTDs San Telmo and Almirante Brown are both a part of a formation that came into being in 2007, the Frente Dario Santillan. This Frente is comprised of those MTDs that are not related to the government or Piqueteros K, but do receive subsidies from the state and organize in neighborhoods in sometimes more vertical ways with regards to distribution of government subsidies. UTD Mosconi has a similar verticality, but is more of a mass movement in itself. Located in the far north of Argentina in Mosconi, near the border with Bolivia, the UTD has thousands of active participants, and in the neighborhoods in which the UTD is organized one gets the feeling, just walking around, that there is a parallel government. Food, barter, healthcare, childcare, beauty parlors and so forth are all organized by its participants. In order to receive their subsidies through the movement participants must be involved in a micro-enterprise. The movement holds individuals accountable for their participation, and the result is a high level of participation. The depth of *horizontalidad* is a question, and the movement organizes itself with a great deal of hierarchy, but it is not a party either. It is in a middle ground between the more autonomous movements such as MTD Solano and MTD Allen that I go into depth within this book, and the other extreme of the Peronist Piqueteros K. A number of movements still reside in this space. (In Chapter 6, the origins and histories of a few of the unemployed workers' movements are described.)

Recuperated workplaces

The dozen occupied factories that existed at the start of the 2001 rebellion grew in only two years to include hundreds of workplaces, taken over and run by workers without bosses or hierarchy. Almost every workplace sees itself as an integral part of the community, and the community sees the workplace in the same way. As the workers of the Ceramica Zanon factory in the south of Argentina say: 'Zanon is of the people.'

Workplaces range from printing presses, metal shops and medical clinics, to cookie, shoe, and balloon factories, as well as a four-star hotel, school, grocery store and daily newspaper. Participants in recuperated workplaces say that what they are doing is not very complicated, quoting the slogan that they have adopted from the Landless Movement in Brazil: 'Occupy, Resist, Produce.' *Autogestión* is the way that most in the recuperated movements describe what they are creating and how. The vast majority of workplaces have equal pay distribution and use *horizontalidad* as a way of making decisions together. The few workplaces that have variations in pay and use representational forms of decision making are almost always the newer recuperations, with workers who have not had as many years together in the workplace, and generally have not had to resist government repression to defend their recuperation (Hibachi, in Ballve and Prashad 2006). This reflects the deep connection with levels of militancy, trust, and radical democracy. The recuperated workplace movement continues to grow and gather support throughout Argentina, despite threats of eviction by the state and political and physical intimidation by the previous owners. So far, each threat has been met with mobilization by neighbors and various collectives and assemblies to thwart the government's efforts.

Over time, recuperated workplaces have begun to link with one another, creating barter relationships for their products. (Chapter 6 delves specifically into a number of workplace examples, explaining the history of recuperation and the level of day-to-day functioning, grounded in the new forms of social relationships and values being created.)

Art and media groups

Dozens of art and media groups emerged in Argentina after the rebellion and as a direct result of it. The media in Argentina is corporate-controlled, and the main network, Clarín, is one that Fairness and Accuracy in Reporting (FAIR) ranks among the top corporate-controlled media in the world (McChesney 1997).

Activists and movement participants knew from experience, or learned quickly, that the media was not going to cover their activities – and in fact that most of the time it would give out misinformation, preferring instead to cover person-on-person crimes such as robbery and assault. Within months of the popular rebellion, hundreds of groups began to form to create their own media. Some of these were relatively small, such as newsletters for neighborhood assemblies, blogs, email lists and websites for movements.[10]

In addition to the alternative print media, art groups and collectives came together to tell stories of what was taking place, as well as to participate in public discourse through intervention in public space. This took, and continues to take, the form of graffiti, sometimes referred to as 'public art' within the movements and their supporters. Groups such as GAC might stencil commentaries such as an empty plate with a fork and spoon and the words, 'Nada', or an image with a police person hitting a smaller person with a baton. Groups also came about to make documentary films and various other artistic video pieces. Plays and public performances were staged with political meanings, as well as dance pieces, performance art, painting and sculpture. However, of all the art forms photography seemed to take off the most, and is one of the forms that continue to this day.

Below are short descriptions of those art and media groups that are either discussed in this text, or whose participants were interviewed. This is merely a small sample of the many more that existed and continue to exist.

Indymedia

In the first months of the popular rebellion, activists from Brazil and Italy came to Argentina to help people who were interested in setting up an independent media source. Established in 1999, in conjunction with the global justice protests in Seattle, WA against the World Trade Organization, Indymedia (www.indymedia.org) was founded to be an open media source to report on people's movements and activist activity. From November 1999 until 2002, the time that Argentina Indymedia was established, many hundreds of Indymedia sites had been set up around the globe, from large cities in Europe and the USA to small towns in Eastern

Europe and Asia. The facilitating group of each Indymedia outlet operates horizontally and is run by volunteers. Most often Indymedia facilitation groups comprise young people who are a part of the movements, and Argentina was no exception to this. A core group of activists, some identifying as anarchists, began Indymedia Argentina with global support. For the first few years after its founding, Indymedia played an important role in sharing media and updates as to movement activity with participants within Argentina and around the world.

Indymedia also played a role in educating activists in how to tell a story or use a camera. Many of those participants who collaborated with Indymedia are now in other photography collectives or groups, such as Sub-coop (Cooperativa de Fotografos, www.sub.coop) and some work with other progressive media, such as MU and Lavaca.

For the most part Indymedia is still an active tool for movements, but much less than in its initial years. This is due in part to political parties on the Left, particularly the Trotskyist, attempting to take over the collective so often that most people have given up the fight and moved on to other projects (conversations with Sebastian 2006, and Nicolas 2009, in Buenos Aires).

The 19th and 20th

The group and monthly newspaper, *The 19th and 20th*, came about in the months following the popular rebellion and, inspired by what they experienced on those days, named their new paper after it. *The 19th and 20th* was run horizontally, using forms of consensus decision making, seeing itself as a part of the movements. The artwork and articles in the paper, for the few years that it existed, covered protests, occupations, new movements and networks, and helped to be a tool for movements as well as a reflective forum for discussion and debate.

Argentina Arde

Formed exactly one month after 19 December 2001, on 19 January, Argentina Arde came together as a group for 'counter-information'. Comprising various subgroups, including video, photography, screenings and newspaper distribution, Argentina Arde is still going at the time of writing. At its high point Argentina Arde had close to 100 people collaborating with it in various working groups, with each group meeting separately and then together monthly as a larger assembly.

Lavaca – MU

> Lavaca is a workers cooperative created in 2001 with the objective of generating tools, information and knowledge sharing that helps facilitate the autonomy of people, their organizations and movements. The way we understand autonomy is: The *autogestión* of personal and collective projects. The free flow of new forms of thinking and doing. The exercise of freedom, understood as a form of social power. So as to develop these objectives we have created a series of tools.
>
> (Lavaca 2009b)

Coop Foto

Coop Foto is a collective of photographers who met during the weeks and months after the rebellion. Most were involved with independent media and photography groups such as Indymedia and Argentina Arde, and in 2006 and 2007 they came together to form a cooperative. Coop Foto describes itself as 'HIJOS of the 19th and 20th' ('Children of the 19th and 20th'), meaning that it has internalized the new forms of social organization and is using them now in the way in which its organizes together with Sub.Coop. It describes its group and ways of relating thus:

> We equally divide the money that comes into the cooperative between paying all of us and using it to pay the rent and paying for travel and other things that help facilitate all of us working. The internet and our website plays a large role in allowing us to do all of this. We are the owners of the tools and we invent the methods. Most of all, we have the idea that we intend to reflect on the photography that we do. We produce reports, essays and news as well as have a photo archive: something similar to an agency.
>
> (Sub.coop.com)

HIJOS

As mentioned in Chapter 1, HIJOS (Hiyas y HIJOS por Identidad y Justicia y contra el Olvido y Silencio – Daughters and Sons for

Identity and Justice against Forgetting and Silence) was established in 1995 by the children of the disappeared, the victims of state terrorism during the dictatorship that governed the country from 1976 to 1983. The name HIJOS resonates with the names of other related human rights organizations such as the Madres de la Plaza de Mayo or the Abuelas (Grandmothers of the Plaza de Mayo).

Mesa de Escrache

The Mesa de Escrache works with others, specifically HIJOS, to intervene in society and public space on issues related to dictatorship, memory and forgetting. Similar to HIJOS, participants in Mesa de Escrache speak to society, rather than looking to the state to solve society's problems or even to hold those who tortured accountable.

Grupo de Arte Callejero

Grupo de Arte Callejero (GAC) may only have eight core members, but the effect of its work can be felt all over Buenos Aires and beyond. GAC also includes many dozens of volunteers in the creation of all of its projects. The core members are designers and photographers who use everyday communication tools to communicate social and political issues, often related to state repression and memory of the dictatorship. As mentioned previously, as with HIJOS and Mesa de Escrache, GAC is for memory and against forgetting. It collaborates with dozens of human rights groups, the unemployed workers' movements and recuperated workplaces.

Conclusion

Most of the above groups and movements could be book topics in and of themselves. I cannot possibly give justice to what each group does and desires. However, this chapter is the beginning of a discussion of the various movements so as to create a general outline of what they are creating and how, what they are breaking from, and ways that relate to questions of longevity and the success of social movements and new social relationships.

THREE
Horizontalidad

'*Horizontalidad*', 'horizontality', 'horizontalism', 'commons', 'flat spaces of communication', 'from below and to the left', 'where the heart resides'[1] – all are words and expressions that have come to embody the social relationships and principles of organization in many of the new autonomous social movements throughout the world. Some social movement thinkers use variations on this same idea, with concepts such as radical democracy (Day 2005), direct democracy (Chatterton and Pickerill 2010), participatory democracy (Polletta 2002), and other forms of popular or people's power (Esteva 2008). Most recently this has been seen with the Democracia Real Ya! movements in Spain, the movements in Greece that are using ancient Greek to speak of direct democracy, and the Occupy movements throughout the USA and globe now calling themselves horizontal or, in a number of US cities, speaking specifically of horizontalism.

This chapter describes what this new social relationship is, often using the words of the people creating these relationships, and analyzes its longevity and challenges. It is this new practice, combined with the creation of alternative means of exchange and value (De Angelis 2007), located in a space that is a liberated territory (Zibechi 2008a), that forms the new revolutionary politics that is creating new subjectivities in the day-to-day. People making decisions together is an integral component of the day-to-day revolutions taking place. Without flat planes of communication for decision making, new social relationships and subjectivities cannot be created. It is only with the desire for, and walk towards, open participation and nonhierarchy that people are able to create themselves and their communities anew; where the future desired can be prefigured in the present.[2]

The movements I discuss in Argentina articulate these new social relationships as both means and ends, like the utopia

Photo 4 Solution – Autogestión (self management/administration)

painted by Eduardo Galeano[3] and repeated by so many in the new movements:

> Window on Utopia
> She's on the horizon, says Fernando Birri. I go two steps closer, she moves two steps away. I walk ten steps and the horizon runs ten steps ahead. No matter how much I walk, I'll never reach her. What good is utopia? That's what: it's good for walking.
>
> (Galeano 1993: 326)

This walk that Galeano describes is how people see the process of changing as a part of the change itself. It reflects the need for decision making and new relationships to allow for this walk. This concept is expressed also by the Zapatistas with the idea of *Caminando preguntandonos* ('walking we ask questions'), which originated in a Mayan folktale and a story that they retell regularly. While in Chiapas, I too heard people refer to this story as a way of explaining how the Zapatistas make decisions:

Many stories ago, when the first gods – those who made the world – were still circling through the night, there were these two other gods – Ik'al and Votán.

The two were only one. When one was turning himself around, the other would show himself, and when the other one was turning himself around, the first one would show himself. They were opposites. One was light like a May morning at the river. The other was dark, like a night of cold or cave.

They were the same thing. They were one, these two, because one made the other. But they would not walk themselves, staying there always, these two gods who were one without moving.

'What should we do then?' the two of them asked.

'Life is sad enough as it is,' they lamented, the two who were one in staying without moving.

'Night never passes,' said Ik'al.

'Day never passes,' said Votán.

'Let's walk,' said the one who was two.

'How?' asked the other.

'Where?' asked the one.

And they saw that they had moved a little, first to ask how, then to ask where. The one who was two became very happy when the one saw that they were moving themselves a little. Both of them wanted to move at the same time, but they couldn't do it themselves.

'How should we do it then?'

And one would come around first and then the other, and they would move just a little bit more and they realized that they could move if one went first, then the other. So they came to an agreement that – in order to move – one had to move first, then the other. So they started walking, and now no one remembers who started walking first because at the time they were so happy just to be moving …

And they were going to start walking when their answer to choose the long road brought another question: Where does this road take us?' They took a long time to think about the answer, and the two who were one got the bright idea that only by walking the long road were they going to know where the road took them. If they remained where they were, they were never going to know where the long road leads.

(Marcos 2001: 17–20)[4]

So, walking they ask questions, or questioning they walk. This is the inspired way of doing things, in both the autonomous communities in Chiapas and the autonomous movements in Argentina. It is also in this way that the forms of decision making and governance take place. There is no rigid structure except that all participate, and over time participate increasingly; through participation we find new modes of participation. It is an open process that allows for more participation and agency, yet more and different participation, then changed people which, again, leads to new forms of participation.

Emilio, a participant in the movements in Argentina, described this process of decision making, and *horizontalidad* in particular, as something that is both a 'tool and a goal', reflecting that full participation of equals cannot happen yet since society is not equal; he says that these processes are used to try to create a situation where people can become more free and the process more meaningful. In this way *horizontalidad* is a tool for liberatory relationships. Emilio ended our conversation by saying that full achievement of *horizontalidad* would mean true freedom, with decision making and participation being central concepts to the creation of that freedom.

This is the rupture, and as it manifests itself in how people are relating to one another day-to-day, it is the base from which they relate to one another. Past practices of having a leader occur less frequently in movements in Argentina. It is often not so much a collective decision (to no longer have hierarchy) as much as an emergent way of relating directly with one another. As Claudia, a movement participant and an alternative media activist and organizer, explained:

There are more than 100 similar communities that not only organize as assemblies, but they also are engaged in impressive struggles, deeply interesting, and they don't speak of autonomy or autonomous people, neither do they speak of *horizontalidad*, there is not pompous discussion of *horizontalidad*. Instead, they do it – they engage in it in practice. There are no leaders and everyone is equal to each other. They do not talk and talk about the theory of struggle – they do it. I think that these ideas – *horizontalidad* and autonomy – function and continue in lived experience, and I also think, paradoxically, that there are many people who were active in 2001 who do not see this, or do not understand: they do not see that there are all these new phenomena that are a continuation of the practice from the 19th and 20th of 2001 – they are continuing to do in practice what others are still talking about.

(Conversation in downtown Buenos Aires, late 2009)

In each country and region there is a unique rejection, specific to that region and history, but what is in common is the rejection of political parties, from the Left and Right, dictating how things are to be done. It is a rejection of aspects of representative democracy, whether manifest in voting for a progressive or Left candidate, or in rejecting a system of clientalism or *caciques*, as seen in Argentina and Mexico respectively. It is a rejection of homogeneity. It is a rejection of imposed values, ideas and decisions. Emergent is active participation, sometimes outside formal government organizations, sometimes with some relationship to them. At the heart of this rejection and various levels of participation lies the question of how the movement avoids dictation from above. El Vasco, from MTD (now renamed Movement for Social Dignity) Cipolletti, explained the relationship to the state and the struggle to maintain autonomous forms of decision making as a conscious process:

It is a complicated relationship, it is a difficult one, but there are certain questions that for us are really clear in this respect. With the state, what we can take from them we are going to take, and while we are taking what we can we are not going to allow the state to place any conditions on us or our practice, and our own social construction. In this we have something like a red light that goes off, an alarm. Whenever we feel that there is any sort of conditioning happening, we run fast the other way.

(Conversation in Cipolletti, Patagonia, late 2009)

Practicing *horizontalidad*

Neighborhood assemblies

People in the neighborhood assemblies first met to try to discover new ways of supporting one another and meeting their basic necessities. Many explain the organization of the first assemblies as an *encuentro* (a gathering or 'finding each other'). People were on the streets, they began talking to one another, saw the need to gather, and began, street corner-by-street corner, park-by-park, intersection-by-intersection. As Pablo, a middle-aged participant in the neighborhood assembly of Colegiales, explained:

> This did not obey an ideological decision; people simply met on a street corner in their neighborhood with other neighbors who had participated in the *cacerolazos*. For example, in my assembly in the neighborhood of Colegiales – and I know many other cases – someone simply wrote on the sidewalk in chalk: 'Neighbors, let's meet here Thursday night.' Who wrote this, no one knows. In the first meeting there were maybe fifteen people, and by the next week it was triple that. Why did it increase in this way? It was not an ideological decision or an intellectual, academic or political one. It is like asking, why did the people go out to *cacerolas*? It was the most spontaneous and elemental thing, to go out in the street and meet others on the corner. It is not that there was a decision to be horizontal, it is not that there was a decision to use direct democracy because there were people who thought up direct democracy, it was not a decision. We simply came together with a powerful rejection of all that we knew ... and with a specific decision that 'we are going to do things for ourselves'.
>
> (Conversation in Colegiales, Buenos Aires, 2003)

The space of the assembly, as the holding of a space and opening of a territory for creation, is a key part of the new movements' politics. The occupation and use of space by those in the movements, along with horizontal practices, is a part of what allows for the creation of these new revolutionary social subjects. Martín describes this as follows:

> The feeling shared by those of us who want to engage in politics is that there is no political scene, that there is no place to make the move – that's the impression. This is why the assembly is held on any street corner. Since there are no institutions, not even a club, church, or anything, the assembly meets on any corner, and in the street even. When this new form of politics emerges it establishes a new territory, or spatiality. It is at first

defined by a single moment in time and space, with the first minimal number of coordinates necessary to build a territory.
(Conversation in Colegiales, Buenos Aires, 2003)

As mentioned previously, neighborhood assemblies all began with people meeting on street corners, often occupying the street itself, at an intersection. Over time some assemblies moved into buildings that they occupied or into parks, but most of the hundreds that emerged the first year or two involved the holding of space in the street. What this looked like is dozens or hundreds of people standing in a circle, sometimes a few people deep, sometimes with a microphone or megaphone, though often not, all looking at one another and talking about what they desired, and making plans to meet their own and each another's needs. When the weather got colder assemblies would often light fires in the intersection, both warming those participating as well as notifying people in the neighborhood that the assembly was taking place.

Inter-assembly coordination: interbarrial

In the first two years after the 19th and 20th, there were attempts by those in the neighborhood assemblies to network with one another and form an assembly of assemblies, using forms of *horizontalidad*. There were numerous *interbarriales* (inter-neighborhood) gatherings held generally in the central park, Parque Centenario, in downtown Buenos Aires. This experience points to one of the areas where *horizontalidad* can be weakened or challenged if alternative methods of dealing with disruption are not organized.

In the first months after the creation of the neighborhood assemblies the Left political parties ignored the gatherings. The assessment was that they were middle class, and even when they were not middle class, they were not located in workplaces and therefore had no real power to change society. However, over time the parties changed their line, and neighborhood assemblies became a project for the parties to 'enter' and try to either win over into their party or to destroy. This was done first with the *interbarrial*, and reflects some of the challenges to the particular form of *horizontalidad* used in the assemblies:

The gatherings were run with a facilitator, but with very few rules or guidelines set out by those participating in advance. This resulted in all sorts of chaos and disruption, for example with regard to the agenda. Topic areas way outside the purview of the gathering would be raised, such as a call for the end of US imperialism, that political party members then would insist was agreed upon at that *interbarrial*. Of course most participants were not pro-imperialist, but neither had they gathered to discuss US policy. Sometimes a debate on whether or not to add something to the agenda would go on for an hour. Then, if it was added to the agenda, a similar lengthy debate on the topic and the exact language to use could last another hour or two. It was through maneuvers such as these that the parties would dominate or sidetrack conversations. The ways in which the parties participated in the *interbarrial* was also insidious. They would invent neighborhood assemblies where only they were participants, and since there was no 'rule' as to which neighborhood was allowed to participate, these false assemblies entered the gatherings. Over time, people from the neighborhoods just stopped attending the *interbarrial*. The political parties, combined with a lack of process within *horizontalidad* to deal with disruption, destroyed the *interbarriales* by attrition.

Some people also shared the perspective, usually upon reflection, that there was too loose a consensus process and not enough structure to the *interbarrial*. As of 2006, one began to see more structure in assemblies, as well as people participating more confidently in simply calling out disruptive behavior. In some instances the political parties were told that they could not participate after being disruptive.

Unemployed workers' movements

At the *piquetes* (road blockades), people used direct forms of decision making and began creating new social relationships, which in many places evolved into what are now generally known as MTDs, or a similar variation such as UTDs (Union of Unemployed Workers). From the *piquete*, many groups became movements with many other visions and projects.

An event took place in the north of Argentina in the late 1990s that has taken on mythical proportions. A *piquete* was taking place, successfully shutting down a major roadway to the city, and the city agreed to negotiate with the *piqueteros*. When the city asked for a representative with whom to negotiate, the group responded that they must all be negotiated with directly. At the end of the standoff the mayor of the city flew to the *piquete* in a helicopter to negotiate directly with the group, and the *piqueteros* won. In it many of these experiences and forms of organization in the 1990s are precursors to the forms of *horizontalidad* that so many of the MTDs use now and began to use in massive forms after the 19th and 20th of December.

In almost all of the MTDs there are forms of *horizontalidad*. In those that consider themselves autonomous, the use of *horizontalidad* is paramount and linked to other forms of social creation and new relations being developed. As Maba from MTD Solano explained:

> The movement is organized under the principles of *horizontalidad*, direct democracy and autonomy. We're against vertical structures where there is someone who commands and others who obey. Everything is decided in assemblies, with consensus, always trying to reach consensus.
>
> (Conversation in Solano, 2004)

The way that participants in an unemployed workers' movement in the south of the country, in Santa Cruz, describe their form of *horizontalidad* is that there are no leaders in the group, they all make decisions together, and the way that they do this when it is time to negotiate with officials – in this instance, often the bosses of the oil refinery that laid them all off – is to have a *voz* (voice) and two *orejas* (ears). The role of the voice is to communicate only that which the group has previously empowered the person to do, and the ears are to listen and make sure that is how things are communicated. It is the ears that report back to the group as a whole, not the voice. They always send three people to negotiate: two to listen, and one to speak. In addition, they have struggled quite a bit with the question of gender division and representation, directly speaking to the fact that women often play a leading role in organizing but somehow are not proportionally represented when speaking publicly. To answer this question they now have a quota where half of all speakers must be women. This is also true when selecting the ears and voice for the group in negotiations: one or two of the people must be women. In this way they believe that a more horizontal space can be facilitated.[5]

There are countless examples of the various ways in which people in the movements are finding ways not only to make decisions together, but to use the process of *horizontalidad* as a means to create new social relationships and, in the process, create new people.[6] Neka from MTD Solano explains this process beautifully. She is a participant in the movement and was one of the founding members. She is a leader in the movements but not in the way that leadership is often understood, reflecting one of the many things that is changing. Her leadership is not reflected in talking very much or always being the one on the frontline, but by actively listening to individuals and the group, and helping the group hear themselves and one another. She has profound insights and is incredibly articulate. She argues that her insights are based in this politics of listening. The idea of listening and organizing spaces so that each person can speak and be heard is at the heart of the movements. The understanding is that we come from societies where people are not really heard, and so to listen to one another is part of creating alternatives. It is through this process that we can find common solutions and hear what each another's frustrations and desires are. Talking itself is not sufficient, but listening and hearing one another is. One of the many reasons that *horizontalidad* is not only so powerful but is being used by millions around the world, is that it is a form of making decisions together that is based on each person speaking and listening: it is a politics of listening without judgment rather than creating power over one another. Listening and facilitating the space so that people can speak and be heard is something that is respected, and often respected more than giving a compelling speech: leadership emerges from those who really listen, not just from speech making. When someone does speak in a compelling way, it opens up a path for this sort of *active* listening.

It is a remarkable thing to see, this new form of leadership. In Neka's example, she does not occupy the space but when she speaks, people listen with a depth that that is reminiscent of how the Zapatistas speak of listening and learning, which is with the heart. In explaining *horizontalidad* and what it looks like in the movement, she shared:

First we began learning something together, it was a sort of waking up to a knowledge that was collective, and this has to do with a collective self-awareness of what was taking place within all of us. First we began by asking one another and ourselves questions, and from there we began to resolve things together. Each day we continue discovering and constructing while walking. It is like each day is a horizon that opens before us, and this horizon does not have any recipe or program – we begin here ... The beginning of the practice of *horizontalidad* can be seen in this process. More than an answer to a practice, it is an everyday practice.

(Conversation in Solano, 2004)

Recuperated workplaces

Over the course of the years that I spent time in Argentina I developed a special and deep affection for certain places and people. Candido and Ernesto are two such people, and Chilavert is one such place; late one evening in 2006 I was asked to attend a meeting with them. Language is very important here, particularly in the new movements. There is a conscious attempt to reflect new experiences and relationships within language, so often even a word as simple as 'meeting' is changed to either 'gathering' (*encuentro*) or people talk of 'getting together'. 'Meeting' is a word used to describe political parties and boardrooms.

When I arrived and saw Candido and Ernesto, I knew that something was wrong and that I was somehow involved. One can just feel these things sometimes. We sat down, no *mate* on the table.[7] Candido immediately said that the workers at Chilavert were frustrated with me: my process of inviting people to the upcoming World Social Forum in Brazil was a problem, and I had not respected the horizontal decision making within Chilavert. Then there was a pause.

This conversation took place in December. The background is that I had realized at some point in early December, soon after arriving in Buenos Aires, that certain movements and groups were planning on attending the World Social Forum, since they had either planned to in advance and had fundraised for it, or they were being sponsored by other international groups. However, in 2006, most of the recuperated workplaces were not that globally connected, and even within Argentina their focus was on other workplaces, and less on other social movements, nationally or globally. The World Social Forum was not on their radar, and it was not a priority. Workplace functioning was the priority.

Having participated in previous World Social Forums, and knowing the diversity of people and social movements involved, I felt very strongly that people from the recuperated workplaces should attend. I knew that there would be people there from other recuperated workplaces that were growing throughout Latin America, many of them inspired by the Argentine example. So, rather than try to convince participants in the recuperated workplace movement to make it a priority, and feeling that time was of the essence with the Forum taking place in January, I decided to reach out to the networks of people that I knew in the USA, Canada and Europe who might be able to come up with some funding. I had come to know Naomi Klein and Avi Lewis while they were living in Argentina and working on the film *The Take* (First Run Icarus Films, 2004), based on the recuperated workplaces there. I spoke with them specifically; they agreed that people should be attending the Forum from the movements, and that they would help financially. Together we came up with the funds and they invited a few workers that they had been working with over the years from two other workplaces. I invited Candido, as one of the leaders of Chilavert, and his wife Maria Rosa, as well as two other workers from a recuperated medical clinic. My feeling was that the process of the recuperation of workplaces is one that requires the support and participation of the entire neighborhood and community. Family is key in this, and I felt that as a leader among those supporting the workplaces, Candido's wife would be a perfect part of the delegation. Also, to be truthful, I knew that they had never traveled outside Argentina and thought that a trip would be special for them personally. I knew that I was not respecting the horizontal process of the workplace. I had all sorts of explanations as to my motivations, the lack of time involved, and so forth, but in the end I made the decision that I thought was best and did not consult with the workers. I realized that I was in a bad situation.

That is how I found myself sitting before two of the workers from the factory, who were telling me that they had had an assembly and that people were quite frustrated with me. It turned out, after much discussion and debate, that they decided to keep the decision as it was but to let me know that I was way out of line, that it was disrespectful, and that Candido and Ernesto were assigned to reiterate to me their horizontal process. I was told that I needed to respect it. They make decisions together. Each has a voice and participates in all decisions related to the workplace, from who is assigned particular jobs, which bills to pay, how much to pay themselves, which events to endorse or allow to take place in the factory when it is closed. All decisions are made together, and each person participates. They are horizontal. It is *horizontalidad*.

In some recuperated workplaces, such as the pastries factory at Grissinopolis, the workers decided to move their machines into a circle so that they could face each another throughout the day, and be in a situation of horizontal assembly whenever they desired. Not all of the recuperated workplaces use *horizontalidad*, but the vast majority of them do. Those that do not still use forms of democratic decision making processes and generally avoid hierarchy, but they do not call their process *horizontalidad* (Zibechi 2006c).

In a study by the Department of Anthropology at the University of Buenos Aires, it was found that the more militant the struggle is to take over a factory, the more likely the workers are to use *horizontalidad* (Ruggeri 2010a). The same is also true for the length of time that people have worked together in the workplace. Where there are workers who have worked together for many years and established stronger relationships, the more likely it is that the workplace will use *horizontalidad*. This speaks again to the importance of trust and social relationships in the process of creating and continuing *horizontalidad*.

Challenges to decision making within *horizontalidad*

As a new form of relating and one that is dynamic, *horizontalidad* opens up a great deal of space for people to relate and make decisions, but it can also create confusion and challenges. Below I will discuss such challenges.

Horizontalidad as a process

> It's like we were saying today, in the *encuentro*.[8] We are all so full of the habits of capitalism, and it is hard to shake them off. And well, sometimes there's a *compañero* that has just joined the movement and has never felt like a protagonist, and suddenly they're elected as a delegate and misunderstands

this and thinks they're the boss. But, as we were saying today, autonomy, direct democracy and *horizontalidad* are built. We don't say 'Today we are all autonomists, we are all horizontalists', and it's a rule or law that has to be complied with – it is a process.

(Conversation with Maba, MTD Solano, 2004)

Here, Maba describes this confusion with the idea of *horizontalidad* and roles, and the process of understanding it. *Horizontalidad* is a process, and it is a challenge and new way of relating and being together, and by saying this alone it does not create the relationship. It is dynamic. It is not only not a thing, but a process that is constantly changing and requiring constant attention to make sure that it is both the intention and goal of those participating in the process. However, this is not always true – so then what?

In different assemblies disagreements and consensus are reflected and resolved in various ways. Sometimes informal discussions are organized with people to help explain the process. Sometimes behavior is called out in the middle of an assembly or process of decision making: as mentioned previously, something that has increased over the years, with more overt attempts by political parties to disrupt.

In one of the neighborhood assemblies that I participated in regularly for more than a year, Colegiales, the way in which they would reflect agreement was to sing the song from the popular rebellion, '*Oh, que se vayan todos, que no quede ni uno solo … ohhh, oh oh oh oh oh, que se vayan todos*', sometimes with people singing higher and lower and others harmonizing, making the song more melodic and generally more fun to sing, then everyone would applaud at the end. This created a wonderful unity. Sometimes the song was sung where there was disagreement too, and was used as a way of reflecting why everyone was there, helping everyone to feel a part of the process – making whatever disagreement feel less contentious, even if it still existed. It was a reminder of the process of building new relations.

Of the overall challenges to *horizontalidad* the question of what it is – a thing or a process – seems to be one of the largest. The idea that *horizontalidad* can be a thing, something that exists by stating that it does and therefore by its invocation that it is then in practice, is a massive challenge. By seeing it as a noun and not in the gerund (the '-ing') can make it stagnant, while the gerund form turns it into a moving practice. So when movement participants talk about, as Neka does (see previous chapters), the hierarchicalization of autonomy or *horizontalidad*, she is speaking to this: that declaring something horizontal does not make it so; in fact, it can do an even bigger disservice to those participating, because if they then have a disempowering experience and believe that it is part of a horizontal process, they might not continue to strive for that relationship.

Concrete nature of assemblies and the question of time

For example, something that is generally a challenge, and really difficult in my neighborhood assembly, is the amount of time it can take to come to a good or right decision, however that is defined. It often takes more time, and the decision might end up the same, but it is the process of discussion that creates real participation. To quickly come to a decision may seem more expeditious, to just vote and be done – but then you lose the most important part, which is the walk, the process of arriving at a decision.

(Conversation with Eziquiel in Paternal, Buenos Aires, 2004)

A question often raised with regard to *horizontalidad* and direct democracy is that of time. Often, people are concerned with the amount of time that an assembly can take. Interestingly, when in the form of a complaint, most of these criticisms come from those not actively participating in horizontal forms of assemblies. This is not to say that the assemblies do not take a great deal of time, because they do – and this is a real challenge – but that the critique that 'regular' people cannot participate because the assemblies go on too long often comes from the outside, not from the participants. While they may be long, for many the process as described by Ezequiel above is a part of the very democracy being created. However, there are some exceptions that can be made here, and in particular with the neighborhood assemblies and the *interbarrial*. In the recuperated workplace movements, as with the unemployed workers' movements, assemblies take a long time, or sometimes even take place in an on-and-off way over the course of days, but those participating continue in each assembly and there is not the same critique. So, what is it about the neighborhood assemblies that is different?

As described earlier in this chapter, some of the recuperated workplaces see themselves in a state of constant assembly. They are making decisions about the running of the workplace, and those decisions need to be made all the time. This happens in smaller workgroups, and sometimes with the entire workplace. By using horizontal forms of decision making all the participants speak and are involved in decisions about what to do. Workers have reflected that by participating in this way they are more, rather than less, invested and involved in the production: they are more likely to carry out a decision in which they have been an active participant. This is also the case with the unemployed workers' movements: assemblies are based on the concrete needs of the neighbors and community, and coming together horizontally is a way to meet their needs. These are survival-based needs, but also the need for affective relationships (as discussed in Chapter 4). So again, there is actually more of a desire to have assemblies, even if they are long, over not having them at all. Some participants have articulated this desire and even need – partly regarding decision making about the projects in the neighborhoods, and partly the need to find each other – to speak and really be heard, especially in a society that says your opinion does not matter, and that as a poor person or woman for example, your voice does not count. In the assemblies people find their own voices and find new ways of listening to each other. This is a fundamental part of the social creation taking place.

As mentioned previously, the projects under discussion relate to concrete matters and day-to-day living, as well as being geographically based in the neighborhoods where participants live and often do not leave; unemployed neighborhoods and workplaces also can be in the same location.

With the neighborhood assemblies the situation was a bit different. Neighbors came together as a part of the crisis and at first it was about meeting needs, and finding one another and one's voice. Within a few years the neighborhood assemblies were less about meeting concrete survival needs, in part due to the economy recovering a little for the middle and lower-middle classes, and also due to the collapse of the barter network, so while they continued as spaces of discussion, they became less concrete. This distinction with concrete productive projects is what in part led to the challenges with *horizontalidad* and the assemblies meeting at all. The complaint around assemblies meeting and people talking with nothing being accomplished became a more regular critique – and, in fact, it was true: much less was getting done. Those neighborhood assemblies that do continue are often in occupied buildings where there are regular projects and activities, or are related to workplaces, organizing *bachilleratos* (high school diploma) or other forms of classes and projects.

Additionally, the infiltration of Left political parties, as described in the sections on the *interbarrial*, led to countless assemblies that were dominated either by that particular Left group or party, or by the struggle not to allow them to dominate. The other outside disruption came from the state, at the city level usually. As is discussed further in Chapter 7, the state would offer things to the assemblies, from space to concrete goods, such that the assembly's agenda became dominated by the state's agenda, and as with the political parties, the time was consumed either with this outside agenda or resisting it. These processes took up a great deal of time, which created a real frustration that resulted in many not returning to the particular organizational form of the neighborhood assembly. To be clear, this did and does not mean an abandoning of the horizontal process, as is seen repeatedly with new groups, but it does speak to the decrease of the neighborhood assemblies as a particular form.

Leadership and power

Horizontalidad is not simply that we all have the right to speak and all have the right to vote. This is one of the components of *horizontalidad*; the rest of the components have to do with what we all can do to realize this right. Because if you have the abstract right to speak, but each time you open your mouth I insult you, and I am in a position of moral authority, or I am a guy and in this context I have more … well, you do not have the right to speak in the same way that I have, even if formally you do, so it seems that it is a culture that implies just this, to see and understand this dynamic. That for as much as you formally or in theory have the same right as I do, the form that I use every day actually deprives you of this right. It is here that we need to change the culture completely.

(Conversation with Ezequiel, Cid Campeador assembly, 2003)

Another challenge to horizontal forms of decision making and the creation of horizontal spaces is the question of leadership. Especially in the first year or so after the rebellion, people in all the different movements spoke of how this was a movement or movements without leaders. That *horizontalidad* meant, among many things, that there is no one leading. On the one hand, this was and is true: in the more autonomous and horizontal movements there is no formal hierarchy; but on the other hand, there are people who, for various reasons, hold positions of more respect, and this respect often looks like leadership. Respect of this sort might be the worker who has been around the longest and is the most talented at their job, or it the person who used to stand up to the former boss the most. In a neighborhood, with the older generation, it is often those people who resisted the dictatorship. It also can be those people who are known for standing up for the community, such as Neka and Alberto in MTD Solano, or sometimes it is as simple as the person who is really friendly and people just like because they are open. Regardless of the reason, it usually is grounded in something concrete: when this person speaks, they are listened to in a different way than others. Perhaps the person's ideas carry more weight, or maybe they are just the person for whom no one leaves the room or circle when they speak. Maybe they are the person whom individuals go to with questions in-between assemblies. The fact is that these sorts of people do exist and they are heard differently, so it is important to take this into account when discussing nonhierarchy and horizontal forms.

Over time, especially in the unemployed workers' movements, a discussion opened up in relationship to leadership, although it remained uneven. I am not arguing here that there needs to be no leadership, but that when it is not identified collectively then there can be confusion, and people might feel left out of a process or wonder why their voice is not being heard in the same way as another's. I have seen this happen in a few places: for example, when a new worker is brought into a recuperated workplace. They are joining an assembly of workers often who have known one another for years, and have most likely battled police together in defense of their workplace. They have a respect for one another that is pre-established, and the new person has to gain respect over time. If this is not discussed then, as has been expressed to me a few times by similarly situated people, the new person might feel that there is a hierarchy. Even worse, in some cases, an informal leadership that is not identified emerges, often among people who are similarly situated, which can look more like a clique or unofficial yet real leadership body. This is one of the issues addressed by Jo Freeman in her article 'The Tyranny of Structurelessness' (1972), an oft-cited work by critiques of horizontal forms of decision making. This work makes profound points in this regard, but points that – when movements are conscientious of them, such as identifying informal leadership and what to do about it – can be overcome. I have seen this conversation on leadership emerge over the years, especially in the unemployed workers' movements, and I believe that this is what has allowed some of them to grow in such breadth and depth, particularly with regard to their democratic process.

Structure of horizontal decision making spaces

Horizontal spaces do not just occur spontaneously. People come together, sometimes spontaneously, but to create a space where all people can speak and be heard with the same equality and intention requires organization and structure. How much structure and organization varies depending on the group, how long they have known one another, their relationships to each other, and so forth. For example, in the workplaces and unemployed neighborhoods there were often past relationships between people, which in many ways allowed for a more loose form of structure for the assemblies. In the neighborhood assemblies, most people spoke of meeting one another for the first time, and thus one would think that there might be a more structured assembly; but what actually happened was that, especially at the start, they did not have much structure beyond a facilitator and timekeeper. It was the unemployed neighborhoods and workplaces that created more roles in an assembly. This was in part due to the necessity of structured subgroups working on everything from production in the workplace, to bread baking, farming, house construction, direct action organizing and so forth. I found the unemployed assemblies to be more organized based on concrete areas of work, and the neighborhood assemblies a lot more free-flowing. However, when there is less organization in a horizontal space, some people try to use that openness to dominate. While I am a huge advocate of structure, there were many instances where the people dominating the discussion, or attempting to dominate it, were handled with informal consensus. For example, on a number of occasions I witnessed a facilitator asking the person dominating the discussion to please pass the microphone (real or figurative). When they refused and continued to talk, others in the assembly would let the person know that they were not going to listen any longer if they did not respect the process, and would do so in an open and fun way, sometimes by singing together, breaking into small groups to talk and take a break, or just turning around, showing their backs to the person talking. This might seem to be a hostile or aggressive tactic, but from all of my experiences of seeing this done, it often led to laughter and broke the tension that one person silencing others can hold. Sometimes the person who was monopolizing the floor would appear offended, but later they went back to participating as if nothing had happened. I also witnessed in a number of movements a similar problem: someone dominating the discussion space but with variations in the response. In these cases the person was directly called out on it during the assembly and told to stop dominating. Then later, I overheard that person being teased as being a chatterbox (*dar a la sin hueso*) or just being teased as not being able to shut up. It is a tease with an edge, but everyone seemed to think that it was funny, including the person who dominated. Granted, this means of dealing with someone disrupting an assembly requires some community or movement so that a base of trust is already established from which teasing can take place. With the movements in Argentina that are discussed in this book, this was often but not always the case.

The above described ways of handling disruption often work, but when the challenges within the assembly become larger, it is possible that they might not. Having structure, such as agreements for behavior towards one another, as some of the unemployed workers' movements have, can go a long way in helping to remind people of how to act towards each another.

Horizontalidad continues as a tool and goal

Horizontalidad is a living word, reflecting an experience that is ever-changing. Months after the popular rebellion, many began to speak of their relationships as horizontal, as a way of describing the use of direct democracy and consensus in striving for dignity and freedom. Now, years after the rebellion, those continuing to build a new and revolutionary movement speak of *horizontalidad* as both a goal and a tool. It is a goal in the sense that there is a clearer understanding now that all of our relationships are still deeply affected by capitalism, and thus by the sorts of power dynamics that it promotes in all of our collective and creative spaces, in how we relate to one another in term of gender and 'race', information and experience, and so forth. In addition, horizontalism is a tool in the sense that a danger is recognized more clearly now that language may become the politics and relationship, rather than a reflection of a living process. This is an active conversation with participants in the movements.

Horizontalidad continues to emerge in various groups and movements in Argentina, from the ways in which high school students are organizing, to the protests that emerged in 2005 against the government after a disco filled with teenagers burned down, taking the lives of dozens of teens. The families that mobilized and continue to organize on the streets around this tragedy insisted on *horizontalidad* as a form of relating to one another. Many speak of *horizontalidad* as an assumption in organizing. In this group in particular, when Left political parties came around and tried to take over its political leadership, the participants aggressively refused. Some even referenced their experience in neighborhood assemblies as a reason for distrusting these groups, as well as the forms of organization that they advocate and embody.

A very similar story was told to me by participants in a political prisoner support network that emerged a few years after the rebellion. Those who created the group and were doing the work, refused to allow Left political parties to dominate the space, sometimes to the point of active confrontation in meetings. I attended one such meeting and was happily surprised to see the power of horizontal decision making united, not allowing vertical disruption. Over time it would seem that some of the lessons from neighborhood assemblies have taken root, and just because forms of decision making are flat and horizontal does not mean that any person can come into the space and try to create another agenda. The use of *horizontalidad* is seen repeatedly in the new political groups and spaces that have been emerging since 2001. The most recent example from 2011 is of those people in the countryside living along the Cordillera in the Andes region, who have been resisting the attempts of international mining companies, and they way that they are doing this is with dozens of horizontal assemblies, using direct action and direct democracy to resist attempts to destroy their land.[9]

As Raul Zibechi explains, in a conversation reflecting on ten years since the 19 and 20th, where he lists a few of the hundreds of new groups and horizontal formations in Argentina:

> The 19th and 20th continues to occur. It happened in 2002 on the Pueyrredon bridge, and it continues, to a large extent, over this entire past decade in thousands of small actions, in the assemblies against the mines, in the popular *bachilleratos*, in the mobilizations against the criminalization laws, in the number of people against the repression. There are a ton of things that show that the 19th and 20th continues. Facts that did not have the same scale of 2001, but could have it if the conditions were there ... All this shows that the political situation is in a constant state of reconfiguration and reshaping ... continuing.
>
> (Zibechi 2010)

FOUR

New subjectivities and affective politics

Protagonism, subjectivity, and a new language for politics

This chapter brings together the emotional and subjective aspects of the new social relationships forming within the movements. These are some of the most inspiring, and for many in the movements, some of the most powerful reasons why the movements continue, and at the same time it is the area with the least amount of theoretical work in the social sciences. Perhaps it is no coincidence, then, that many of those same social scientists who dismiss the importance of emotion and subjectivity also claim that the movements have not succeeded (this is central to the discussion in Chapter 8 on the meaning of success).

One of the moments in my life when I felt the thrill of witnessing new social relationships and subjectivities in action was in the autonomous Zapatista community of La Garrucha in 2008, at the first ever women's *encuentro* of the Zapatistas. The event was organized, facilitated and completely run by women, with the exception of cooking food and cleaning, including the recently dug latrines, all of which was done by the Zapatista men. Each presentation consisted of women from the different autonomous communities presenting on various topics, from healthcare and education to organizational forms and relationships with other movements in Mexico and the world. The vast majority of the women who spoke read their pieces, all collectively written, in quiet yet confident voices. At times one had to strain to hear, even with the microphones. Then there was the participation of the new generation of young women and girls. They held themselves differently, they spoke differently – they are the new generation born of the rebellion. Much of the Zapatista artwork, particularly that year, depicts seeds being planted and new growth, things such as corn, but in place of the ear of corn is the small face of a masked Zapatista. The idea of planting seeds so as to create the new world while in this world is an often referenced metaphor in Zapatista territory. A nine-year-old who spoke, Maria Linda, is that face in the corn – she is the new seed planted that has germinated. Rather than speaking in a quiet voice from a prepared statement, Maria Linda spoke loudly, confidently and even played with the crowd of hundreds of women from all over the world. Speaking personally and directly, she began:

> I'm going to tell you about my own life and about my rights. As a girl – I have the right to do all the things that I want to. My parents have given me the right to study in the autonomous schools, so that I can learn. And they have given me the right go outside, to play, and to sing, and dance – because I think it's necessary to have fun.

The faces of the older Zapatista women behind her looked up and looked proud, and the hundreds of women filling the *galpón* (shed) broke into loud and joyful applause.

Being an actor in one's life, a protagonist, a subject and a new person are all ways in which participants in the movements in Argentina and the Zapatistas of Chiapas speak of what they are doing at the individual and collective levels.[1] As a participant in the Chilavert recuperated print shop, Candido, clarified for me in a conversation once, when I remarked how much more political he was, and that so many people seemed to be from what they were before; he shook his head and said: 'No, no Marina, I am not "political", I am "an actor and protagonist" in my life.' This movement participant was speaking about what he does and how he feels about what he does as it relates to other people, not just about the politics of doing.

Chilavert, like hundreds of other occupied factories, functions as a direct democracy, using *asambleas* (assemblies) to make decisions collectively on, for example, equal pay to questions about what to produce and how much. Clearly what they are doing is political, but for them, and many in the autonomous movements, politics alone does not suffice to describe what they are doing. They do not call themselves activists, but rather protagonists or social subjects. This is in part because the political frame as is has no space for them, for this way of creating, but also because the newness creates a need for a new language. As Emilio from an assembly and occupied bank explains:

> We're historical subjects. We are no longer passive subjects, as the system tries to make us, that same system that pushes us to vote. We are no longer marginal subjects, empty and excluded, but are now historical subjects, active subjects, participating subjects. We are actors in our own lives.
>
> (Conversation in Jujuy, near Bolivia, 2004)

It is a politics described in language based on their social relationships rather than an overarching theory, based in turn on horizontal decision-making, and what cannot be separated from this is their role as individual protagonists. The conversation on protagonism and new subjectivity was just as widespread in the *asamblea* movement. To see oneself as an actor, when historically one has been a silent observer, is a fundamental break from the past. For many in the *asambleas*, remembering the days when they did not even know their neighbor's name, let alone talk about their children or parents, simply to meet and speak to their neighbor about conditions in the neighborhood or the economy has been an enormous step. As Paula explained:

> The best part about the assemblies is that they let people do politics in a different way, one that is not partisan. This new relationship has given way to very deep changes in people's subjectivity ... If the assemblies disappeared, it wouldn't be so terrible. I say this because there's something happening in people right now, a real change – and this is really important for building whatever kind of future, it doesn't matter what kind exactly. I think that this is the most important thing with respect to the neighborhood assemblies, which is that they have created a profound change in people's subjectivity.
>
> (Conversation in Paternal, Buenos Aires, early 2003)

In neighborhoods with unemployed workers' movements there has been an equally powerful shift. A new protagonism is evident even in the way in which certain words have been given new meaning. As discussed previously with regard to Peronism, for example, the idea of 'dignity' was the idea of the 'good worker', the one who goes to work, comes home, returns to work the next day, and feels pride in this relationship to their job and selling their labor. As Peter Winn described in his book *Americas: The Changing Face of America and the Caribbean*: 'But beyond the material rewards that Perón gave to Argentina's workers was the restoration of their dignity after years of the oligarchy's distain ... Perón also gave Argentina's workers a sense of self-worth' (2006: 149).

The unemployed workers' movements have retaken the idea of dignity as one of their organizing principles under the banner of 'Dignity, Horizontalism and Autonomy'. Dignity is not related to working for an employer or anyone, it is related to one's own sense of self, what one is creating and doing with others, autonomously and collectively. This is reflected in the conversation below between two women in MTD Solano (who did not wish to be identified), who begin to describe how they broke from dependence on the state and into autonomy and dignity:

Compañera 1:　We started getting some money from the state with these protests, but in the assemblies, we discussed fighting for more than the tiny amount of subsidies they threw at us ... and that's where the whole idea of fighting for dignity emerged, fighting for freedom, fighting with *horizontalidad*.

Compañera 2:　We found each other, met each other, and started to love each other as neighbors. We discovered that we were a lot happier when we were confronting the crisis together, and a new potential developed, a new subjectivity, no?

(Conversation in Solano in 2003)

Both of these participants discuss a new sense of dignity grounded in their new individual and collective subjectivity, combined with affect, with 'love', in the words of one participant. Their discussion also reflects the need for a group to help facilitate and house this new development of emotion and politics. In discussing HIJOS and the new subjectivity arising there, Benegas puts forward the idea of the need for a group or movement to keep hold of this emerging protagonism and affect:

However, this highlights the value of the organization as a factory of subjectivities. One of the many purposes of H.I.J.O.S. is to give its members a place to be – a social space where to become social agents. Organizations complete our secondary socialization and shape our subjectivity in the specific terms of the institutions of our society. H.I.J.O.S. is not only an association to voice grievances but also an original project of building new democratic subjectivities. It is an experiment in organizing and building a network with political efficacy without forgetting the voices of its members. It gives society a generation of activists, professionals, workers, and leaders who choose to train themselves in non-hierarchical decision making and in respect for dissent – perhaps precisely what state terrorism aimed to take away.

(Benegas forthcoming)

As each new social practice and social relationship is described in this book, a deeper and more profound protagonism and subjectivity is reflected through people in the movement's growing agency and continued changing subjectivity. An individual and collective re-creation of people's ways of being that is revolutionary, that is transforming people's ways of thinking, doing, being and feeling. This new social relationship is what revolution is about, and why the social movements in Argentina are revolutionary in their day-to-day practice. As Neka from MTD Solano explains, this sense of revolution is something affective and relational:

This experience brings you in and makes you commit right from the start. Something that made a profound impression on me, related to the idea of affective politics, was listening to Luis Mattini speak on his participation in the struggles in the 1970s. He was giving a self-critique and said something like: 'We have fought against and attacked the capitalists, but we did not know how to combat capitalism. If we don't combat our way of relating, which reproduces all these things, it seems as if we are fighting an empty battle.' I think that's also one of the differences today. This day-to-day practice we constantly talk about means combating and simultaneously building other alternatives.

(Conversation in Solano, 2004)

As Rebecca Solnit so eloquently described in March 2011 for *Tomdispatch*, 'for what changes in revolution is largely spirit, emotion, belief – intangible things, as delicate as butterfly wings, but our world is made of such things. They matter' (Solnit 2011).

Affective politics

Indeed, I would go so far as to say that freedom and love constitute the foundation for spirituality, another elusive and intangible force with which few scholars of social movements have come to terms. That insight was always there in the movements I've studied, but I was unable to see it, acknowledge it, or bring it to the surface. I hope to offer here a beginning.

(Kelley 2003a: 1)

In his book *Freedom Dreams: The Black Radical Imagination* (2003b), and in subsequent interviews and articles, Kelley speaks of the importance of the use of 'love' in movements. Below is a response to a question that an interviewer asks with regard to the characterization of his work on love in movements as 'New Age'. This sort of characterization is a reflection of how many, particularly in the academic and more scholarly world, see the politics of affection and subjectivity. It is often cast as not serious, as Ellen Wilkinson (2009) describes and argues against in her article, 'The emotions least relevant to politics?', or at best as something that has use value but not standalone value, such as emotion for the purpose of mobilization (Tarrow and Tilly 2001). Kelley grounds the concept here:

I'm talking about the collective, how to deal with the community, how to change people's relationships to one another. I do invoke the term 'love', not because it's a new thing and not in a New Age way, but because it's an old thing that is rooted, I think, in a long tradition of black Christian, communitarian, radical movements. In other words, the love I talk about is the love that Dr. King invoked.

(Kelley 2003b: 60)

In the movements in Argentina, particularly in the unemployed workers' movements and neighborhood assemblies, many have used the term *politica afectiva* (affective politics) to explain part of the base from which their organizing and motivating derives. I have translated this as 'affective politics' based on the context in which participants in the movements use the term, with 'affect' meaning affection and love, a relational emotion based on one's own feelings but not separated from the group or collective.

A new area of study has emerged in the past 20 years, in particular in the USA, that deals with the question of affect. This new area includes an analysis from fields as diverse as humanities and sociology to neuroscience and business. To link as well as distinguish the politics of affection in the movements in Argentina from the wider discussions is useful in helping to gain a more specific understanding of what is meant by affective politics in Argentina. Below is a comment from a 2010 symposium on the 'Turn to Affect', which took place at Duke University (Altaf Mian 2011) – an institution where a number of scholars, including Michael Hardt, both research and write about love and affect, among many other things. In this description from the symposium, emotion generally, and individual emotion in particular, is taken out of the concept of affect. In Argentina, the emotion of the individual as well as collective is, of course, at the heart of the idea:

> Affect has become one of the key themes of contemporary
> critical thought over the past two decades. Humanities scholars
> working on affect pointedly distinguish it from emotion,
> feeling, or sentiment. The turn to affect throws full light
> on human and animal bodies, sensation, and potentiality.
> The Affective Turn has generated a rich constellation of
> perspectives on and practices of ontology, ethics, aesthetics,
> and politics. Distilling the philosophies of Spinoza, Bacon, and
> Bergson, the thought of Gilles Deleuze is at the forefront of this
> nascent turn to affect.
>
> (Altaf Mian 2011)

A different sort of description and experience of affective politics in Argentina is explained by Martín, from the neighborhood assembly of Colegiales. Through looking at affect and love from the perspective of the Argentine experience, we can begin to come to a deeper understanding of the framework and base for organizing, and hopefully contribute to larger conversations

on affect and the importance of emotion and love in the process
of affective politics:

> I feel like a different person, happy, although still with
> uncertainties ... I have a lot of faith because some of the things I
> am saying, I hear other people saying all the time too, and I feel
> like I'm part of a time of change. When people feel like there
> are others who are feeling similar things to us, especially when
> coming from different situations and places, it helps us feel more
> comfortable, it really is an amazing feeling. This new political
> action is based on trust and wakes up people's emotions. I
> believe that this is the revolution that's happening now.
> (Conversation in Colegiales, Buenos Aires, 2003)

This description is all about individual and collective feelings
of affect and love. When speaking about love, Michael Hardt
resonates more with the framework of affective politics in Argentina than the previous discussions on affect. For this reason, this
section, which relates to the work of Hardt, will do so regarding
his discussions of love rather than affect. It may be useful here
to bring the writing of Hardt and Negri on love together with
the Argentine concept of affect, thus arriving at more of a com-
plimentary understanding. Hardt and Negri's book *Multitude*
(2004) ends with a passage that grounds the ideas around which
they are organizing in a base of love – a passage that sounds very
much like it could have come from a participant in an autonomous movement in Argentina:

> We can already recognize that today time is split between a
> present that is already dead and a future that is already living
> – and the yawning abyss between them is becoming enormous.
> In time, an event will thrust us like an arrow into that living
> future. This will be the real political act of love.
> (Hardt and Negri 2004: 358)

I describe below an example of the discussion of affective
politics guiding a particular event in which I participated in
Argentina. In January 2004, close to 1,000 people participated
in four days of horizontal discussions and exchanges. This
gathering, called 'Enero Autónomo' (Autonomous January)

took place on a dozen acres of occupied land outside Buenos Aires. 'Enero Autónomo' was a space for sharing practices and ideas in the different movements throughout the country, as well as with some invited guests from movements such as Bolivia's Mujeres Creando (Women Creating), Brazil's Movemento Sem Terra (MST, Landless Movement), the Mapuche of Chile and the Mexican Zapatistas, to name but a few. The intention of the four-day exchange was to do exactly that – exchange and gather – and perhaps deepen some experiences and relationships along the way. The guiding principles were *horizontalidad* and *politica afectiva*. Autonomy was a theme, as was *autogestión*, but the ways of facilitating and motivating these relationships was based in open, direct communication, grounded in trust and love. The gathering was incredibly successful, from the new relationships developed, the ways in which each discussion was handled, to how food, clean-up and camping was coordinated. Below is something I wrote with a *compañero*, which was distributed around the world on activist websites, listservs and email. It is because of the widespread circulation of this dispatch that I include it here; it speaks to the global resonance of the love and affective base in social creation:

Imagine nine hundred and forty people sharing practices and theories in a truly horizontal manner. Imagine that all are participants in anti-capitalist struggles representing more than ten countries. Now imagine that all consider themselves and their practices autonomist. All are gathered to share in the love and passion of changing the world from a base of direct democracy and horizontalism. Imagine women and men, Indigenous and European, young and old. Imagine hundreds organized in Unemployed Workers Movements (MTDs) from Patagonia, Buenos Aires, and Salta, in neighborhood assemblies from Buenos Aires to Mendoza, in indigenous movements of Mapuche in the South of Argentina and Chile to Guarini in the North of Argentina, together with a myriad of autonomist collectives from around the globe, including Mujeres Creando (Women Creating) from Bolivia and the Landless Peasants Movement (MST) in Brazil. Imagine all of this and so much more ... You are now in the Ronda de Pensamiento Autónomo (Gathering of Autonomous Thinking),

in Roca Negra, Argentina, otherwise known as Enerno
Autónomo (Autonomous January) ... The depth and variety
of conversations about autonomy, freedom, horizontalism,
and consensus is beyond description for us, as it is still, quite
literally, beyond our imagination ... One of the things we have
all been learning is the power of collective imagination. As
difficult as it can be to place one's self in a single experience
of another, when we collectively discuss, learn, listen, and
exchange, we begin to be able to imagine in a new way. It
is no longer the 'I' or the 'me', but a new we, a new way of
imagining. As one compañera so eloquently closed one of the
last workshops, 'In these four days ... in our imagination ... in
our creation ... we are another world.

(Sitrin and McCrossin 2004)

In a dialogue between Michael Hardt and Lauren Berlant in
2011, during an event under the title, 'On the Commons; or,
Believing-Feeling-Acting Together', both scholars and writers
spoke on the question and importance of love in politics and a
love-based politics. Hardt, responding to the question 'What is
it about love that makes it a compelling or politically interesting
concept?', responded in part:

Another thing that interests me is how love designates a
transformative, collective power of politics – transformative,
collective and also sustained. If it were just a matter of the
construction of social bonds and attachments, or ruptures
and transformation, it would be insufficient. For me it would
have to be a necessarily collective, transformative power in
duration.

(Hardt, in Davis and Sarlin 2011: 1)

Berlant's response to the same question was as follows:

I often talk about love as one of the few places where people
actually admit they want to become different. And so it's like a
change without trauma, but it's not change without instability.
It's change without guarantees, without knowing what the other
side of it is, because it's entering into relationality.

(Berlant, in Davis and Sarlin 2011: 2)

Both descriptions of love as transformative, relational, and a part of the creation of new subjectivities is how those in the movements also speak of affective politics. Diego Benegas, a participant in HIJOS, wrote a book on the new forms of politics and organizing within the group, linking it to the new, more autonomous social movements in Argentina. Central to his argument is the importance of affect and the new subjectivity that is actively created in the movements and groups. While much of his work is psychoanalytic, dealing with questions of recuperation from collective trauma, the centrality of affect to this as well as radical forms of direct democracy, as with *horizontalidad*, are useful for this book. With regard to the question of affect, he wrote: 'In turn, we might find a different sense of what it means to do politics if we look at the affective aspects of political intervention' (Benegas, forthcoming). His work is ethnographic and participant-observer, and contains many firsthand observations and quotations. Of one conversation he relates:

> 'H.I.J.O.S. is an affective-political organization', a member of H.I.J.O.S. Cordoba told me in 2002. I would learn later that it was a much-discussed issue: the 'affective' component has a central, crucial place ... For example, providing emotional support for its members can be an original and powerful political intervention, for, in order to change global structures of economy and politics, it is imperative to start building new subjectivities – which implies changing affective structures. This under theorized aspect of H.I.J.O.S. political action is indeed an attempt to 'change the world by changing the people', an approach going beyond traditional political work.
>
> (Benegas forthcoming)

Members of HIJOS whom I interviewed explain their motivations in a way that is very similar to what Benegas found. As the conversation below reflects, they speak of a love and trust-based politics from which they organize and live:

Paula: Our understanding of the idea of *el compañero* enables us to shield ourselves when we're up against a difficult situation, to come together with such great unity that we can withstand anything. We've taken some really hard hits. We were born of a rupture, and it happened to us again. We've endured all of this partly because of our profound political conviction, but humanism is the real key. We really believe that the only way we can achieve a revolutionary process, unleash a revolution, is by changing as human beings first. We try to build within ourselves that which we're trying to achieve for society. We believe that if we don't live our lives in the way we desire and seek to live, then we'll never achieve our goals.

Gonzalo: Above all, what we have come to understand is what Che used to say: a revolutionary is moved by great feelings of love, and we must create this love between *compañeros*. Love is the link, because what we're struggling for is of such great importance – it is so important that it is only natural to feel love among ourselves.

(Conversation in Once, Buenos Aires, 2004)

This change, towards seeing the importance of affect with love and the creation of new relationships and new subjectivities, is seen with HIJOS and in Benegas' work. Specifically, the importance of affect and trust as a foundation allows us to see a before and after, a change in the ways in which groups were organizing, and the intentionality behind this organizing. By way of example, a HIJOS participant who filmed one of the *escrache*s observed:

After the escrache, the demonstrators walked south, silently, folding their flags. Solana made a short film of their feet walking away; she does not know why. She only says it was a moment strongly charged with affect and intense feelings. Once released, the escrache's 'sweeping power' (Mesa and H.I.J.O.S. 2003) leaves the participants in a particular affective state. In her 30s, Solana had a long history with H.I.J.O.S. and organized several escraches. This one felt different; it was like a reunion with dear friends. She was also happy for the neighbors' support. She felt them to be warmer than previously; many were out, greeting them.

(Benegas forthcoming)

This change that Solana observes is the difference in reception that HIJOS received after 19 and 20 December 2001. They began to organize *escraches* in the late 1990s (as described in Chapter 2), but it was only after the popular rebellion that people came out to participate in their action, and if not to actively participate, then at least to support them. This change in support is part of the break with past ways of relating in society. It is a part of breaking with fear of the dictatorship – the *no te metas* described previously. This change in people is a part of the intention behind HIJOS' actions, to change the way that people in society see and relate to each other. The role that affect plays is internal to the organizing in HIJOS as well as meant to be a much broader relationship to and for society more generally. This approach to doing politics goes beyond traditional political organizing, which attempts to change society without changing the subjective structures that reproduce it (Bourdieu 2000). Pierre Bourdieu (2000) criticizes traditional Marxism and feminism for their exclusive trust in 'raising consciousness' in order to produce social change; he argues that changing deeply embodied structures of domination requires practices of counter-training that, by repeated rehearsal, confront the habitus' powerful inertia. It is precisely this that the movements are doing, not in the order in which Bourdieu writes of it; it is not using affect to change structures of domination, but as the movements become grounded in affect, supported and facilitated by *horizontalidad*, those structures begin to fade.

For the new social movements, changing social relationships, and doing so based on trust, love, and creating new people, is at the heart of the movement, which they state explicitly:

> For now, we will say that affect is the building block of this utopian construction where everyday practices and relations are conceived as the site for a social intervention that consists mainly in trying, exploring, and inventing, new forms of sociality.
>
> (Benegas forthcoming)

As Martín reflects, expressing not only the heart of affective politics but also the openness and newness of it all, as a process to be created and discovered:

It's about being able to create a new relational mode. What happens is that no one knows exactly how to do it, no one knows – and it requires a collective process, it's not like someone is going to come over and tell us how. One thing we have called this is 'affective politics', politics of affect, politics of affections ... When this new form of politics emerges it establishes a new territory, or spatiality ... and how is this sustained? It cannot be supported through ideology. In the beginning, the assembly consisted of people from all walks of life, ranging from the housewife who declared, 'I am not political', to the typical party hack. But there was a certain sensibility, I don't know what to call it, something affective, and that generated a certain kind of interpersonal relationship between people. It generated a way of being and a certain sense of 'we', or oneness that is sustainable ... Speaking of affective politics, we are talking about a lot of different things for which previously there were no words. It's a new language, and this new language constitutes a new space.

(Conversation in Colegiales, Buenos Aires, 2003)

Decision making and affective politics: the Southern Non-Violent Coordinating Committee and the feminist movement

These new social relationships based on trust and creating new people are inextricably linked to horizontal forms of decision making. For example, as a *compañero*, Toty, from MTD La Matanza explained:

This new way of relating is really important to us. It permits us to have a really diverse movement. There are many compañeros who do not think like many others, compañeros with distinct positions and ideas, but this is not a problem in any way since we love each other. We can have really difficult discussions and disagree, but we all stay part of the organization. We try to love each other. It's difficult. Imagine being in a neighborhood like La Matanza, which is full of really tough men, men who have lived and still live a violent, macho life, and we're talking about new loving relationships. No, it isn't easy, not to talk about or even practice. This is part of our changing culture, and as we change we notice how much we really need to. There's a huge desire to all be together in the movement and to continue creating together. In some ways this is the most important step that we've taken, because we're conscious of what we're doing, and that makes us realize how necessary it is.

(Conversation in La Matanza, 2004)

Toty refers here and throughout our various conversations to the importance of decision making and participation in social transformation. This is also true for the other MTDs and neighborhood assemblies. *Horizontalidad* as a tool and goal for new emancipatory relationships is key, and affective politics is fundamental to making this possible.

Benegas (forthcoming) describes the reasons behind the use of *horizontalidad* in HIJOS as integrally linked to the base of affection and trust: 'Horizontality emerged from the conviction that the only way to change structures of power at high levels (state, national institutions) is to change structures of behavior, feelings.'

The connection of directly participatory decision making and new subjectivities cannot be discussed without a discussion of the Civil Rights Movement in the USA, specifically the Southern Non-Violent Coordinating Committee (SNCC), and the early radical women's movement. As Frances Polletta puts forward in the book *Freedom is an Endless Meeting: Democracy in American Social Movements*:

> The process of decisionmaking makes for a greater acceptance of the differences that coexist with shared purposes. In fact, consensus often aims not to arrive at a position or policy agreed to unanimously in all its particulars, but to delineate a range of individual positions that are consistent with a group position.
>
> (Poletta 2002: 9)

Later in the book, she goes on to describe:

> Finally, friendship was the main interactional model for participatory democracy in SDS [Students for a Democratic Society], in early women's liberation collectives, and among SNCC staff. The striking thing in these democracies was the informal quality of decisionmaking and its intimacy.
>
> (Polletta 2002: 19; emphasis in original)

Both SNCC and segments of the radical women's movement of the late 1960s and early 1970s, in various ways and at various times, saw either beloved community or prefigurative politics creating the desired future relationships in the present as a core part of what they were doing. Decision making was one part of this new social relationship. The role of caring, trust and active listening as an integral part of the politics is something that both movements strove towards. Moreover, in both instances the social science literature makes a great many references to these topics, and there would seem to be a general consensus that emotion was involved in the movements; however, at the same time, there is little in-depth work on either the issue of beloved community as a means and method of organizing or motivating the participants in SNCC, or a profundity (i.e. detail) in the literature of the Second Wave feminist movement.

This second example is even more strange since it is the movement that is most attributed to bringing 'emotion' and subjectivity into discussions of social change and creating new social relationships. The phrase 'The personal is political', one of the slogans of the radical feminist movement, is quoted so often but rarely explored in its meaning, intention, and practice. It is beyond unfortunate that these two areas have not been explored in greater depth in the literature, since I believe that social movement actors and students would benefit tremendously from analysis of how affect and subjectivity were a part of organizing day-to-day, and where they were not.

The personal is political

As mentioned previously, 'The personal is political' is not only a radical feminist phrase, but also one that is often repeated with regard to the movement, although the intention behind those quoting it, and the original meaning put forward by Carol Hanisch in her 1969 article under that title, are quite different. I am not sure that it matters that much that the intention and the interpretation are different, because in the end I do believe that the radical feminist movement did believe very much in the importance of changing subjectivity in the movement, as well as seeing the importance of personal relationships in political organizing and movements. That said, the original article written by Hanisch addresses the consciousness-raising groups in which women were involved:[2] groups that addressed each woman's daily existence in society, at work, in her personal and familiar relationships, and then this was interpreted in the various oppressive ways that it can play out – thus women's personal lives were in fact political (Cahill 2006). This is in fact true. However, it is also different from arguing that we need to make our political relationships more prefigurative, therefore adding a personal component to the political. Based on the women's movement organizing separately due to oppressive relationships, one can infer that the subjective is key in organizing: that we need to actually prefigure the relationships that we desire, and that the oppression of women is not a part of this. Ultimately the conclusion that 'the personal is political' is one that many feminists would agree with, and in the interpretation that the movement we need to build must include subjective personal relationships that are based on trust and love. (Again, it is important to clarify that this was not the original intent of the slogan.)

Taken together, the beloved community and trust base from which SNCC organized, and the importance of social relationships in the women's movement, provide a strong base for understanding the desire for affective politics and new subjectivities in the movements in Argentina and around the world today.

Beloved community

> But SNCC's participatory and consensus-oriented style also reflected a powerful ideological impulse. From the beginning, the group sought to operate as a beloved community that would transcend race as well as hierarchies of all kinds. To operate in radically democratic fashion was to prefigure the radically democratic society SNCC wanted to build on a grand scale, to make the means reflect the ends.
>
> (Polletta 2006: 275)

In the past few years, Grace Lee Boggs, a lifelong activist in numerous struggles including civil rights and black power, has begun to re-examine some of the basis for organizing in the Black Power movement, and specifically is looking at the concepts of beloved community as an area that today should be explored more deeply:

> In the 1960s I didn't pay much attention to Martin Luther King, Jr. My own social change activities unfolded in the inner

city of Detroit. So I identified more with Malcolm X than with Martin. Like most Black Power activists, I viewed King's notions of nonviolence and beloved community as somewhat naïve and sentimental. Thinking back over these years, I can't help wondering: Might events have taken a different path if we had found a way to infuse our struggle for Black Power with King's philosophy of nonviolence? Is it possible that our relationships with one another today, not only inter- but intra-racially, would be more harmonious if we had discovered how to blend Malcolm's militancy with King's vision of the beloved community? Could such a synthesis have a revolutionary power beyond our wildest dreams? Is such a revolutionary power available to us today? King constantly pointed out to those in the freedom movement that their refusal to respond in kind to the violence and terrorism of their opponents was increasing their own strength and unity. He reminded them and the world that their goal was not only the right to sit at the front of the bus or to vote, but to give birth to a new society based on more human values ... This is what true revolutions are about. They are about redefining our relationships with one another, to the Earth and to the world; about creating a new society in the places and spaces left vacant by the disintegration of the old; about hope, not despair; about saying yes to life and no to war; about finding the courage to love and care for the peoples of the world as we love and care for our own families. King's revolutionary vision is about each of us becoming the change we want to see in the world.

(Lee Boggs 2004)

As if responding to Lee Boggs's reflections, Neka from MTD Solano discusses the importance of love and affect in what they are creating in the movement and how:

We have put all of this together with patience and a lot of love and affection. Without this foundation, it would be impossible. To get together, get to know one another, and know that we struggle together, creates a lot of affection. This is really powerful and important. I believe that if there's one thing that sustains us in the movement, it's this relationship of affection. Sometimes we quarrel, but since we love each other, we can move forward.

(Conversation in Solano, 2004)

FIVE

Power and autonomy: against and beyond the state

It is the evening of 21 December 2001. Hundreds of thousands of people are in the streets of Buenos Aires, watching the president and Minister of the Economy take off in a helicopter. They have resigned. Dozens of government officials and members of the judiciary have resigned. If they appear anywhere in public they are followed and harassed. Despite the state of siege, the people dominate the streets. They are singing and greeting one another. They are helping each other escape police repression. Cafés and restaurants open their doors to everyone in the street. Food, water and refuge are provided. Many thousands of people are in the square in front of the Pink House, the same square where the Madres de la Plaza de Mayo have been walking twice a week since the dictatorship of the 1970s, bravely demanding the appearance of their children. These protestors, now both young and old, are survivors of the dictatorship and children of the dictatorship, they are all in the same square. All children of the same history. They are proudly and bravely demonstrating. In a flash, seemingly out of nowhere, police move in on a few hundred protesters, those closest to the Pink House ... the protesters run. They jump over the fence to the Pink House and get close to the doors. There is no one blocking the doors. The president has fled. Who is the government? What is the government? Should they go in? Should they take over? Is that where power is? ...

They stop.

They turn around.

They go to back to the neighborhoods, look to one another and begin ...

This chapter examines what movement participants mean whey they say that they are rejecting power, creating alternative power, and doing so autonomously. It will discuss the definitional

Photo 5 Woman worker from FaSinPat (Factory Without a Boss)

and sociological meanings of these terms, and then distinguish and expand upon these definitions. It also begins to engage with social scientists who critique the movements largely because of their different analysis of and strategy towards power.

Power

Power was no longer located in the Pink House, nor in the state. Power was (and is) being created in and among the people within the new autonomous social movements. Power – the sort of power that they desire and the power they are creating – is not located in or embodied by the state or formal institutions of power. What they are creating and theorizing are new and different forms of power. It is a living and changing power, it is power as potential and capacity. Some people have come to call it *potencia*, distinguishing the relational and active interpretation of the word. Others simply put it that power is a verb and not a noun. The state holds power as a 'thing', something to wield over others, when really power is or can be a verb: something that one creates, uses, and shares. However, there are others who say that they want to destroy power – all forms of it. Within their definition, power is seen only as something that is used against or over others. Over the past ten years, many in the movements in Argentina who first argued for the destruction of all power have arrived at a more nuanced interpretation of it (as a verb), seeing it as something positive if used in a horizontal way.

'Power over' is a form of power that has been the most widely discussed both historically and within the social sciences. It is the power held by a subject or institution, over another subject or institution. Steven Lukes defines three dimensions of power in *Power: A Radical View*:

> A may exercise power over B by getting him to do what he does not want to do, but he also exercises power over him by influencing, shaping or determining his very wants. Indeed, is it not the supreme exercise of power to get another or others to have the desires you want them to have – that is, to secure their compliance by controlling their thoughts and desires?
>
> (Lukes 1974: 23)

Here, Lukes alludes to Robert Dahl in the way that he defined power: as A having power over B to the extent that he can get B to do something that otherwise B would not do. This understanding of power is seen as a product of conflict used to determine who wins and who loses, and is based on who has the power to make decisions, including who has the potential to access decision making positions. This question of access is placed by Lukes in his category of the second dimension of power, but remains within an overarching vision of power as a 'thing', something that one can wield over another. The third dimension is similar to the second, however within this dimension power can withhold the other's ability to speak, in a sense making them unaware of the potential of their own voice. These three intricate dimensions carry different intentions; nonetheless, ultimately within these conceptions there is always someone who gains and someone who loses.

There are countless theories of power but for the purpose of this chapter, placing arguments and articulations on power in slightly more generalized categories is useful for an understanding of the ways in which it is used or created by the movements. For a common definition of this widely articulated view on power we can turn to Max Weber: 'By power is meant that opportunity existing within a social relationship which permits one to carry out one's own will even against resistance and regardless of the basis on which this opportunity rests' (Weber 1990[1962]: 117).

Frances Fox Piven also uses this definition as a starting point for a conversation on alternative forms of power, as she explained in the 2007 president's speech to the American Sociological Association. The talk, entitled 'Can Power from Below Change the World?' addressed many of the very same issues as this chapter: the new forms of power and power relationships being created and acted upon in countless places around the globe. In her address, published in the 2008 issue of the *American Sociological Review*, she asks, 'The potential for the exercise of power from below must, I believe, command the attention of sociologists. But are our intellectual traditions and institutional locations suited to conduct such inquiries?' (2008: 3).

In response to this question I would argue 'yes', but a 'yes' contingent on our listening to what is taking place within these autonomous communities. This chapter will outline what these new movements and communities are conceptualizing and acting upon, how they are implementing power from below, and how the creation of new social relationships (new autonomous ways of creating, living, and being), is a part of this new power. In addition, it will challenge various social scientists who have arrived at conclusions without enquiries into forms of power from below.

There are a few social scientists and movement thinkers who have been developing concepts of power to explain these new ways of being. One of the most well known and contentious is John Holloway, author of *Change the World Without Taking Power: The Meaning of Revolution Today* (2002). The widespread international popularity of this book cannot be overstated: many global justice groups, from Europe to South Africa and throughout Latin America, have discussed it. Holloway has been invited to speak at demonstrations, gatherings, universities, and in debates all over the globe, from Chiapas and Buenos Aires to Rostock and Tokyo. His book addresses many similarities of the issues and points that participants within the movements have been thinking about and/or doing. His book has helped to give voice to these actions. This does not mean that movement participants have begun speaking in the language of 'anti-power', or specifically about breaking the 'social flow of doing', but clear articulation of the proposition of power as potential has been pivotal to the developing discussion:

> Power-to, therefore, is never individual: it is always social. It cannot be thought of as existing in some pure, unsullied state, for its existence will always be part of the way in which sociality is constituted, the way in which doing is organised. Doing (and power-to-do) is always part of a social flow, but that flow is constituted in different ways. Power-over is the breaking of the social flow of doing. Those who exert power over the doing of others deny the subjectivity of those others, deny their part in the flow of doing, exclude them from history. Power-over breaks mutual recognition ... History becomes the history of the powerful, of those who tell others what to do.
>
> (Holloway 2002: 15)

Fox Piven, like Holloway, offers another definition of power that is also based in social relations rather than force:

> I propose that there is another kind of power based not on resources, things, or attributes, but rooted in the social and cooperative relations in which people are enmeshed by virtue of group life ... This kind of interdependent power is not concentrated at the top but is potentially widespread.
>
> (Fox Piven 2008: 5)

Argentina: power as verb

Distinct from the Zapatistas in Chiapas, where alternative power and autonomy are created in one specific geographical location, in Argentina the creation of alternative power is happening in pockets throughout the entire country. Neka from MTD Solano explains their concept of power as emerging from their reality:

> The issue isn't just physical confrontation with the system. Everyday we're forced to confront a system that is completely repressive. The system tries to impose on us how and when we struggle; the question for us is how to think outside this

framework. How to manage our own time and space. It's easier for them to overthrow us when we buy into concepts of power, based on looking at the most powerful, based on something like weapons or the need to arm the people. We're going to build according to our own reality, and not let them invade it. I think this idea of power as a capability and a potential, not a control, is a very radical change from previous struggles.

(Conversation in Solano, 2004)

This is seen with the movement creating various means for self-sufficiency, from participants building their own homes on occupied land to growing their own crops, raising livestock, and creating alternative medicine, healthcare and education – and not only creating these things together, but doing so through relationships based in *horizontalidad* and *politica afectiva*.

When discussing the unemployed workers' movement of Solano, Raul Zibechi distinguishes two forms of power: hierarchical power, and power as capacity, arguing that the movements have been breaking with the former and are now creating autonomous power. He argues against the idea of 'empowerment' as a way of describing what the movements are doing; instead, seeing it as a break with former pre-established ways of relat-ing, and 'jumping' ahead with the 19th and 20th, viewing that moment as a 'before' and an 'after', with the autonomous nonhierarchical creation as the 'after':

And people continue despite the state giving out resources or trying to get in the middle of the new projects. The sociologists call this power 'empowerment'. This is a word I do not like. It is this capacity to do things from below that broke free from all the pre-established organizations, and leapt into the public arena on the 19th and 20th.

(Zibechi 2010)

Nicolas, a young photographer who became involved in the movements after the 19 and 20th, explained:

Power used to be talked about as an enemy – power, like that of the state. But they didn't consent to this attribution. Power is seen more as a daily practice. For example, in each neighborhood there is a very bureaucratic health center that until now has been where milk is given out. But the milk never arrives, or no one knows how much milk is coming, or it is bad when the people get it. So the assemblies – I'm talking about my neighborhood assembly, which has the Córdoba and Anchorena Health Center – they observed that the health center wasn't functioning, or only worked for the people who worked there who didn't do anything, and that took away people's motivation to go to the health center. So they began to take over the health center peacefully, to begin to control it over time, to put pressure on the doctors there and on the managers to do their jobs – and they spoke of power in that way, the power of the neighborhood. Not of taking government power, or fighting from one side, but a daily power.

(Conversation in Downtown Buenos Aires, 2003)

Power and the state

Soon after 19 and 20 December 2001 the Colectivo Situaciones, a militant research and writing group in Buenos Aires, edited a book entitled *ContraPoder: Una Introdución* (*CounterPower: An Introduction*, 2001). It is a compilation of writings from a number of scholars who are involved in the autonomous social movement in Latin America and Europe. The book addresses power, what it is, and how different forms of power can be used to create freer societies. It is a book that includes tactical and theoretical arguments, many of which address specifically the question of state power.

The question of power is integral to the movements and to those thinking about change. Here, I would like to point out the theoretical importance of what the movements are creating *in practice*: as they broke with hierarchical forms of power and began creating power with one another, autonomously, they began to discuss the practical and more theoretical aspects of what they were creating. These discussions were, and continue to be, grounded in what the movements and communities are *doing*, as opposed to an abstract conceptualization of relationships to the largest power-holder in each situation: the state. This break from seeing the state as the agent of change, or even as a place for any progressive transformation, was the entry point for this new politics of power. The break with *punteros* and clientelism came hand-in-hand with the creation of new social relationships, such as *horizontalidad* and *politica afectiva*, and the development of a new value production, as seen with *autogestión*.

Theory versus practice: challenging the 'other' power of the movements

Despite the fact that social movement actors in dozens of movements and groups, representing tens and hundreds of thousands of people, clearly state that their aim is not to take state power, there are still a number of social scientists who argue that the movements have failed since they have not done so, and neither have they even attempted to create a political party that might counter the government. This argument tends to be grounded in the contentious politics framework (a paradigm that is challenged as insufficient in Chapter 8).

It is important to note that many of the people making these arguments have had little and sometimes no direct relationship to the movements. By relationships with the movements, I mean ongoing relationships where the person writing about the movement actually goes to Argentina and spends time with movement participants, in the location that they are organizing in and from: for example, in an unemployed neighborhood or recuperated workplace.[1]

The sociologist James Petras has contributed significantly to the literature on Latin America over the past thirty years; in particular, in his analysis of US foreign relations and discussions of the more contentious social movements have been important. However, his analysis is based only within the contentious framework and this, coupled with a predetermined view of what success would mean for a movement and for society, means that his perspectives on the autonomous movements have little room for maneuver. Rather than attempting to understand what the movements are doing and why, Petras' analysis begins within the context of his own goals. This limits his ability to hear and see what is really taking place and does an enormous disservice to the movements, casting them in a light that is of his creation, rather than theirs, at times even arguing that they do not exist at all. For example, in an article three years after the rebellion in Argentina, he surmised the following:

The question of state power was never raised in a serious context. It became a declaratory text raised by sectarian leftist groups who proceeded to undermine the organizational context in which challenge for state power would be meaningful. They were aided and abetted by a small but vocal sect of ideologues who made a virtue of the political limitations of some of the unemployed by preaching a doctrine of 'anti-power' – an obtuse mélange of misunderstandings of politics, economics and social power.

(Petras 2004: 29)

Earlier in the same article, with regard to the unemployed workers' movement, he notes:

Ironically the system of local personal patronage relations has been justified by referring to 'horizontal structures', an ideology popularized by the 'anti-power' ideologues. The failure of the 'horizontalist' to achieve democratic control is in large part a result of the lack of class-consciousness ('a class for itself'), which is a necessary development to exercise democratic control. Democracy in the *piquetero* movement without class-consciousness, did not lead to a sustained assembly-style political process. Instead the popular rebellions and initial militancy led to a narrow focus on immediate consumption, social dependence on local *piquetero* leaders and in some cases to political bosses. The emphasis on 'autonomy' and 'spontaneity' of the *piqueteros* by the anti-power ideologues at the time of the rebellion was the other side of the coin to the subordination of the *piqueteros* to the new local regime bosses in its aftermath. Both phases reflect the absence of organized class-conscious political education.

(Petras 2004: 23)

Then on the question of revolution, meaning in his terms, the taking of state power, à la the storming of the Bastille, Petras continues:

The leaders of the *piqueteros* rode the wave of mass discontent; they lived with illusions of St. Petersburg, October 1917, without recognizing that there were no worker soviets with class-conscious workers. The crowds came and many left when minimum concessions came in the form of work plans, small increases and promises of more and better jobs.

(Petras 2004: 28)

During my time in Solano I raised the question of power on a particular occasion: 'And what of power?'

Neka: We want to take power. [everyone laughs]

Alberto: What we believe is that transformation occurs when one begins to relate differently to one another, and begins to have other values ...

Our principal struggle is this: the generation of new subjectivities, new relationships, and ones that have to do with the new transformations. We don't think this will come about because of a revolutionary president or a revolutionary group like we've seen historically, in Russia and China for example, where they fought for values and ideals but ended up continuing the same oppression, and freedom remains absent from their lives.

(Conversation in Solano, 2004)

These two perspectives are so disconnected that it is hard to take on board the 'failure' to which Petras refers; his judgment is based on what he perceived to be the movements' goals, rather than what they actually were. There was never a desire to create a revolution like that of Russia in 1917.

When interviewed by the website Venezuela Analysis under the title 'Changing the World by Taking Power', Tariq Ali, a prominent Left political writer and intellectual, was asked: 'Without adequately addressing state power, what alternative to neoliberalism is the global social justice movement offering?' His response:

No, they have no alternative! They think that it is an advantage not to have an alternative. But, in my view that's a sign of political bankruptcy. If you have no alternative, what do you say to the people you mobilize? The MST [Movemento Sem Terra] in Brazil has an alternative, they say 'take the land and give it to the poor peasants, let them work it.' But the Holloway book of the Zapatistas, it's – if you like – a virtual book, it's a book for cyberspace: let's imagine. But we live in the real world, and in the real world this book isn't going to work. Therefore, the model for me of the MST in Brazil is much more interesting than the model of the Zapatistas in Chiapas. Much more interesting.

(Ali, in Jardim and Gindin 2004)

Similarly, for an article in *Monthly Review*, Petras stated that the goal of the movements is to take power, therefore all questions regarding success or strategy must stem from this overarching objective:

Many questions remain unanswered. Is it possible for these new movements to unify into a national political force and transform state power? Can alliances be forged with employed urban industrial workers and employees and the downwardly mobile middle class to create a power block to transform the economy? Can local assemblies become the basis for a new assembly-based socialism?

(Petras 2002)

In many ways it is difficult to argue against these writers, not because their argument is such a strong one, but because it begins in a place that is completely different from where the movements are and what they desire. Let me draw a parallel: a person may argue, for example, that my life is a failure since I do not own a home but, in fact home ownership has never been my intention or goal. There are of course strong arguments as to why I am not in a position to own a home, but how am I to engage with all of these critiques? They are in fact true – I do not have these things and there is clear evidence of that – but what about the fact that these are things I never desired? How should I enter this conversation? Am I even a part of it? Similarly with the movements, what they are doing is rethinking revolution and creating alternative paths to social and political transformation – a change that is envisioned as total, but not in the same way that Petras and others frame totality. This does not mean that the movements do not want to replace the state with something else, only that they do not want to use old and tired forms and tools of change, taking existing institutions of power and merely changing the individuals that constitute them. They clearly articulate that they are breaking away intentionally from this form of change. However, this position is not a politics of nonengagement with the state, neither is it one that argues for eliminating it; rather, it is a position that chooses to form alternative powers and new social relationships within the present, prefiguring the future.

El Vasco, from the Movement for Social Dignity in Cipolletti, responded directly to attempts made by various thinkers at conceptualizing the movements. He explained that writers and intellectuals 'fall into the trap' of framing the movements as a part of 'the political' – meaning the formal political structures of institutional power within the state, the sphere that is seen as the traditional place for politics. (This separation of the political and social spheres distinguishes the ones governing from those who are governed, which is fundamental to traditional state governance, and precisely what the movements are refusing to accept – hence the denial of representation and party politics.) El Vasco explained that, perhaps contrary to popular belief, the movements are 'political actors' within their own lives, and within their collective communities. What the movements are about is breaking down this division between the political and the social and creating a politics in everyday life.

William Robinson is a sociologist whose work focuses on the problems of global capitalism, often using the specific example of Latin America (Robinson 2008a). Unlike Petras and Ali, Robinson goes into much more detail with regards to the new movements, and his challenges address specific activities and forms of organization. However, his conclusions are much the same in that they are based in the same framework for social change. Petras' allocated goal, and the starting point for his analysis, is the taking over of the state through a political party based in the working class:

> It is quite true, as the Argentine autonomists point out, that political parties are bankrupt and corrupt and that local and global elites control the state (*'Que se vayan todos!'* – 'Out with them all!'). Yet the *autonomist* movement, with its strict horizontalism, has come no closer to challenging this structure

of elite power, nor has it been able to hold back the onslaught of global capitalism.

(Robinson 2008b)

This line of argument comes from a long tradition of social scientists and intellectuals who view power as something to take, use, and wield. For them the only way to make lasting change is through taking over formal institutions of power. The danger with this argument is not that it is inherently wrong – and of course many in the movements want to stop the 'onslaught of global capitalism' – but it is the movements' approach and method that is different. That one wants to transform society does not, and should not, mean that one must either create a political party to do so, or only see the agents of change as the traditionally organized working class. One of the main problems in the social sciences, and especially those who study social change and social movements, is that they often do not allow one to listen or see what is actually happening in particular circumstances. This is precisely because most intellectuals begin first with theory, or their analytic framework, and then look at the practice, when, in fact, theory and practice need to have a relationship that is recip-rocal (Gramsci 2000). The result of this current state of affairs is that many thinkers are negating the existence of hundreds of thousands of social movement actors.

My friends in the movements tell me not to worry about this negation of their experience, theory, and practice – that it is not a big deal – they encourage me to 'ignore these people'. The movements are continuing to create on their own agenda, within their own time, creating their own power. However – and this is where I disagree with my *compañeros* in the movements – in a world where it is all too often the academic or scholar who has the final authority on whether something is 'legitimate', and whether it should be included in the history books (something about which I have considerable critique), not engaging in a debate that insists on your obsolescence is a huge error.

Rejection of the state?

Of course, the autonomous movements' rejection of traditional, centralized and hierarchical forms of power and organization did not originate in response to the theories of people such as John

Holloway, Raul Zibechi or Colectivo Situaciones. As Emilio suc-
cinctly stated in 2003, 'We don't need anyone to impose a new
Communist Manifesto on us.' These scholars, among a number
of others globally, have played an important role in helping
to bring out the theories that are being developed in practice.[2]
Zibechi, in his book *Geneología de la Revuelta* (2003), discusses
the daily changes taking place in the Argentine movements, and
breaks down the dichotomy between reform and revolution to
discuss the new politics and new revolution. He explains:

> The state cannot be a tool for the emancipation since one
> cannot structure a society of non-power relations by means of
> the conquest of power. Once the logic of power is adopted, the
> struggle against power is already lost.
>
> (2003: 21)

Similarly:

> [T]he past century puts in relief the impossibility of advancing
> from power to a new society. The state cannot be used to
> transform the world. The role that we attribute to it should be
> revised.
>
> (2003: 202)

As emphasized previously, people in the movements desire
and are creating forms of self-management and alternative
values, using forms of *horizontalidad* and direct democracy:
they are meeting basic needs, providing food and healthcare,
with minimal relationship to the state. They are asking of one
another, as they look from side-to-side, not by looking above: as
the Zapatistas say, 'from below and to the left'. As El Vasco from
the Movement for Social Dignity in Cipolletti explains:

> Yes, I believe that the relationships with the state were always
> complex, the fact of putting forward autonomy necessarily
> implies not being trapped in the state agenda, but to look to
> satisfy concrete needs that you have and to take from the state
> all that we are able, as long as it does not get in the way of our
> sovereignty.
>
> (Conversation in Cipolletti, Patagonia, late 2009)

Autonomy

Autonomia (αὐτονομία) is the Greek word for autonomy, the combined word roots 'auto' and 'nomos' meaning 'self' and 'law' – self-governance and self-legislation. Autonomy as used by the movements in Argentina is an evolving term, as is *autogestión*. Autonomy, as discussed by contemporary social movement and social change scholars, is posed in a number of ways. One is as a positive process of self-valorization, as discussed in the writing of Antonio Negri (1996); another is in the creation of spaces 'beyond capital', as with Massimo De Angelis (2007) (as will be discussed in Chapter 6). However, a third interpretation may be seen as a negative reaction, or negation that then creates the positive, as is the case with the movements in Argentina and as articulated by John Holloway (2002).

Ana Dinerstein, a scholar who has done research with the social movements, including with the more autonomous movements such as MTD Solano, explains:

> Recently we have witnessed the emergence of autonomy as a central demand in political struggles. Autonomy is usually defined as self-determination and independent practices vis-à-vis the state. Autonomy asserts itself as organisational self-management. It is also based on the assumption that that autonomous practices can actually offer an alternative to economic and political capitalist practices and relations.
>
> (Böhm et al. 2009)

Many people I have met in the movements speak of being autonomous as something instinctive; it is a relationship, being autonomous from something, and then over time this relationship becomes something in itself and one desires autonomy as an active form of being rather than as something solely oppositional to the state. As with *horizontalidad*, autonomy comes from practice, it is a theory or an idea based in a way of being and necessitated by that new relationship. Again, necessity is a part of the creation:

> In the past we were told what projects we had to complete by different ministries. We had no autonomy to explore our own interests and do what we wanted to do. Not until we fought for

and created our autonomy were we able to do and create what we desire. We have an alternative economy, which we were able to create through this autonomy.

(Conversation with Maba and Orlando in Lanus, outside Buenos Aires, 2003)

It is this autonomy, as described above, that people are creating, an autonomy that is collective. The emphasis here is the *construction* of autonomy, not just the *response to power* using autonomy.

Argentine autonomy

I don't believe there was ever a time when we said, 'Yes, we're autonomists. This is our identity.' At one point, we were pressed to produce a more concrete definition of ourselves. I believe this was the moment when we said we wouldn't allow ourselves to become any '-ist' or '-isms'. What we're doing is constructing an experience-based practice, and it is precisely this experience-practice that speaks for itself. Since this is an open movement and one that's territorially based, with ours located in the neighborhood, we're constantly discussing what *horizontalidad* and autonomy are and what they mean for us here. It's an open and ongoing discussion.

(Conversation with Neka in Solano, 2004)

The argument on autonomy in Argentina is not that the entire country is trying to function based on their own agenda, not engaging with the state except when absolutely necessary, and, in fact, the movements discussed here are a minority of the experiences. However, there are many tens to hundreds of thousands of people involved in small, medium and large-scale autonomous social projects across Argentina, and it is these experiences that are the most interesting when examining alternative forms of power and construction.

Emilio, a former neighborhood assembly participant and now radical environmental activist, put forward a clear perspective shared by many in the movements. He is arguing for a fluid politics, one that is ever-changing, based on practice, meeting necessities, using new social relationships, and thus creating autonomy:

'What is it that we want? What is our project?' The good thing is we have no program. We are creating tools of freedom. First is the obvious: to meet our basic necessities. But the process of finding solutions to meet our basic needs leads us to develop tools that make us free. For me, that's the meaning of autonomy. If you start to think about what constitutes autonomy, and you then start to discuss the notions of *autogestión*, self-sufficiency, web-like articulations, noncommercial exchange of goods, horizontal organizing, and direct democracy, you eventually end up asking yourself, 'If we achieve all these things, will we then be autonomous?' Autonomous from what? No. If one day we achieve true autonomy, we will not be autonomists, or autonomous – we shall, in fact, be free.

(Conversation in Jujuy, 2004)

Similarly, Orlando and Maba from MTD Solano continue with the discussion of autonomy that is a social creation:

Orlando: We are not a movement about making demands, but rather about creation. We are creating projects that don't necessarily produce material goods to sell, but instead they build knowledge and professional and vocational skills. *Compañeros* learn a trade, *compañeros* in the health field strengthen their capacities to perform their work rather than assume the easy way out by simply giving a pill, and hey presto. This consists of discussing with *compañeros* the problems they are experiencing and preventing illness or whatever else ails them. Not just illness prevention in terms of 'I have a cold, a fever', etc., rather, illness prevention in all aspects of life, including the illness of capitalism. When you are ill, you go to the doctor, you are prescribed a remedy, and you take that remedy – and that remedy then gives you an ulcer. There might be something else you can do that does not affect you that way, remedies that are more natural – let's find those alternative remedies. These are things we discuss.

Maba: It's not as if the movement is responsible for solving our problems, but rather it is the workshops and skill-sharing in the movement where each *compañero* understands that he or she is the movement.

(Conversation in Lanus, outside Buenos Aires, 2003)

Autonomy and conflict resolution

As a part of the creation of autonomous ways of being, the movements are finding ways to resolve conflict without involving the state or police. I have participated in numerous assemblies, discussions, and later, reflections on the processes of conflict resolution within the movements. Here I would like to share two such processes in order to give a sense of what conflict resolution can look like within them.

Three neighborhood assemblies and two community groups, all but one of which emerged after the popular rebellion, came together in late 2002 to occupy a four-story abandoned warehouse next to the train station in Lomas de Zamora. They named this space 'La Toma' ('The Taken') after the Julio Cortazar story, 'La Casa Tomada'. Lomas de Zamora is a poor, working class neighborhood, and it is not especially safe. When a movement participant went to wait for a train at night, the assemblies usually suggested that two other people go and wait with them. In this neighborhood the various assemblies came together to open this space as a community center, holding events similar to many other assemblies such as popular education, popular kitchens, activities for children, and so forth. It is also a space where neighbors work with street teens, conducting training and education as well as simply providing a place where they are respected, listened to, and can hang out without harassment. This is not without a great deal of challenges. Many of the young people who are now participating in La Toma have never had any structure or experience of accountability, and while a few of the assembly participants have various sorts of psychological or social work training, it is by no means uniform. The process described below took place in late 2003 while I was living in Argentina.

La Toma organized frequent social activities, including evening musical performances and dances. Similar to the Zapatista communities, and later some of the unemployed neighborhoods, alcohol and drugs were prohibited in the space. The night after one such party a young woman from the neighborhood and an assembly participant approached a few members of the assembly and shared with them that she had been sexually assaulted right outside La Toma by one of the teens who recently had begun to attend the social events. The assembly members who were told decided, together with this young woman, that this was an issue to take up in the assembly and not, at least for now, to take to the police.

I participated in the assemblies for the next few weeks where this issue was addressed. The young woman came to the assembly with a few friends and had a few assembly people sitting with her in the circle. The accused young man also came to the assembly, having been told of the accusation. Similarly, he was there with a few friends, and a few assembly people sat with him. For the next few weeks discussions were held where each person was able to explain what happened and their feelings about it. Eventually, proposals were made and agreed upon for a sort of restorative justice. Among those resolutions were that the young man agreed to get support for his alcohol misuse, that he would not go to any of La Toma's parties until his alcoholism was under control, that he would meet with counselors on issues of sexual abuse, together with a few participants from the assembly who would go along to support him. He also had to meet with a few volunteers from the assembly on a weekly basis for the next few months, keeping them posted as to his participation in the various groups. If he failed to attend any of the agreed upon meetings he would not be permitted to enter the space of La Toma.

The end result was a very positive resolution where everyone concerned seemed satisfied and heard. The process was a lot more complex then space here allows me to describe. Included in the tensions and challenges were such things as the young man claiming that the young woman 'asked for it' by the way she was dressed, and that women usually push men away when they mean yes, etc. His friends who were with him were in complete agreement regarding these questions – at least at first. It was an amazing shift to see this tough street teen begin to listen to people around him on questions of gender and power, and that his desire to be a part of the assemblies and the occupied space was so great that he was willing to seek treatment and go to support groups with others from the assembly.

This is one of many examples of mediation and restorative

justice that I witnessed in the movements. It reflects the actuality of autonomy within the movements with regard to conflict resolution without state or police intervention. It also reflects the deep level of integration that the movements have achieved within their neighborhoods – that participants choose to bring problems and issues to them for resolution.

Another example of autonomous justice in which I participated was in the Movement for Social Dignity in Cipolletti during 2009. At the time I was staying with participants in the movement, going to the collective space each morning, participating in various activities and workshops. On this particular morning, as everyone was drinking *mate* and forming a circle to discuss the day, one of the older members of the movement asked about a younger one, wondering where she was. It was then that we learned from one of her friends that this young woman and her little sister were not coming to the space because they were too afraid to leave their house. They lived in one of the villas, and as was explained, their neighbor had begun to terrorize the young women. He was throwing things into the window of their home, yelling and following them when they left the house, he had even thrown rocks at them a few times. He was well known for violence, robbery and assault. The girl's father was afraid of the neighbor, as were most people in the neighborhood. As this story began to emerge in bits and pieces from a few of the teens in the movement, it was decided that we, the movement, should call the house to hear from the girls what the situation was. It was the girls and not the father who were in the movement at the time. After a long phone conversation, it was revealed that the girls were not only being threatened by this man, but that their father would not call the police because he knew that the man was a good friend of many on the local police force. The police are perceived as being incredibly corrupt in this region, allegedly often being involved in criminal activity and violence, so people in the neighborhoods cannot go to them for support or help.

The group began to talk about this particular issue. It was agreed that the girls were a part of the movement and therefore anything that threatened them was an issue for the movement: it was totally unacceptable that these girls could not leave their home because of fear. After lengthy discussions it was decided that we, as a large group, would go to the girls' house, show our support for them and, together with them, leave the neighborhood. It was also decided that a group of people from the movement who lived close to their house would continue to go there and walk the girls wherever they needed to go, whenever they needed it. This was decided after a few hours of discussion and debate, which included some of the teen boys suggesting that we beat up the neighbor, go there with bats, patrol with guns, etc. It was a long process of achieving consensus.[3]

There was also a long-term plan to make flyers to hand out in the various neighborhoods about violence and neighbors taking action, organizing events in the small local park and a few other longer-term suggestions that were to be discussed in the upcoming assemblies. The longer-term goal was to make the neighborhood a safer place through an active and visible presence.

In the meantime, we were all going to the house of these girls. With no small amount of trepidation on behalf of many movement participants – myself included, I must admit – we departed for their house together. We knew from conversations with them that the man was armed, although he had not yet attempted to shoot at them. It was of course, the being armed part that I most feared, but in a group of about thirty we went to their home. Everyone but the two people who went into the house waited in the street outside, showing that the girls were supported. I interviewed one of the adult participants later that afternoon. He reflected:

> If we are not generating new feelings and new relationships then we are basically being complacent. We know how the police will respond if we do not act in this other way – they will respond with violence – and if we act in violence to support our *compañera* then we are just reproducing what the state wants us to do. What we are doing is rejecting and negating that way of being, those ways of creating justice, negating the police and affirming ourselves – our capacity to avoid that and create something else. The idea to do something came about immediately from some of the teens in the group. They wanted to act and to act fast, and act together ... we act from our collective power, and at the same time it is what gives us strength to act. I think it's an example of this we trying to build.
> (Conversation in Cipolletti, Patagonia, 2009)

The above are two examples of how conflicts are resolved internally and are consistent with countless other such experiences. There have been other occasions of conflict existing between one movement and another, or between participants in different movements, and a fully participatory way to resolve such conflicts is yet to be developed. However, as of 2010, movement participants were beginning to discuss various ways in which this could occur, ranging from circle justice concepts to assemblies comprised of participants from various movements, but this has yet to be formally established. It is seen as a challenge, but one that is an active discussion and a next step.

Conclusion

Hierarchy and 'power over' (whether *punteros*, workplace managers, or delegates to an organization) will not create freedom, and taking over the state is not the way to change society: this is the case when the desired changes are new, horizontal, emancipatory, social relationships. These are some of the core ideas that the autonomous movements in Argentina, as well as the Zapatistas in Chiapas and numerous other regions throughout the world, are practicing. This notion of autonomy is not a simple concept and is even more complicated in practice. However, what is so inspiring and interesting about these movements is that despite these challenges, they continue what they are doing. Many tens of thousands of people throughout Argentina are creating alternative means of sustenance and survival that are based on their own agendas, not those of the state or institutional power, even if they choose to engage with or take what they can from the state (as will be addressed in detail in Chapters 7 and 8). Power is not something to take, but something to create. This is the case if one sees process as integral to what may constitute a desired end:

> Still, the defiant movements from the bottom that are fueled by interdependent power hold at least the hope that the needs and dreams of the great masses of the planet's people will make their imprint on the new societies for which we wish.
>
> (Fox Piven 2008: 12)

Many criticisms can be made of the autonomous movements, and when these critiques are well intended and constructive, they are useful; however, looking at alternative ways of organizing, creating, and engaging is crucial if we are to move ahead in the theory and practice of social change, social movements, and revolution. When an eight-year-old girl from the unemployed workers' movement of Solano demands an assembly because she feels that her parents yell at her too much, something is happening. She feels power. Then when the movement resolves this conflict, among many others, with some much larger (except perhaps to this little girl), there is an autonomous creation taking place that cannot be ignored:

> Sociologists have a contribution to make in fostering interdependent power. Our sociological preoccupations equip us to trace the contemporary patterns of social interdependence that are weaving the world together. We can describe these patterns in ways that reveal the contributions to social life of the majorities of the world's people.
>
> (Fox Piven 2008: 12)

Ultimately, in conclusion, the movements want to and are creating alternative power and carefully negotiating their relationships to institutional power, as stated so clearly by El Vasco:

> We take from the state all that we are able, as long as it does not get in the way of our sovereignty.
>
> (Conversation in Cipolletti, Patagonia, late 2009)

SIX

Autogestión, territory, and alternative values

The autonomous movements in Argentina, like the Zapatistas of Chiapas, are *autogestiónando*, self-managing, and self-organizing many aspects of their sustenance and survival. However, it is not just that people are making food together and doing so using *horizontalidad*, running factories together, producing metal and ceramics, creating new schools and forms of cooperative education, they are creating new relationships to production and in the process creating a new set of value relationships – ones that push and break with the rules of capitalist forms of production. Value is, perhaps, no longer something that is defined by the capitalist market or economic relations. The value of what is created and how in the autonomous communities is not measurable by the market or the system of value exchange. As seen with the system of barter (described in Chapter 3), the value of a good or service exchanged is decided by those involved in the process and on their needs, rather than the market value placed on that particular good or service. Equally, where the unemployed workers' movements have built schools, what is taught and how is decided by the movement and the community, and the only 'cost' of education is participation. This is also true of the recuperated workplaces where, time and again, solidarity is the choice over extra labor hours, or even in place of labor time. These formations are still quite new, still exist under capitalist relations; but as will be discussed in this chapter, these new forms create new ways of being, both individual and social, and demonstrate the beginning of breaks in the capitalist mode of production.

This chapter will detail what *autogestión* is, what the specific movements are developing using *autogestión*, and then reflect on the possible meanings and implications with respect to capitalist modes of production. The movements discussed are as follows:

Photo 6 Entrance to Zanon/FaSinPat (the sign reads 'Zanon is of the
People')

- recuperated workplaces created within the spaces of a
  factory or workplace;
- unemployed workers' movements, created on and within
  urban peripheries, building homes and producing various
  forms of self-sufficiency;
- neighborhood assemblies, focusing in particular on the
  elaborate barter network developed, where goods and
  services are bartered by millions of people; and
- *autogestión* in day-to-day creation with art and media
  groups.

The chapter then goes on to explain the importance of territory as specific geographic location in this creation. Finally it will
show that taken together, *autogestión*, *horizontalidad* and the
creation of new subjectivities within territories creates a new sort
of value production: one that sometimes falls outside the system
of capitalist domination, breaking from the profit motive, alienation, and capitalist relationships in day-to-day relationships to
production.[1]

Conceptualizing *autogestión*

The etymology of *autogestión* is both Latin and Greek. *Auto*, from the Greek *autós* (self or same), and *gestión* from the Latin *gestio* (managing), which in turn comes from *gerere* (to bear, carry, manage) (Vieta 2008). Taken together, the words *auto* and *gestión* create the inadequate English term 'self-management'. In the case of contemporary movements in Argentina, not only is the most direct translation not sufficient, but as with so many other words *autogestión* has taken on additional meanings when one combines it with *horizontalidad* and the goal of creating new subjectivities. Despite its ambiguities, it is a word that I believe should continue to be used, reinterpreted, updated, and retaken. The history of workers' self-management and attempts at worker control are a part of a tradition to which the recuperations in Argentina belong.

Autogestión was first articulated in Europe in the early nineteenth century by the utopian socialists, for example Charles Fourier (1971), whose concept of self-managed communities was based on production and concern for one another. Robert Owen's concept of 'federations of cooperative communities' (Horvat 1982) is also part of the base from which the concepts of *autogestión* have emerged. From the libertarian tradition there are Pierre Joseph Proudhon's (1970) writings on mutualism and equal systems of exchange, 'collective properties of workers' associations', and Peter Kropotkin's (1989) articulation of 'mutual aid', among others. In particular the libertarian or anarcho-syndicalist tradition had at least an early influence on the labor movement in Argentina (as described in the Introduction to this book), and is referenced sometimes as a continuity to which the current experiences of *autogestión* belong.

Other historical and theoretical examples include council communism, anarcho-syndicalism, self-management in the former Yugoslavia, European workers' councils, the Shora in the Iranian revolution, worker-soviets in the Russian revolution, and contemporary workers' cooperatives (Ness and Azzellini 2011). As will be explained in the rest of the chapter, while these historical examples are useful and what has been occurring in Argentina is a part of this tradition, it is also unique to the particular politics and circumstances of the movements contemporarily in Argentina.

What autogestión looks like in Argentina

Empresas recuperadas

The writer and public intellectual Naomi Klein spent more than a year in Argentina after the popular rebellion. Her mission was to make a documentary with the filmmaker Avi Lewis, reflecting on what people were creating, not just what they were against. The result was the award-winning film, *The Take*, based on the experiences of recuperated workplaces. In an article she wrote in 2003, titled: 'Argentina's Luddite Rulers. Workers in the Occupied Factories Have a Different Vision: Smash the Logic, Not the Machines', she states:

> Here in Buenos Aires, every week brings news of a new occupation: a four-star hotel now run by its cleaning staff, a supermarket taken by its clerks, a regional airline about to be turned into a cooperative by the pilots and attendants. In small Trotskyist journals around the world, Argentina's occupied factories, where the workers have seized the means of production, are giddily hailed as the dawn of a socialist utopia. In large business magazines like *The Economist*, they are ominously described as a threat to the sacred principle of private property. The truth lies somewhere in between.
>
> (2003: 1)

Origin in Argentina

The process of recuperation of now more than 270 workplaces in Argentina arose from desperation resulting from economic crisis and a total lack of response from managers, owners, and the state. Hundreds of thousands if not millions of workers lost their jobs in the years leading up to and after the economic crisis, and thousands of workplaces were closed. After the popular rebellion of 2001, as with so many other things, people took the situation into their own hands. 'The workers acted not as a result of ideological debates, but out of urgent need' (Zibechi 2006b: 338).

This need to which Zibechi refers stemmed from a total lack of work and possibilities as the result of economic crisis borne out of decades of privatization and speculation. The Argentine economy was in ruins, and so as a result workers responded in one workplace, then another, and then another decided that they were not going to permit this to continue. They did not refuse factory closure by protesting or staging a sit-in; they decided to occupy it – not only to occupy though, but to recuperate it as well. The people took over factories and ran them together without the bosses or owners. The language of recuperation is key here: workers came together to take back and run a workplace. It was not an occupation with demands and from the beginning the idea was to keep producing, thus the slogan of the recuperated workplace movement became 'Occupy, Resist, Produce.' No one else was going to do it for them, so they recuperated what they could and began producing.

Esteban Magnani, an Argentine scholar and writer who worked with Klein and Lewis on *The Take*, has continued to study and write about the recuperated factory movement. In explaining its origins as well as the overall politics of *autogestión*, he writes:

> Among the many feelings that emerged during those months, [referring to the popular rebellion] there were at least two that would produce a qualitative change in our society. The first was the general certainty that if people themselves did not set things right, nobody would, and the second was that whichever way out was chosen, it would have to be taken democratically and as a group. Out of this conviction there emerged new ideas such as the neighbourhood assemblies. But above all, these convictions served to generate the consensus that those who fought for a better world had the right to overlook the laws of a system, which had lost legitimacy and only offered poverty and humiliation. This ingredient of social legitimacy, added to many workers' firm belief that they would never find work again (facing a 25 per cent unemployment rate) if their factory went bankrupt, gave momentum to a phenomenon which had until then been rare: the recovery of factories.
>
> (Magnani 2005)

Numbers of groups

The main arguments in this book are not about statistics and numbers, and in fact they are generally to the contrary, arguing that while numbers are important, most significant is what is being done and how, and this often falls outside the framework of statistical analysis. In the case of the recuperated workplaces this is also true; however, in their case the numbers in the phenomenon are an important part of the conversation. While they are important, if the experiences of workplace recuperation were that of only a handful of places or something that occurred only in the first year of the rebellion, they would not have become a topic for this book. Over the course of ten years since the popular rebellion (at which time there were fewer than five recuperations), the number of recuperated workplaces has grown to more than 270. This is a number that continues to increase, with a large majority *autogestiónando* (self-managing) with *horizontalidad* – and that is significant. In a recent article published in *Pagina* 12, an important progressive newspaper in Argentina, Magnani writes:

> The third national survey conducted by the Open School Program of the Department of Philosophy and Letters (University of Buenos Aires) on the recovered companies throws light on the numbers and characteristics of the phenomenon. The study recorded the existence of 205 recuperated workplaces, with 9,362 workers. The figure reflects the dynamics of this socio-economic labor process when compared with 161 companies and 6,900 workers surveyed in 2004. This is a strong indicator of its validity as a tool in confronting corporate crisis.
>
> (Magnani 2010)

The numbers of recuperated workplaces reported ranges from 200 (Ruggeri 2010a) to 270 (Antón et al. 2010). Much of the difference in numbers depends on what exactly those studying the workplaces consider to be a full recuperation. For some this is based on legal recognition from the state, while for others it depends on levels of production and if salaries are being paid. Because there are a minimum of 270 workplaces that have been taken over and are at some level of production, even if only 200 are recognized by the state as legitimate, I am going to use the figure of 270. I base this figure on how those in the recuperate process identify, not on an external legal definition. For the most complete list of all the workplaces, as well as what they produce, when they were taken over, how many workers participate, their locations, and many other details, one needs to look to both the book *Sin Patron* (2004), by the Lavaca collective, and at the website created by Ruggeri and his research team. *Sin Patron* was published in English in 2007 and since then the website www.lavaca.org has updated the information regularly, being one of the most reliable sources on workplaces. It is also, not coincidently, an alternative media collective, working together with the social movements.

The most recent study conducted by Andres Ruggeri is published at www.recuperadasdoc.com.ar (2010b). Ruggeri organizes an independent project on recuperated workplaces within the University of Buenos Aires. One of the many tasks of this group is to gather information as well as organize conferences of workers and intellectuals on the question of *autogestión*.[2] Ruggeri (2010b) states that the recuperated workplaces have not only not disappeared, but have become an option – with all their difficulties – that workers recognize as valid, rather than resign themselves to the closing of workplaces.

The fact that the vast majority of recuperations continue is also a crucial point. As the report by Ruggeri illustrates, 90 per cent of recuperations have continued, and some of those that are no longer recuperated workplaces have not closed but instead chosen a different path, one that they believed would continue production based on worker power, paths such as *estatization* (nationalization or being under state control) (this is discussed greater detail later on in this chapter). As Ruggeri states:

> So far the study indicates that of the 161 companies surveyed in 2004, 22 have disappeared, changed to some other form of operation (such as the nationalized Medrano Clinic) or could not be contacted. This indicates that the survival rate is quite high: nearly 90 per cent, or more if you include those that survived in another form, other than *autogestión*.
>
> (Ruggeri 2010b)

Organization of recuperated workplaces

Horizontalidad, decision making, and income distribution

It is a common assumption that recuperated workplaces use *horizontalidad* or, as defined previously, horizontal forms of organization. When asking a worker in a recuperated work-place how they organize, they will reply that this takes place in assemblies with everyone having a voice, or will use the term *horizontalidad* to talk about how everyone makes decisions together. Magnani (2005) states this fact in his writing on the movements: 'Therefore, already more than 200 recovered factories are carrying out their productive projects under horizontal forms of organization.'

More than 71 per cent of recuperated workplaces have egalitarian remuneration practices (Fajn 2003; Zibechi 2006b), a practice that is not shared with more traditional workers' cooperatives around the world, barring a few exceptions (Vieta and Ruggeri 2009).[3] This same percentage of workplaces also practice equal or rotating job descriptions: this means that either workers rotate jobs so as to avoid hierarchy in tasks or, when the jobs are more trade or skill-specific, workers do not designate hierarchy of position, even if one job requires a great deal more training than another or more years on the job. For example, at Chilavert, the printing press, all workers are considered equal cooperative members, although they carry out different jobs with different levels of experience. Shared in common (although this is not a conclusive reason for egalitarian wage and job distribution) is the level of struggle involved in recuperation of the workplace, as well as the length of time that workers have worked together in that specific place (Zibechi 2006b; Vieta 2008). Similarly, 60 to 70 per cent of those workplaces that practice *horizontalidad* or similar forms of direct decision making have had to struggle, sometimes with police confrontation, so as to gain control of their workplace (Ruggeri et al. 2005).

Some 88 per cent say they hold regular assemblies. Forty-four per cent have a weekly assembly and another 35 at least once a month. This *horizontalidad* is also reflected in income: in those where all work the same number of hours, 73 per cent have the same remuneration (equivalent to a salary in a cooperative). In cases where they do not receive the same, 33 per cent explained it by differences in the type of work and 30 per cent by the number of hours worked.

(Magnani 2010)

With regard to the wages received compared to nonrecuperated workplaces, according to Magnani (2005), wages are higher in the recuperated factories, especially if they have been functioning under worker control for three years or more. As Candido from Chilavert describes:

> But now I know, looking back on our struggle three years on. Now I can see where the change in me started, because it begins during your struggles. First, you fight for not being left out on the street with nothing. And then, suddenly, you see that you've formed a cooperative and you start getting involved in the struggle of other ERTs [*Empresa Recuperada por sus Trabajadores*; Recuperated Workplaces by the Workers]. You don't realize at the time but within your own self there's a change that's taking place ... You realize it afterwards, when time has elapsed ... Then, suddenly, you find yourself ... influencing change ... something that you would never imagine yourself doing.
>
> (Gonzalez 2005)

Relationships to neighborhoods and community

The vast majority of recuperated workplaces, if not all, have involved the community and neighborhood in the process in one way or another.[4] In those cases where there has been confrontation with the police and previous owners – 60 to 70 per cent of recuperations (Vieta 2008) – defense of the workplace has come from the workers and the community (with 'community' here defined loosely as those who believed in the takeover and sided with the workers). This is a significant sector of the Argentine population, and locally, this is usually the majority of the neighborhood in which the workplace is located. As will be outlines below in descriptions of a few workplace recuperations, not only did neighbors come out into the street to support workers when the police attempted to convict them, but sometimes they insisted on being on the frontline. Neighbors and the community would volunteer with 24/7 monitoring so as to know if the police were coming – something that often happened late at night; and in the early months of the recuperations, when workplaces were yet to function and produce, neighbors would bring lunch, sometimes daily.[5]

This relationship with the neighbors and community is important background when looking at a workplace today and seeing how the vast majority also doubles up as community center-like spaces. It is not the workplace opening itself up to neighbors, but rather that the workplace has become a part of the neighborhood and community since the process of recuperation. When the people of the city of Neuquén, where Ceramica Zanon is located, say 'Zanon es del pueblo' they really mean it: 'Zanon is of the people', and the people are Zanon. Some of the workplaces, such as the huge IMPA metalworks and the Hotel Bauen in downtown Buenos Aires, opened as community spaces in the first weeks of their recuperation before production began. Some of the others, such as Chilavert and Nueva Esperanza, slowly morphed into community spaces: beginning at first with a few evening events each week, then some weekend events, and now holding daily activities for the community organized by neighbors in collaboration with workers. These community events range from music and dance performances and political talks and films, to classes in everything from tango and salsa to computer usage and basic writing. It is up to the neighbors' desires and capabilities. In many ways the recuperated factories are housing many of the activities that the neighborhood assemblies once carried out; and in many cases, from my personal observation and discussions, they are many of the same people.

Community education programs

'In the classroom we are all equals', says Marisel, a woman of around 40 who is already a grandmother. We are in the shanty town of Las Tunas, built by its occupants on an enormous rubbish tip 40 kilometers from the centre of Buenos Aires. Marisel is participating in a *bachillerato populare*: an informal educational system for which the literal translation is 'popular baccalaureate'. 'Everyone is involved in creating the lesson', adds Rossana, who works as a cleaner in one of the residential neighborhoods that surround the 'misery townships' – as Argentineans refer to their slums. Most of the people studying are poor women who have not completed school. The system emerged six years ago, in the factories rescued from closure by workers who took them over and ran them themselves. The *bachilleratos* spread into poor neighborhoods and there are now 40, some of which have gained state recognition, with 5,000 students.

(Zibechi 2010)

Raul Zibechi wrote the above in an article for which he had done research in early 2010. One year later, the number of *bachilleratos* is estimated at almost double his statistic, with close to 10,000 students (lavaca.org). This is not an ordinary alternative high school program: not only because it is generally held after hours in a recuperated factory, but because of the type of education being provided. Students can choose a path for their diploma, with subjects such as cooperativism (the study of how a cooperative works) being particularly popular. The way classes that tend to function is via face-to-face meetings, influenced by or using direct democracy, attempting for full participation and doing so without hierarchy. The size of the groups range from ten to thirty people, with each group choosing what they will study, how, where, and then what they will do at the end of the study process (Zibechi 2010). For example, the first class to graduate, having met in Chilavert, decided to print notebooks using the skills of cooperativism to gift to the next *bachillerato* class.

In 2009 I was invited to a graduation of a *bachillerato* class. It was actually the graduation of four classes, all of which had been held in Chilavert. Two different people from two different backgrounds invited me to the graduation, reflecting for me the widespread nature of the *bachilleratos.* One person who invited me was a cooperative member at Chilavert, and the other, a woman who was a member of HIJOS. Her husband, formerly a neighborhood assembly participant and an unemployed teacher, was one of the facilitators of one of the graduating classes. She was quite proud of what he had been doing and wanted to share the importance of this graduation, the first class from Chilavert. I had no idea when I left the apartment where I was staying with friends that I would arrive at such an elegant event. Granted, it was held in the street that the neighbors had shut down, and the chairs were a mix from the factory and people's homes, and the stage a makeshift wooden construction with a hand-held microphone, but the people attending were so elegant. The seats overflowed. Hundreds of people filled the streets. Some came from work, and others, who had loved ones graduating, were there with cameras, dressed in their best clothes. The women graduating looked like they were going to their proms in elaborate dresses and high heels, although many of course were decades older than prom age. The spirit, joy, and pride on their faces and those of their families and neighbors was palpable. It was incredible. The pride was for graduating high school: something many people in these poor and low working-class neighborhoods do not get to do. For me, the joy of course was sharing in their pride at graduating, but also in recognizing how 'regular' this had all become for the community. The graduation took place in the street in front of the recuperated workplace where the students had been studying for months: a street that the workers and families had shut down because they needed to. It was all so normal – normal in the revolutionary sense of normal. Che Guevara once said, 'When the extraordinary becomes ordinary, that is when the revolution has begun.'

Relationships to other workplaces and recuperated workplace networks

The vast majority of recuperated workplaces receive help from other similarly situated workplaces. This help can range from the following:

- physical defense of the workplace, in the case of police threat of eviction;
- financial support for getting the business off the ground when first recuperated;
- participation in occupying the workplace; to
- support in the process of deliberating whether or not to take over a workplace.

This type of support is particularly important with people, finding the direct experiences of workers who have gone through similar processes the most compelling and most helpful.

Each workplace decides internally how it is going to help other workplaces, in many cases by establishing 'press centers' or 'external relations'. When these groups exist within a workplace they tend to deal with all visitors and receive, what in US union language would be, 'release time' to do solidarity work. In a recuperated factory this is part of the experience of rotating jobs.

All the workers agree that the person in the press office is to be paid an equal salary, and their job includes external relations as well as solidarity work. When I arrived at the Ceramica Zanon factory (FaSinPat, short for *Fabrica Sin Patron* – 'Factory Without A Boss') in Neuquén, even though I had made an appointment with all three of their press people (since FaSinPat is so large, receives so many visitors, and is asked to do so much solidarity work such as training, etc., it found the need to increase its press team to three full-time workers), they were not at the factory, and a further twenty other workers had been released from their jobs for the rest of that day. A nearby workplace had been recently occupied by its workers and was in the process of being recuperated; they had sent word that the police were due to arrive that day to evict them. FaSinPat, along with other workplaces and unemployed workers' movements in the region, immediately mobilized to defend this workplace (through this solidarity they were able to successfully defend the occupation). In the meantime, I arrived for a tour and to conduct some interviews, and found the press office empty. However, one of the workers who met me at the entrance, who was recently off shift, decided that he would show me around and help me interview workers on the shop floor.[6]

Many examples exist such as the one mentioned above, where workers under threat send out the call and recuperated workplaces from all over the region respond. As Candido describes below, this incredible level of solidarity is central to these communities. It is not insignificant that he began to cry during this conversation, and that what moved him was the discussion of solidarity, not hardship:

In Chilavert, you could lift your foot and out would crawl an *asambleísta* [assembly participant]. They were everywhere. It was amazing, the support we got from everyone. People that didn't even know us were there, on the frontlines, being clubbed. Everyone fought to be on the frontline. It's really emotional [eyes tearing]. Today it's a little calmer. Now we talk about the day-to-day running of the print shop. But when you struggle for something, it's your obligation to fight for what you want, and that moves you. People you don't even know, who you've never seen before in your life, are fighting for you [starts to cry].

(Conversation in Pompeya, Buenos Aires, 2003)

From my observations, the vast majority of networking between and among recuperated workplaces is done informally and through solidarity and friendship networks. Workers telephone one another and share information in person and gatherings as well traveling from workplace to workplace, making requests or sharing information face-to-face. Email and the internet are also used, although much less so; face-to-face and voice contact communication dominate by far. There are quite a few networks of recuperated workplaces: the network of each organization is different, but the main idea of all of them is to help in the process of recuperation, including speaking with workers before they decide to take over their place of work, helping to connect workers with free legal representation, and connecting them to other workplaces. Some of the networks were founded by former workers and workers in the recuperation process, although some are not. The two most well known networks (in part I believe because they are located in Buenos Aires, and the vast majority of research done on the movements is in the capital city), are the Movimiento Nacional de Fabricas Recuperada por su Trabajadores (National Movement of Worker Recuperated Factories) and Movimiento Nacional de Empresas Recuperadas (National Movement of Recuperated Workplaces). The support that they provide is similar, although there is some difference in strategy and political outlook between the two networks. While some academics studying the process of recuperation find the political differences with these two networks to be significant (Ranis 2005) – and it is true that there has been some serious discord – I do not think at this time that this is a central question for the movements.

Disagreement and discord is part of the political land-scape in Argentina. A fundamental point of disagreement among recuperated workplace networks is how much to engage in politics of the formal kind; also, for example, how much to challenge capitalism actively. It is a disagreement not dissimilar to that of the two Madres de la Plaza de Mayo organizations, where one group focused solely on the issue for which they had come together, and the other has taken up more political and social issues. Ultimately both networks support workplace processes, both mobilizing and providing active support, and overemphasizing their difference does not reflect the day-to-day reality of the process of worker recuperation in Argentina. However, a different question, that of national and global coordination between and among workplaces, *is* much more significant (and is addressed later on in this chapter). At the time of writing there have been some further developments in networking and it may be that another umbrella network will emerge.

Legal relationship to the state

The statistic of the majority of recuperated workplaces being organized under the legal rubric of cooperatives was 95.3 per cent in 2004. However, while this is an impressive figure, it is also somewhat misleading (Ruggeri 2010a: 22).[7] During the first months of recuperation there was no legal status for the workplaces within them. During the rebellion, as the number of recuperations continued to grow (as did the outpouring of support for them), the various transitory governments appeared to be at a loss as to how to handle the growing situation. Often forms of direct repression were used, sometimes at the behest of the previous owners, but they were always met with resistance from workers and the community, and attempted evictions were rarely, if ever, successful. With the election of Néstor Kirchner, the government made the establishment of 'legitimacy' a top priority. One of the ways in which this was attempted was by the government reaching out to the social movements, encouraging them to participate more directly in government. Many social movement actors were offered government positions, although these were never decision making roles, and more likely created in order to demobilize the alternative construction. This attempted incorporation and cooptation was successful on occasion, but in the case of the workplaces there was no obvious way to include them in government, so new laws of cooperativism were introduced. The new recuperations could and had to be recognized through the state. In many ways this was merely a formality to appease the state.

There are some benefits for recuperated workplaces receiving cooperative status: these include the possibility of taking out loans from the state as well as the state freezing the debts that the workplace had at the time of recuperation. Although beginning with large loans and agreed-upon debt can appear to be a potential burden for workers taking over a factory, it is not. Generally workplace participants are dismissive of these debts; in fact, many do not see them as legitimate and feel no sense of responsibility towards the debt. Additionally, under current Argentine cooperative law, members of a workers' cooperative cannot have their personal property seized if the cooperative should fail.

The cooperative law poses some specific challenges to the movements, demanding that part of their agenda must be to respond to state demands. The question then arises: should groups respond to state demands, hope for a positive response, and only then start production, or should they 'Occupy, Resist, Produce' and then ask the state to ratify what already exists? As of 2011 both paths were being followed, with a recent example of a little of both. A group of 130 women from a recently closed garment factory, in the working-class neighborhood of Flores, Buenos Aires, took over their factory and went to the judiciary to request cooperative status. While hundreds of people from other recuperated workplaces and the community had mobilized their support for this, the judge declined their status as a 'legal' recuperation. In response, this group of women, with no real prior political experience, took over the courthouse until finally the judge agreed to their demands, and they are now a 'legal' cooperative (Lavaca 2011).

Challenges to autogestión

Production and productivity

Most of the recuperated workplaces operate at between 20 and 60 per cent of production capacity compared to their production runs when they were capitalist firms (Ruggeri 2010a). For some workplaces, particularly those at the higher end of the percentage, this is not a tremendous problem since there is no longer a boss or management structure taking a huge percentage off the top. However, for others, their desire is to increase operation. The main factors involved in this lower level of operation, according to the studies done by Ruggeri et al. (2010b), are a lack of adequate machinery, lack of specialized workers, an aging workforce, difficulties in accessing markets, and lack of investment capital.

The workplaces are dealing with these challenges and are

finding ways to get the training they need. As mentioned previously, within many of workplaces people rotate jobs, and so are learning the various roles and skills necessary to run the workplace. With regard to materials, there is now a considerable amount of recycling taking place in the factories and service-providing workplaces.[8] As it turns out, although some of this was done at first for political reasons, there is also some monetary gain to be had in some cases: for example, for print shops and metalworks this can be considerable. Workplaces often produce only what they need, when they need it, and in turn this can save a great deal on potential costs. When agreements are made for production, workers will ask the client for the cost of raw materials upfront: this is called *al façón*. This allows for more immediate production without the workplace needing a large reserve of funds.

In some workplaces, the physical structure or organization of production has been changed so as to facilitate conversation. In recuperated workplaces such as Grissinopolis, workers have moved their machinery to face one another so that they can be in assemblies and discussions whenever they desire, thus limiting the amount of time needed to break for conversations about production and running of the plant. Similarly, having a horizontal mode of assembly creates constant conversation on production issues, and with more conversation comes more creativity and thus changes that can increase productivity. At the most base level, with more breaks, lunches together, *horizontalidad*, and affective politics, workers are happier, and, as many studies have found, even in capitalist enterprises, when workers are more content and feel they have more of a say in production, productivity improves (Hodson and Sullivan 2008). There are, however, a number of important distinctions to make here. With examples such as Volkswagen and FIAT, where workers are more a part of the discussions with regard to production, they do not have any ultimate decision making, as the workers in a recuperated workplace obviously do. Additionally, workers in a participatory – non-recuperated – capitalist workplace have to meet levels of production no matter what, whether a worker is sick or solidarity actions are desired. In recuperated workplaces, the standards and levels are decided by the workers and are flexible based on the workers' needs and desires. Production could be reduced or, as with many of the workplaces, there is job rotation, so workers are in a better position to take time off and so on – all horizontally decided. This also relates to the question of alienation, and how under capitalist models of production workers are not ultimately involved in the decisions about what is produced or how, even if they are a part of the conversation; they are not the decision makers, therefore they are alienated from the labor produced. In the recuperated workplaces, however, there is much less alienation, since all decisions are made together and the relationship to their labor and questions of production within the workplace are decided by them.

In recent years international solidarity and 'Fair Trade'-type organizations have shown an interest in recuperated workplaces' products: these groups often organize tours of recuperated workplaces and sometimes even set up ongoing relationships to purchase some of the goods produced, such as drinking glasses from one, or balloons from another; however, as yet it is unclear what this might mean for production. Of course, this does strengthen global ties with workplaces, as well as giving encouragement to the workers themselves.

National and international coordination

One of the greatest challenges faced by workplaces (and this reflects my personal hopes for them) is their lack of national and international coordination. While a great deal of communication and networking does take place, as well as barter and a few international gatherings, there is still no day-to-day or even month-to-month overarching communication or information exchange. I believe that for recuperated workplaces to move ahead, meaning to continue and expand, this is essential. This does not mean the forming of one organization, but a network, or networks, that can share all information and experiences. Along similar lines, national and international communication with other social movements and groups would be tremendously helpful. But this goal of national and international coordination is one that I envision for the workplaces, and is linked to my personal vision of a post-capitalist society. The recuperated workplaces are creating new values and new social relationships, ones that are breaking with capitalist modes of relating, but this does not mean that they are actively striving to eliminate capitalism. As of yet, the slogan does not go beyond 'Occupy, Resist, Produce'. Through struggle this may change, but for now international coordination is not on the agenda. As discussed previously, on the one hand, the government has expressed support for workplaces by offering legal cooperative status to legitimize their way of existing; but on the other hand, it allows the police to attempt to evict workplaces and to create countless obstacles, both legally and through the use of force. A prime example here is the fact that currently the state does not permit recuperated workplaces to barter with other similarly situated groups internationally, arguing that this violates international commerce law.

Five specific recuperated workplace examples

In this section I examine five recuperated workplaces in which I have spent a great deal of time over the past eight years; specifically I reflect on diversity in production, numbers, gender, and geography.

Ceramica Zanon (FaSinPat)

FaSinPat (www.ceramicafasinpat.com.ar) is perhaps the most famous of all the recuperated workplaces. It is the largest in physical size and number of employees; in terms of production it is the most profitable in capitalist market terms and has the most militant history of all the workplaces, as well as being the most frequently visited. Documentary films about FaSinPat have been made in Basque, Dutch, English, French, German, and Spanish. They have a guest room for special out-of-town visitors, such as representatives from the movements in Brazil or the Government of Venezuela. Their indoor theater is used for assemblies, public events, and concerts. They have featured some of the most popular rock bands in Argentina, such as Bersuit, and some of the most popular folk (*nueva trova*) artists in all of Latin America, such as Leon Geico. Almost all of the concerts are fundraisers for the factory. There is even a popular song by one of the most famous Argentinian rock bands, Attaque 77, that celebrates FaSinPat with lyrics such as:

Espíritu setentista vuelve hoy,
Gente que no puede decir:
Hey, hey, no te metas

En Neuquén resiste Zanon
Lucha obrera, movilización
Los bastones acechan, también voy yo.

FaSinPat produces ceramics as well as a very specialized sort of ceramic which in part has helped it to succeed in the capitalist market. It is the largest recuperated workplace, employing close to 500 workers as of 2011. In December 2009 FaSinPat won a bill of expropriation, which it had been demanding, making it legally the workers'. This is a massive victory for the recuperated factory movement, even for those workplaces not calling for expropriation. As one worker explained, 'The state needs to make laws so that workers can work. In eight years we haven't asked the state for anything other than an expropriation law' (Trigona 2009).

The struggle within the factory began in 2000 after years of a business union collaborating with bosses; workers began to fight within the union to make it more democratic. Then later in 2000 a young worker was injured: while there was supposedly a medical kit on site, it was empty and the young worker, Daniel Ferraz, aged twenty-two, died. The workers believed that if proper medical equipment had been in the factory, he would have lived. That instance sparked the first big fight. From there the workers fought and won a new union under their own control. This was the result of a number of job actions and strikes, creating an environment in the workplace of worker dignity and increased hostility from the owner, Luis Zanon. After a lengthy strike by the workers in 2000 for issues including layoffs and refusal to pay back pay or current pay, Zanon locked out the workers who still were due months of back pay. As a result, the now extremely organized workforce decided to take over the plant. The factory that they took over had been left with more than US$75 million dollars of debt.

In the process of a lengthy struggle, with the workers always going to the community for support, the courts ruled that the workers could sell off the remaining stock so as to pay their back wages. In March 2002, with the remaining stock gone but with workers who could run the factory and who were organized and unemployed, the workers created an assembly and decided to begin production together. At this point there were only a few dozen workplaces that had been taken over by workers: a few such as Chilavert were already running, although most were in various stages of occupation and struggle.

FaSinPat began the running of the factory, or, as they say, they 'turned on the ovens' in March 2002. At the start of the takeover there were 240 workers – a number that progressively increased to 400 by 2004 and in 2009, 470 workers (lavaca.org). On 5 April 2002, the first production of 20,000 square meters of tiles left the factory. Three months later they produced 120,000 square meters, already half of what the company had produced under the previous owners. The workers decide everything, from production decisions to who they will *incorporar* (incorporate or hire) as a new cooperative member collectively. At first this was done by all the workers, and now it is done by one of the many 'worker commissions', the name of the working groups within the factory. FaSinPat has a bi-weekly general assembly, where all 470 workers come together and make all binding decisions, and in-between these assemblies each work area makes decisions for the day-to-day running of the factory, decisions that are then shared with the entire workforce in the assemblies.

In their pamphlet 'Zanon Under Worker Control', Ceramica Zanon workers explain their methodology:

> We are interested in letting you know that behind each ceramic tile there is a history and a reality that has made it possible for the wheel to keep on turning. All processes and decisions are in the hands of the workers. We are the ones who decide what to buy, how to sell, what and how to produce.
>
> (Zibechi 2006a: 355)

As with many of the workplaces taken over by workers, the desire to make decisions together horizontally was what dominated the earliest forms of organization. However, while this worked for smaller factories such as Chilavert, for example, having only eight workers, FaSinPat found that having all the workers make decisions on all matters was too time-consuming. Therefore, they decided to organize into work commissions, with each area making day-to-day decisions regarding a specific area of work, and organizing meetings each Monday to outline the work for the week. There are thirty-six such work areas, each having three eight-hour shifts of workers. Each area elects a coordinator, and every few months the coordinators rotate so that after a certain amount of time, each person has had a shift as coordinator. Then once a month there are day-long factory-wide assemblies where all big decisions are made, from solidarity action to the type of protective gear needed on the job, to questions of production and quality. As the workers explain in their pamphlet:

> The social, political, and production aspects are all discussed ... we will not adjourn the meeting until every last issue is agreed upon ... It is exhausting, but it is productive because you find solutions to all of the problems debating them with everyone.
>
> (quoted in Zibechi 2006a: 356)

Counter to capitalist business models, the workers have found that through long discussion and debate, production has risen. As Carlos, a worker in Ceramica Zanon states:

> Hours no longer mean what they used to. Back then, I worked 12 hours and returned home feeling exploited and destroyed. Now, if I return home tired, it is a different kind of tiredness. Because inside you is a stream of satisfaction that is sometimes difficult to explain ... Now I stay longer even when I don't have to ... Back then, I would pass a ceramicist on the line, and he was just a ceramicist, period. Now, each ceramicist that I pass on the line is like something of ours in its rightful place, something that belongs to you.
>
> (quoted in Zibechi 2006a: 357)

Along with growing numerically, FaSinPat has diversified a great deal. At the beginning of the takeover the only women who worked in the plant did so in a support capacity such as cleaning or cooking. Now there are more than a dozen women working on the shop floor. They have even organized a women's commission to make sure that gender issues stay central to the workplace as well as more generally in the region and society. One of the many things that the gender commission has changed within the workplace is that women are entitled to one additional sick day per month due to pain with menstruation, which is no small matter in a male-dominated industry and society. In addition they have brought in a large number of workers from the local unemployed workers' movement, which was out in the streets supporting worker control from the beginning. Not only does this change the composition of the workforce (by bringing in workers not traditionally from the working class), but it also racially diversifies the workplace. Many of the poorest sectors of society in Argentina have indigenous roots. In the south of Argentina this is generally Mapuche, while in the north it is Guarani. Many of those from the unemployed workers' movements identify as Mapuche, and/or have physical traits that are more identified as indigenous. This generally means slightly darker skin.

The workers have transformed the relationship of the factory to the city of Neuquén where they are located. Prior to being run by the workers, the factory had little relationship to the city aside from being a place of employment for a large number of families. Often the factory was responsible for having a negative impact on the region: for example before the workers occupied the factory the previous owner would go into the countryside and take the raw materials needed for the ceramics. The people from whom this land was taken are Mapuche, indigenous communities who have few (if any) rights or protection under Argentine law. While much of the material taken was removed legally, the Mapuche had little legal recourse to challenge this set-up. After the workers took control of FaSinPat, one of the first groups they reached out to were the Mapuche, promising to pay for any raw material that they were permitted to extract. In addition, as this relationship developed, the FaSinPat workers together with the Mapuche developed a whole line of ceramics with Mapuche designs.

Another relationship that is new since the takeover is that to the University of Comahue in Neuguén. The university has been working with Ceramica Zanon to help update its technology, and has been successful to a large extent (Zibechi 2006a). Ceramica Zanon workers have a weekly radio program that is broadcast from the university, and students regularly come to visit the workers as well as being on the frontlines when the factory has needed defending.

Naomi Klein and Avi Lewis's film, *The Take*, does a fantastic job of showing the massive community support for Ceramica Zanon. This is done through images of the thousands who come out at every potential attack on the factory, but also through random interviews with people in the city. Cobblers, hairdressers and regular neighborhood people are interviewed, and they all say the same thing: 'Zanon es del Pueblo.' One of *The Take*'s compelling images is filmed on the roof of Ceramica Zanon. It shows a worker practicing with a slingshot, shooting perfectly smooth, round, white balls that are made in the factory. Ceramica Zanon produces many thousands such balls for its workers as well as other social movements' members who might need them if attacked by the police. This moment of the film captures the David and Goliath dynamic of recuperated workplaces and the state. The police have mobilized and attempted to formally evict the workers of Ceramica Zanon three times – that is, with a judge's approval – and many more times through 'informal' police mobilization. Each time they are repelled not by bullets, but by the support of the community and the little white balls produced under worker control.

> 'The poetry of life can be larger than the poetry of paper', said the Argentine poet Juan Gelman, upon contemplating 'a square meter of poetry' impressed into ceramic tile that the workers of Zanon take wherever they go as a gift. When he learned his poetry decorated the 25 squares of ceramics, he wrote emotionally: 'Never in my life did I imagine that I would see my poems published on ceramics. Never in my life did I imagine that the workers of a reclaimed factory would interrupt their work in order to make it happen. It appears my imagination fell short.'
>
> (Zibechi 2006a: 358)

Brukman

Another of the more renown recuperated workplaces is the small, majority women garment factory located in downtown Buenos Aires, Brukman. Its location, gender composition, the timing of its occupation and nature of the resistance all came together to make it politically and geographically central to the struggles during the post-rebellion years.

Common to the experiences of all workplaces is that they had been declining economically for years, resulting in lower profits for owners and massive salary cuts for workers. In Brukman

the workers had their low salaries cut from 100 pesos a week
down to 2 pesos a week in the weeks preceding the occupation:
just enough money for a round trip bus fare, as they reflect.
The owner and managers continued to tell the workers that
there would be an increase in salary, and to 'hang in there and
keep working'. The money would come, they were told. In the
context of an economic crisis the workers felt that they had few
other options, and continued to come back to work. Then on
18 December 2001 none of the managers or owners came to
work. This happened within the context of workers' growing
frustration and militancy, although at this stage nothing had
been done apart from demanding some back pay. On that day
the workers met and decided that they would stay in the factory
and wait for the owners and managers to return. They waited
together all night, and on 19 December there was still no owner
or managers. The workers began discussing what to do. Many
wanted just to wait until the bosses came back and insist on their
salaries, as Liliana describes:

> In reality, for us it wasn't a factory occupation. We stayed on
> December 18, 2001 because we didn't have enough money to get
> home – we also decided to stay to see if the bosses would decide
> to give us a little money so we could celebrate the holidays with
> our families. This wasn't an occupation at first, but it became
> one without us intending it ... We waited two months for the
> bosses to come back. We went to the unions, the Ministry of
> Work, all with the intention of getting the boss to come back
> and offer us a solution. He never came. So we decided to work.
> That's how it started, and we were doing a really good job,
> working well ... But what we were doing bothered them from the
> beginning and they came around all the time to harass us. They
> claimed we were destroying the machines, for example, but that
> didn't work since there was a ton of media all around us and
> they saw that nothing was broken. Why would we break the
> machines in the first place? How would we eat? How would we
> pay for everything? We were working, despite the boss's lies. We
> are not political. We're surrounded by politicians, but that isn't
> the type of politics that makes sense to the women workers of
> Brukman. What we want is to work.

(Conversation in Once, Buenos Aires, 2003)

Like most of the factories, Brukman has had the police come, attempting to evict them, and as with the other workplaces the community and social movements mobilized to prevent it – except on one occasion. In April 2003, right around Easter, late one night, when most activists and movements were at home with their families, a huge battalion of police charged the factory, broke down the door, woke the sleeping workers keeping security, and at rifle point forced them out of the factory. This was the beginning of one of the highest profile struggles in Argentina since the days of the rebellion. There was a legal aspect to the struggle, but it mainly took place in the streets as well as in the minds and hearts of the population. The fifty women and men took over the park a block from the factory, put up tents and began a public protest. Soon hundreds of community members joined them, sometimes in tents, always bringing food and other supplies. The workers survived based on the solidarity of the movements. Most of this came from Argentina, but there were also international groups that fundraised, and in one case an activist group in England commissioned the workers to sew red bandanas with a big smile printed on them: these were to be used at the upcoming anti-globalization protests to help protect activists from tear gas. They were protecting their noses and mouths with a smile sewn by the workers of Brukman. They set up donated sewing machines in the streets, and worked.

After many weeks of outdoor protest the workers announced that they were going to re-enter 'their' factory. When that day arrived, tens of thousands of social movement activists and community members came out. I was there with a group of internationals, thinking that since we were foreigners we should be at the front, closest to the workers, believing that the police would be less likely to use brutal force if they saw from where we had come. The previous nights we worked hard at making visible signs with the names of our countries on each, from Sweden, the USA and Israel, to Chile and Mexico. We also built shields, using the experience we had gathered in other global protests resisting police repression. The shields were for the women of Brukman, and the country signs for us. The *piqueteros* were there in force, with tires ready to be burned and Molotov cocktails (in case the workers wanted that sort of support). When the moment was announced the workers, with the support of the movements, moved to take down the huge fence blocking the street where the factory was located. Just as the fence went down, police repression began. Serious repression. There were hundreds of police in full riot gear lined up behind the fence, and as we learned quickly, thousands of others throughout the neighborhood, hiding in dozens of buses and in buildings. All at once the police emerged, surrounding the streets, firing tear gas, rubber bullets and real bullets. It turns out that the real ammunition was fired into the air, but done intentionally so that people would see the casings on the ground and not know if people were being shot, as one falls from a rubber bullet like a real one. Everyone scattered, running in all directions. Our international group quickly dropped our signs so as to run faster and cover our faces better. It was a terrifying situation. Dozens of people were arrested and many hundreds injured. The Brukman workers did not get back into the factory that day. However, the repression backfired: instead of creating more fear, as with the state of siege at the time of the rebellion, it just incensed people, and support for the Brukman workers increased.

It took months for the Brukman workers to win their legal battle and re-enter the factory. In December 2009 I interviewed some of the women; in particular I spoke with an elderly woman whom I recognized from the days of the tent encampment in front of the workplace. She was not a Brukman worker then, but a part of an unemployed workers' movement. She had been out in the streets with them day in, day out, and later the workers voted to bring her into the cooperative.

> Brukman has come to represent a new kind of labour movement here, one that is not based on the power to stop working (the traditional union tactic), but on the dogged determination to keep working no matter what. It's a demand that is not driven by dogmatism, but by realism: in a country where 58 per cent of the population is living in poverty, workers know that they are a pay cheque away from having to beg and scavenge to survive. The spectre that is haunting Argentina's occupied factories is not communism, but indigence.
>
> (Klein 2003b)

Chilavert

Chilavert is a print shop in which I spent hours upon hours, over many years, talking with workers and listening in on some of the assemblies. It is also where I spent three full weeks daily helping with the process of printing the Spanish version of my book, *Horizontalism* (*Horizontalidad*). Of all the workers I became closest with Candido and his family. I met Candido during the Hotel Bauen occupation in April 2003. I had heard that the Hotel Bauen workers were going to re-enter the boarded up hotel, occupy it, resist in whatever way necessary, and then bring it back into production. I decided to go that evening and see if they would allow me to participate in the takeover. Some workplace occupations are carried out only by their own workers, but in this case Bauen allowed quite a few neighborhood assembly supporters and recuperated factory workers to join. While waiting in the lobby, Candido and I began talking. He invited me to come and see his print shop the next day, and I did – thus began a friendship and political alliance.

Candido and seven other workers took over their workplace on 4 April 2002, four months after the beginning of the popular rebellion. This, as with Brukman, came on the heels of a workplace experiencing decreasing production and profit, and an owner who had stopped paying wages. When the boss left Chilavert, the workers met and decided to stay. They finished the jobs already in production and received the money from those sales. Their first job as an occupied print shop was a book entitled *Que Son Las Asambleas Barriales* (*What Are the Neighborhood Assemblies*). During this book's production, a few days into the occupation, the owner had contacted the police and the front of the print shop became a police militarized zone. As Candido tells the story:

> The decision to take the factory was a very difficult step for us to take. Most of us here in the print shop have been working together for forty years. We have always more or less shared in union struggles, and generally we won. We always ended up doing pretty well. So taking over the business, the factory, was really powerful. At first we didn't know what to do, but when we realized that they were going to come and take the machines, well, then we had to make a decision. The time for thinking

had ended and we took over the workplace. That step was reflexive, instinctive. You know that if they take the machines from you, you'll end up on the street. It's a reflex and you don't think about cooperatives, you don't think about anything. Defending your source of work is a reflex ... No, look, I can't explain it to you ... When they came to evict us for real ... The repression was intense. They started with the assault vehicles, the ambulances, everything, with the determination that they were going to remove us. We had already predicted all of this, and had advised the neighborhood assembly of Pompeya, which is around the corner, who mobilized, and the assembly at IMPA [a recuperated metalworks], who defended the factory by standing in front of it, linking arms to make a chain. I never expected to see so many people. There were members of the neighborhood assemblies of Parque Centenario and Parque Avellaneda, everyone from *asembleístas,* and people from other recuperated factories. We were inside during all of this. We were even printing. We were printing the cover for the book *What Are the Popular Assemblies?* That was Thursday, and the book was going to be presented at noon on Saturday in the assembly of Palermo Viejo. The assembly had been doing a series of events, the last of which was the presentation of that book, which was written by participants in the assemblies.

(Conversation in Pompeya, Buenos Aires, 2003)

The workers not only printed the book, but were able to get it to the neighborhood assemblies by passing it through a small cement hole that they had made in the wall on the other side of the building, where *asembleístas* received the contraband books. The Chilavert workers are very proud of this hole in the wall, and the story that it represents. Even though they filled the hole, they placed a wood frame around where the hole once was, reminding themselves and everyone who comes to visit of their struggle and resistance.

Since the beginning Chilavert has had to resist a number of attempted evictions, each of which was defended with the help of community mobilization. Chilavert also has a legal strategy, which is to simply use whatever laws are available or invented to continue under worker control. They have no illusions about the state and no intention of allowing an owner or government official to come into the workplace and make decisions for them, but they have agreed to be a cooperative. Over the course of a few years of existence, most workplaces have opted for this route. One of the things that they have received due to cooperative status is a loan of many thousands of dollars. They see it as a loan, but only plan to pay it back if there are sufficient extra funds to do so. Each year since 2002 the factory has done a little better financially and now has 11 workers. Most of what it prints relates to social movements, from political books and magazines to large art posters for groups such as the Madres de la Plaza de Mayo or the Abuelas. They do not go out and solicit work since they have enough from the movements.

The biggest challenge Chilavert faces is the antiquated nature of its machines. I did not realize this at first, not having been in a print shop before. It looked to me as though the machines were all running fine. But then, one day, I was in the office and looked through the large glass window onto the shop floor and saw a few of the men huddled around what looked like a magazine. The way they were all trying to get a look at it I imagined it must be pornography and felt a little uncomfortable. When one of them gestured for me to come and join them I had no idea what to do. So, hesitantly, I went over. What I saw when I arrived at the little circle was a glossy centerfold of a printer. They all began talking to me about it. 'Do you know how much more we could print with this?' and 'This would never break down, it would not need two people working it all the time like she does' (gesturing to the huge machine in front of me). So, this is what the workers of Chilavert fantasize about, new machines.

IMMEC Clinic and Medrano Clinic

If one runs an internet search for Ceramica Zanon, Brukman, Chilavert or Hotel Bauen, the top results will be articles about the recuperated nature of these workplaces. This is not true for the medical clinics such as IMMEC, Felix Salud or Medrano. IMMEC looks like any other medical center in the world; there is no indication that it is run cooperatively by its workers. IMMEC, as with Medrano, was occupied by its workers after they were told that the clinic was going to be closed due to lack of profits. In both cases it was technicians and less skilled workers, such as cleaners and administrative staff, who moved towards occupation. At both IMMEC and Medrano the doctors stood aside, watching and waiting to see what happened, although on some occasions doctors personally came to the occupied clinic to bring food or small donations.

Both clinics endured prolonged struggle, with the police often attacking those occupying the clinic as well as the neighbors and community members who came to support them. Over time both were put back into production, each contracting with doctors. This made, and in the case of IMMEC still makes, for a complicated relationship. The workers, only a little over a dozen in 2003 in the case of IMMEC, and a few dozen at Medrano in 2002, took over the clinics and in both cases hoped that the doctors would join them once it was clear that they were going to run things cooperatively. Instead, in both cases, the workers who took over the clinic formed a horizontal assembly, dividing all wages and finding new ways to balance jobs where possible, but the doctors were not keen to join the process. At IMMEC the assembly hires the doctors and pays them a much higher wage then the rest of the members of the cooperative. In the case of Medrano this was especially difficult, and because of these financial difficulties the assembly decided to take the government up on their offer to *estatilizar* the clinic (i.e. put it under state control). What happened, however, was once the assembly voted to allow the government to have control, the state immediately shut down the clinic, saying it was only temporary, and placed the dozens of workers in clinics and hospitals all over Buenos Aires, with no two workers in the same place. In the conversations I had with some of the workers after this process, there was a great deal of regret, depression, and anger. In fact, it is the only place where the workers would not do a follow up interview with me.[9]

However, IMMEC is doing well, salaries are being met, production is increasing, and its legal status is stable as a cooperative. Nonetheless, there is a great deal of frustration regarding the hierarchical nature of the workers' relationship to the doctors. It is not just that the doctors make more money, but that they often treat the rest of the staff in a condescending manner. The cooperative is working towards a more horizontal management structure, but it would seem that the doctors continue to desire a more hierarchical system of organization. At the time of writing there are thirteen people who comprise the cooperative and make the decisions for the workplace, then there are more than a dozen doctors and nurses who collaborate with them.

When asked about the most inspiring moment in the process of the clinic's recuperation, Elsa, a member of the IMMEC cooperative, immediately thought of the days after the occupation when the police mobilized to evict the workers. Elsa recalled this being the most frightening moment in her life. She is in her fifties and had never been at a large protest, much less in a situation of police confrontation. However, she was quick to point out that this moment was the most frightening, and yet the most beautiful. She remembered:

> It was beautiful, the response to the police came from all over. The level of support and affect was incredible. It was the most beautiful because this support is what permitted us to open the clinic.

She ended our conversation by reflecting on the situation overall:

> Some people say that history is finished. For us, history is now, history is in the day to day.
>   (Conversation in late 2009 at IMMEC, Buenos Aires)

Hotel Bauen

On the Avenue Callao, at the corner of Corrientes in the center of Buenos Aires, Hotel Bauen could not be more centrally located. It is a five-minute walk to the congressional building, across from which are the school and bookstore for the Madres de la Plaza de Mayo. Corrientes is one of the main avenues in Buenos Aires, known for all of its shops and restaurants.

When the Hotel Bauen workers took the plywood off the lobby window and entered the hotel, their intention was to have the entire hotel up and running within the year. Hotel Bauen has more than 200 rooms and was previously a four star establishment with two pools, a massive bronze-filled lobby which includes a grand piano, a full theater, two restaurants, two cafes, two bars, a basement laundry that takes up hundreds of square feet, as well as a small print shop, and countless offices and other facilities. After months of significant lay-offs and firings in late December 2001, the owners laid off the remaining workers and shut the hotel. Almost immediately thereafter a few workers came together to meet with workers from other recuperated workplaces, including Candido from Chilavert and a representative from the National Movement of Recuperated Workplaces network. Together they made the decision to take over the workplace and run it in common. They began meeting more regularly, and gathered a few dozen of the previous workers to join in the process. In March 2003 they took back their workplace, together with hundreds of supporters as well as neighborhood assemblies, and the community at large. There are now more than 150 workers running the hotel.

The night of the takeover was tense, but also incredibly joyful. People sat chain smoking, waiting to see if the scouts had any news of police movement. Nothing at all – hours passed. At one point a man sat at the piano. I will never forget this moment, I still get chills thinking about it. In fact, I met the man who sat at the piano that night again on a recent trip to Argentina in 2009. During our interview I shared with him how moved I was at that scene, and it was at that moment that I recalled that it was he who sat at the piano. At the same moment he remembered me from all those years ago. His head is full of white hair now, he jokes 'from all the struggle in fighting for the hotel', but his energy and passion remain the same. That night, when we all sat waiting in the lobby, with no electricity except for the few lanterns that people had brought with them, Guillermo sat at the piano and began to play a tune, which at that point was little-known. A song he had written. A song that now is known throughout the country.

It goes:

We are the present and the future
To resist and occupy,
The factory will not be closed
We are going to raise it together
The factory will not be closed
We are going to raise it together.

It continues, and over the years it has been sung with various names of workplaces that are in the process of being recuperated. The chorus is 'To Resist and Resist – and Occupy … then to Resist and Resist – and Produce'.

Sitting in the occupied lobby that night, learning this song, singing with hundreds of other workers in the process of taking over their workplace, was one of the most powerful experiences of my life. Over the years, as I have continued to go back and spend time in Argentina, the Hotel Bauen café has become one of my bases. This is because of what it is, a recuperated hotel, but also because it is so centrally located – and it also is a great place to drink a *cortado* with *media lunas* (espresso with croissants) and watch the world go by. It is a totally different place from that smoke-filled lobby in 2003. However, at the same time the feeling of excitement of being in such a massive and important place run together by the workers, using *horizontalidad*, is ever present. To enter the lobby one would never know this was a 200-room hotel run by its workers. There is a small brass plaque which states that this is a cooperative run by the workers, but it is such that one would not see it unless they knew where to look.

Since the occupation the hotel has faced a great many challenges. During the first months after the recuperation, as Fernando from the cooperative stated:

> The hotel went bankrupt in February 2001, but it was kept open by a trustee until December 2001 when the closure was decreed, everything stopped, and they threw all the employees out. They owe us back wages, bonuses, and vacations. About a month ago, we got in touch with the National Movement of Recuperated Workplaces, who told us it was possible to take over our workplace. Friday of this week was when we took the building. Our principle objective is the reclaiming of our workplace, and then in two months we're going to open the hotel. The idea now is to open it soon, with fewer rooms, maybe seventy or eighty to start, and to begin using the halls, restaurant, and theater, and do all sorts of cultural and social events with the community.
>
> (Conversation in Downtown Buenos Aires, 2003)

Often the gap between the dreams and desires of those in the process of the recuperation and the reality of how those dreams play out is larger than initially thought. In the case of Hotel Bauen, it has been a long process of opening up rooms for outside use. The main focus in recuperation has been fixing the massive lobby, all of the meeting rooms, auditorium, restaurant, café, and now the pools. The rooms that are available are rented out, generally to people in Argentina for reasons of political solidarity, from tour groups on global exchange visits to Venezuelan sports teams. One of the main hurdles in bringing the rooms up to standard is a financial one. While the workers did get a loan from the state, it has been used to repair the ground floor as well as make some basic but crucial improvements in infrastructure and areas such as heating and air conditioning. The hotel has faced various challenges, including the fact that initially the number of participants was too low to effectively run the hotel. Later on, more people wanted to join the process despite not being a part of the first year or so of struggle. This is something that has affected a number of recuperations. The current cooperative law, under which recuperated workplaces are recognized by the state, requires members to allow all former employees who wish to come back to the workplace to do so. For many this is challenging to internal politics, as some workers feel that they struggled and lost a great deal during the process of taking back the workplace, and now previous workers who were not a part of the struggle get to share equally in the recuperation. This is a particularly interesting point when seen from the perspective of remuneration. There is rarely an issue about all workers being paid the same salary, regardless of training, number of years in the workplace, education, etc., but if a worker was not part of the struggle and did not fight the police, then tension often arises when equal distribution is discussed. This tension points to an interesting phenomenon in value production. Here, workers are not arguing for or against remuneration based on work towards production, but on solidarity and political struggle. Again, this reflects the new value that is being created, a value based in social relationships rather than profit.

Bauen has and continues to face challenges posed by the state, but thus far every single eviction attempt has been met with thousands of people, workers from the recuperated workplaces, and others, mobilizing in its defense and support.

Autogestión in the unemployed workers' movements

Our principal activity in the struggle with the state is to negate the power relationships they attempt to force upon us, on the one hand, and on the other to bring forward what we call 'social change' – the development of new social relationships that negate this power over, that negate the principles of authority the state attempts to dominate our lives with ... the state is not going to just disappear; in this case, the capitalist state has as its fundamental essence to preserve the reproduction of capital and capitalist relations, its role is to continue this relationship and to create more capital – and we refuse this form of the reproduction of capital, because capital negates life, denies our humanity as a whole, and leads to increasing confrontations. For us the question is not so much where are we trying to go tomorrow, as in some locations, but for us we are permanently in a place of constantly creating new social relationships that negate capital, that negate the state, value based in the market – and to reconstruct new forms of life permanently. So, it is not that we are trying to get from one place to another, from one day to the next, but rather there are steps and paths that we are constantly taking. Ultimately, we are trying to create a world in which many worlds fit,[10] and this presumes many logics, many ways of thinking and doing, and especially not the logic of the reproduction of capital. It is especially to negate this.

(Conversation with El Vasco in Cipolletti, Patagonia 2009)

Autogestión, the creation of alternative values and new territories, occurs not just in recuperated workplaces in Argentina. Part of the uniqueness of *autogestión* in Argentina is precisely that it is a production-based social relationship that is a broader phenomenon: people are creating together, pushing at the boundaries of the dominant power of the state and the economic dictates of the capitalist market; it is a new social relationship to production, but not one limited to the confines of a workplace or factory.

While the recuperated workplaces are *autogestiónados* and creating value, often pushing the boundaries and even cracking the capitalist form of value production, this is not always being done with conscious intention. In the autonomous unemployed workers' movements, as described by El Vasco above, there is a clear intention behind attempting to break with capitalist modes of production and value. (The question of alternative value will be addressed towards the end of this chapter.)

The unemployed workers' movements focus on a wide variety of projects, forms of production, and organization. However, what they share in common is that they are all attempting to produce things that they need and desire to differing extents.

There are dozens of unemployed workers' movements throughout Argentina. I have spent time with eight of the more autonomous groups and have chosen here to write descriptions of four of them. This is not meant to be an exhaustive list of movements or what they are creating. What this small selection does is provide a little more detail of what the autonomous unemployed workers' movements are creating and how they reflect on this *autogestión*.

MTD Solano

I recently had a conversation with a carpenter friend who was born in the USA, but has lived in Latin America at different times in his life. He had just got back from a long visit with MTD Solano, outside Buenos Aires. He said, 'Marina, you know, I have never been in such a beautiful and revolutionary place.' When I asked for details, he replied, 'I was living in a neighborhood entirely constructed by the people living in it. I felt free.' Sections of the neighborhood of Solano have been taken over by participants from the movement. The land has been divided up collectively, and on each plot people have built and continue to build homes, sometimes for families, sometimes for a few adults living together. The houses are extremely rustic, yet filled with creativity. When I am in the neighborhood I sometimes stay with Neka and Alberto (who are quoted at length in this book). They built a two-story home from materials largely found and recuperated. Some of the window areas are made of old wine bottles filled with water and set in the cement so as to allow in some light, but not leave them vulnerable to the dangers of the neighborhood. Beams are made of recuperated telephone poles, or better said, telephone poles that a former worker 'found' and brought to people in the movement one night in a truck. Much of the cement comes from another unemployed workers' movement that produces cement blocks, among other things. The path that leads from their home to Claudia's, another movement participant, is made entirely of bottle caps, creating a colorful walkway over the earth.

The movement, from its very founding, made surviving, surviving together, and doing so in a way that was totally different from capitalist modes of exploitation and alienation, its objective. This meant *autogestiónando*, people self-organizing their lives. As Neka explains with regard to what they are producing and how:

> When we talk about production, we talk about it in a holistic sense. We're talking about a network of production, not productive groups in themselves, one that is communitarian and collective. For example, we have a people's pharmacy where a lot of *compañeros* work. What's produced there benefits everyone who needs it, like those without an income. We also have a lot of people working in libraries and with the different children's projects. We're trying to become self-sustaining.
>
> (Conversation in Solano, 2004)

The various *autogestiónados* projects within the movement have changed over the years, but the basic aims remain the same: striving to be self-sufficient with food, health, housing and social activities. One of the more recent activities that the movement has undertaken has been the takeover of land to build housing. This began in 2006, but it was not until 2008 and 2009 that these projects began to really have an impact. In 2006, the movement took over hundreds of abandoned hectares of land in an area a few miles from the dense urban sprawl that is the center of the neighborhood. There they began to grow crops such as corn and beans, as well as raise chickens and other small livestock. The goal is to be able to feed the movement from the land, as well as raise larger animals, such as pigs and cows, which can feed the movement and perhaps even be bartered or sold for other goods and materials that the movement needs. Members of the MTD have engaged in exchanges with other groups and movements within Argentina as well as throughout Latin America, sharing experiences and knowledge about the land and self-sufficiency: movements such as the Movemento Sem Terra (MST) of Brazil, the Zapatistas of Chiapas, and urban and indigenous movements in the north of Argentina and Bolivia:

> We believe, and continue to reaffirm our belief and desire to build and continue building, a collective movement that expresses this desire for transformation – but not a partial transformation, one from the root. We desire a profound change beyond the constraints that reality puts on us. We continue and are increasingly convinced of *horizontalidad*, and not as a method of organization, but as a relationship that helps us to recuperate ourselves as active people, bringing back out creative ability, helping to bring new meaning to life. For us this is not an organizational gesture but it has to do with human relationships, the new relationships breaking from the system that tries to hierarchize us, a system that tries to make us passive. We are recuperating our potential as human beings to do things: for us this is what *horizontalidad* is, it is a relationship ... For us the new society expresses itself in horizontal relationships, and this has to do with our no longer being an object of politics and changing ourselves into subjects and protagonists.
>
> (Conversation with Alberto in Solano, late 2009)

MTD La Matanza

La Matanza is located on the outskirts of Buenos Aires. With almost 2 million people, in terms of population it is the size of a city and the most densely populated district around Buenos Aires. Located 20 kilometers from the city, this area was once the heart of manufacturing in the region. Numerous metalworks, textiles, and automobile manufacturers from Mercedes Benz to Volkswagen, all had factories in this region. The area expanded due to high levels of production, but the infrastructure did not. The factories have now been closed for two decades, in some cases three, and the infrastructure remains minimal. More than half the population has no access to formal sewage services or drinking water, with squatted areas being even worse.

It was within this context and these conditions that people began organizing in the mid-1990s. Some of the first organised groups were the *Ollas Populares* (popular kitchens), which distributed food along with clean water and milk for children. Soon thereafter, the unemployed workers' movement was founded, immediately organizing to meet people's needs and demanding 100,000 jobs. As with other MTDs, the demand for unemployment subsidies was won, and some money was distributed to those participating in the movements. For MTD La Matanza, like Solano and many others considering themselves to be autonomous, the desire was not for the government to meet their needs, but rather to become self sufficient – a self-sufficiency, they believed, would arise via the formation of new social relationships such as *horizontalidad* and *autonomía*.

During the founding months of the movement, *piquetes* were organised and food was divided among members. Soon enough, a small bakery was founded, and within two years the group had taken over a few acres of land, created a garden, and were raising small livestock. By 2003 they had begun to build a school and set up a few productive work projects, such as a small garment shop and a larger, more sophisticated bakery. Some of these projects were borne out of a decision to no longer accept the *Planes de Trabajo* (unemployment subsidies), which the movement felt were making them dependent on the state. Furthermore, it had been argued by some in the movement that accepting money from the state was further alienating neighborhood residences from a schedule and relationship to work. Distinct from MTD Solano, La Matanza was not against traditional conceptions of work, or what it calls a 'working class ethic'; it argues that through *autogestión* it has created a new relationship to work: one where work is still valued as such (MTD Solano argues for an entirely new concept of work and exchange). In many ways MTD La Matanza's relationships to work and production resemble that of recuperated workplaces.

With regard to the movement's productive projects, the school is the one of which it is most proud. The school is organized and managed by the movement, but is open to anyone in the neighborhood. The only requirement is that parents must actively participate in the assemblies related to the running of the school. It must be a parent-led and horizontally managed school. The curriculum is also considerably less traditional, with topics such as cooperation, solidarity, mutual aid, and *autogestión* being part of the learning agenda. Even the hopscotch painted onto the cement floor outside the school is different. Instead of numbering one to ten, it begins with *Lucha* (struggle) and ends with *Dignidad* (dignity). As a few women from the movement (who did not wish to be identified) reflect:

Compañera 1: We are creating a model school, not in terms of a model of perfection, but in the sense that there's not another one like it. We are developing the school together in the movement and with neighbors, and without interference of the state: that is to say, we're going to make the decisions that we think are suitable within the school. The goal is to create a true educational community where we can all participate in all of the decisions. Our beginning point is to figure out our needs, what the real needs are of this community, and then from there, beginning to find ways we can begin recuperating and repairing all that the educational system has done to us, and what it is engendering in the children.

Compañera 2: The idea is that this new school would be sustained in the mid-term by our micro-enterprises, like our silk-screen printing, sewing, bakery, and book publishing. The idea is to start to create a different culture.

(Conversation in La Matanza, 2004)

The aim at MTD La Matanza is to begin creating a different culture, as the compañera said, creating a different culture based on different ideas, relations, and values.

MTD Allen/Cipolletti (now Movement for Social Dignity in Rio Negro, Patagonia)

Allen and Cipolletti are two towns outside Neuquén in Patagonia, the far south of Argentina. The groups' new name immediately reflects the construction of new people, new relations, and new values. After a few years of existence as an unemployed workers' movement, its participants began questioning why they would identify as unemployed workers when what they were doing was creating dignity. At a similar time (and as is later discussed in Chapter 8), the movement agreed no longer to accept subsidies from the state. Under the auspices of *autogestión*, the movement shifted from taking money from the state to creating micro-projects to meet its day-to-day needs, ranging from bakeries and collective kitchens to medical and optical care, with the latter two provided by volunteers who worked with the movement in solidarity capacities. Similar to MTD Solano, La Matanza and dozens more unemployed workers' movements, the Movement for Social Dignity of Allen and Cipolletti takes over land in the various shanty areas outside the city and collectively builds housing for movement participants. As of 2009, the movement was in the process of forming a *bachillerato* to help the youth around the movement get a high school education:

> When we started organizing on the issue of health and our own healthcare, we began with a basic premise that capitalism produces sickness – sorry, sick people and sickness – in that order. This is because we live in a society that produces constant necessities and binds the individual to constant and permanent necessity, and from there it generates sick people. Alienation itself and subordination to power are huge aspects of the healthcare situation. So, we cannot create a health project that does not presuppose a rupture with relations that capitalism establishes in you. In the end, we can have a good supply of medicine, we can heal a lot of sick people, but sick people continue to exist. So what we try to do in the movement is to generate new relationships, including new relationships with professionals, not just among ourselves. Now it is the *compañeros* in the movement who manage our own healthcare relationships, all from within the movement. The *compañeros* who are doing this do not necessarily know anything about health, but understand very well relationships of subordination, particularly the relationship between professional and patient.
> (Conversation in Allen, 2003)

Other groups and movements in Argentina which have been using forms of *autogestión* range from neighborhood assemblies to barter networks, some media groups and art collectives. I will mention a few of these below. These examples are not of the same magnitude, neither do they have the same sort of social weight; however, they are also a part of the same phenomenon and rethinking of capitalist value.

Autogestión in the neighborhood assemblies

Most of the assemblies organized into working groups that addressed basic needs in the neighborhood as well as facilitated political and cultural events. For example, food being the highest priority in the first weeks after the rebellion, assemblies organized soup kitchens and collective spaces where food was brought, cooked, and distributed. Medical groups were organized and worked with people from the neighborhood who had medical skills, or invited outside volunteers to help with different forms of medical support. Neighborhood assemblies have not created alternative values with regard to production and *autogestión* in quite the same way that the recuperated workplaces and some of the unemployed workers' movements have; however, their combination of *autogestión* and *horizontalidad* began to change people's experiences. As Martín explains with regard to these changes:

> Imagine a mode of value production that has as its principle the worth of the person – and not what is accumulated – not the equivalent of money. For example, that the value of what is produced has to do with the community, that if the community is better or more content, it would be better, have more value. An individual would be happier in a place where one feels better, in a place involving everyone; this would be a form of power, another power ... to bring about another value. It has to do with love, and with politics and identity, but with a mode of identity that is not only individual but singular and collective.
>
> (Conversation in Colegiales, Buenos Aires, 2003)

Barter

The barter network was and continues to be organized based on 'prosumers': people who have something to promote as well as consume. In order for a barter market to function in a 'multireciprocal' way, all participants must consume in the same proportion in which they supply goods and services: this is known as 'prosuming'. People used a coupon to represent value of exchange. Each person participating decided the exchange value of the good or service they were offering, and others would decide whether or not to exchange with them based on that value. So, for example, empanadas (dough-baked pockets filled with meat and vegetables), a staple food in Argentina, might be valued at four times the amount for a dozen, and two hours of computer repair might be valued at 16 times the amount. Or, as is the case with Nicolas and Gisela, the couple who discusses barter below, Nicolas gave French lessons in exchange for film for his camera, and Gisela baked empanadas in exchange for childcare of their daughter by a neighbor. The barter was formal and took place in physical locations or nodes, but it also became a way of being and relating, so one might exchange something with a neighbor or friend without going to the local barter club to do it. Nicolas and Gisela give a flavor of what the Barter network was like at its height, as well as what might have happened to it. Gisela was a part of the Elipsis-Video group at the time, and Nicolas is a photographer who has worked with Indymedia:

Nicolas: Bartering networks sprung up all over very quickly. First people just said, 'Ok, you're able to do this and I can do this, so, what do we do now?' – and we began. The idea was great, but not totally good. There were times when people used the network just to get things for themselves. But at the same time, it really did help a great deal. In every neighborhood people were able to eat because of this relationship and we were all involved. Also in the barter network there were different relationships that sometimes emerged between the rich and the poor, those that had a lot of nice things to exchange, and well, those that did not. The representation of the exchange was in tickets that were made. Each person would have a quantity of tickets representing exchange. For example, with my photography I was able to go around and take photos of people and then they paid me in tickets, and with those tickets I got a kind of credit. Now these tickets barely exist at all, very few places use them. They exist in a sort of sentimental way, but before they really did, there were many millions of them ...

Gisela: What happened is that there were people who started to counterfeit the tickets, to make fake tickets. Since it was just a piece of paper, it was really easy to counterfeit. So people made fake ones and the barter networks that used tickets fell apart. I do not know who did it, but it seems it was people who had access to printing millions of tickets at a time … people with power … The barter network that used tickets was distinct from the one that exchanged object for object – the difference was in the ticket and idea of credit.

Nicolas: At one point, those tickets helped pay for train trips to Mar del Plata.

Gisela: And the taxes, right?

Nicolas: No, I don't think so, but in some of the provinces and in some towns so many people were using this type of money that the government began to accept it.

Gisela: The municipalities. In the beginning it was in the province, in Avellenada. They even allowed people to pay electric and gas bills with the tickets because people had more of these than money. It's a bartering commission … [reading from the ticket in her hand]: 'The Global Network of Bartering Exchange, this ticket is valid only for those that are a part of the Global Network of Bartering.'

Nicolas: The condition for participation in the barter network was that you had to sell something. Someone couldn't enter into the space where merchandise and services where exchanged if he didn't have something to exchange, if he didn't have something to offer. It did not have to be an object, it could be a skill or craft or trade … anything.

Gisela: Each person decided the value. There was a sort of base, but it didn't have anything to do with the value of money; and not too long after it began, really from one day to the next, when everything with the dollar began to change, the bartering networks changed too. I mean, before a packet of sugar cost, let's say seven credits, and then one month later it cost fifty. It started to become impossible. It began to cost money to buy food to bring to the bartering clubs. Then the clubs fell apart so much that people started to bring clothing and objects from their homes to exchange only for food and not anything else. It became only about food, and there was no more fun in it. Many people were able to eat because of their relationship to the barter networks.

Nicolas: Before you used to buy raw products and then use them to make other products you could sell. For example, you'd buy flour, sugar, and various things to make ravioli or cakes. You'd sell some products and with that you could buy more than just the products to make the cakes again, to bring more to the next barter, but you could also buy fruit and really everything that you'd eat. It worked for a long time. In reality, it worked too well. Really, it got to quite a sophisticated level, and there were exchanges that didn't get taxed or anything. So then, since it began to seriously worry the Ministry of the Economy ... blah, blah, blah ... No one knows what happened with the government, what their position was or if they were trying to break it up. Maybe, no one knows – but some speculate that at some point, the government started to ...

Gisela: To counterfeit.

Nicolas: ... to make thousands and thousands of those tickets. What happened was, you'd go to a block where people got together in each neighborhood where there was a bartering network, and for US$2 you could buy fifty credits. So then, it wasn't worth anything to bring those products, because with US$2 you already had fifty credits and that made the prices ...

Gisela: It was because of money that people boycotted the barter networks. Food products got so expensive that people couldn't invest in goods to then barter with. You could no longer get things that you needed. It broke the balance of the barter economy.

Nicolas: Remember when the Barter network started in 1999? It was soon after that we were invited to participate.

Gisela: Yes.

Nicolas: I teach French classes, and they had invited me to come and teach. They had explained a little bit about what it consisted of.

Gisela: It grew a lot after the 19th and 20th of December, completely. Before, the bartering networks meant going to a fair to buy some lost object, something attractive. After that it turned into something for the basic survival of a family.

Nicolas: This was true for everyone. In the rich neighborhoods, people also created barter networks. If you went to those barters you would notice pretty quickly that they were exchanging things totally different from us.

Gisela: Now, in the poorest, most humble places and also in the provinces, the networks have started to work a bit again – but just a bit, because all that happened with the counterfeiting was disillusioning for people. I'm from the province, and when we used to go to the province to see my family, there were three or four clubs a day, at noon, at night, at times to go shopping for food. It had turned into a supermarket, more or less. Most all of the barter networks were organized by women.

(Conversation in Buenos Aires, 2003)

During the end of 2001 and beginning of 2002, when the barter network took off, there were more than 5m000 *clubes de trueque* (barter clubs, or nodes), with many thousands of people participating in each node regularly (Alcorta 2007). There were also parks and community centers where people bartered through an informal network. The nodes, or more formal spaces of exchange, were located in a wide variety of places and buildings from recuperated workplaces to occupied banks, and even in a center that had been used once to hold political prisoners during the dictatorship.

> The worst blow, however, was the large-scale counterfeiting of vouchers. At one point, Desanzo said, 90 per cent of the chits in circulation were fake ... The counterfeiting undermined the system's credibility, but the lack of basic products, along with inflation – which was almost nine times the level of that in the formal economy – and the inability to obtain vouchers were the main reasons for the system's collapse, Marchini said.
>
> (Gaudin 2003)

Interestingly, though perhaps not surprisingly, there has been a resurgence of the barter networks. While bartering never stopped completely, those facilitating the formal *clubes de trueque* report a doubling in the number of people participating in bartering (this does not include those neighborhoods and groups that have never stopped bartering). During weekends various sections of the park in Buenos Aires are set aside for those coming to barter. However, many of these barter networks no longer use a method of representation for value, but instead barter directly goods for goods or goods for services:

> Some 500 barter clubs operate in Argentina. And although the number of people involved today is far below the three million people who sought support in bartering in 2002, spokespersons say there are twice as many people in the clubs now as there were last year. Organisers have seen a 50 per cent rise in the number of barterers over the last year or so, coinciding with the beginning of a feeling of economic uncertainty linked to the conflict between the government and farmers over a hike in export taxes. Rubén Ravera, one of the founders of the Club del Trueque, or Global Barter Network (RGT) in Argentina [commented] 'It's recommended that the number of participants at each location is no more than 100, because that's the only way to establish face-to-face relations and build up trust between the members.'
>
> (Cerioli 2009)

In 2009 CNN reported on the barter networks, both showing them as an alternative and using them to illustrate the point that the economy was not as strong as it appeared:

> They line up early every Saturday morning at the decrepit gymnasium that houses the La Matanza Barter Club. Club members shuffle in carrying sacks stuffed with everything from homemade clothing to homegrown vegetables, set up their stands and begin a day of bartering. They provide a vital service for people who are short on cash by helping them make ends meet.
>
> (Byrnes 2009)

It is useful to stress the self-organized nature of the barter networks and how the process of coming together to find ways to meet individual and collective needs created, and creates, a new sense of need and a new value on the item for exchange.

The significance of bartering is not found so much in the number of people involved in it, but rather in the culture of exchange that surrounds the phenomenon. Workers in recuperated factories exchange goods for services, and many neighbors now exchange and do for one another in ways that they never would have before. Previously, the market and concepts of capitalist exchange would interfere with relationships, but now, neighbors often look after another's children for a few hours and ask nothing in return, or borrow or lend milk or butter without asking for the same in return. Relationships to one another, and the value of what happens in that relationship and exchange, are mitigated more by *politica afectiva* than by the peso value of that thing or exchange.

Territory

The creation of new social relationships takes place in specific physical locations; often these are created intentionally by those in the movements, for example the recuperation of land upon which to grow crops and build homes, the recuperation of workplaces, and even the weekly assembly meeting on the same street corner, standing in a circle. The use of space as a place within which new relationships are constructed is something that often has been reflected upon (Deleuze and Guattari, 1986; Davis 2006). These spaces are simultaneously sites of protest and creation: for example, *piquetes* are open to assemblies and have become spaces of mutual support where people can get food and medical support. Additionally, these are spaces of nonrepresentation and nonhierarchy, distinct from, say, union occupations of a factory or political parties organizing in a neighborhood; these are spaces organized horizontally, of which active participation and new relationships are an intentional product. This creation of territory necessitates some form of *autogestión*, or autonomous doing, where within that space the group is making or creating productive, transforming relationships and meeting concrete needs (from food, medical, building homes and growing crops to placing whole factories back under production). Taken together, these new relationships and their products create a new concept of territory that goes beyond geographic or political space. Raul Zibechi has contributed a great deal to this literature over the past few years. His argument, building concretely on Davis and Deleuze, is that territory is a physical state as well as a new political category of social relationships, distinct from social movements. First I will address the spatial component of this discussion.

Martín, a participant in the Colegiales neighborhood assembly in Buenos Aires, spoke of the need for people to come together, but to have, in his words, 'a container' for their gathering. At first this container was the assembly, but the group soon realized that it was not just the assembly, but also the meeting of the assembly on the street corner. Here, importance is placed on both taking over space and using a specific geographic space:

> Since there are no institutions, not even a club, church, or anything, the assembly meets on any corner, and in the street even. When this new form of politics emerges it establishes a new territory, or spatiality ... In the beginning, the assembly consisted of people from all walks of life, ranging from the housewife who declared, 'I am not political', to the typical party hack – but there was a certain sensibility. I don't know what to call it, something affective. There was a sense of wanting to change things, a desire for transformation, and that generated a certain kind of new interpersonal relationship, it generated a way of being and a certain sense of 'we', or oneness that is sustainable. I think this is what makes things self-sustaining in the assembly ... Call it whatever you want to call it, but it needs to create a particular affective space. It's as if we live in flux, moving at a certain speed, like little balls bouncing all about, and then suddenly, the assembly is our intention to establish a bay, to momentarily pause time and space and to say, 'Let us think about how to avoid being dragged and bounced about, and simultaneously attempt to build something new ourselves.'
> (Conversation in Colegiales, Buenos Aires, 2003)

As Martín described:

> I understand *horizontalidad* in terms of the metaphor of territories, and a way of practicing politics through the

construction of territory: it is grounded there, and direct democracy has to do with this. It is like it needs occupy a space.

(Conversation in Colegiales, Buenos Aires 2003)

This territoriality, constructed in space, existing in the assemblies as described above, is seen even in the unemployed workers' movements, all of which began in specific neighborhoods, organizing in and for their specific locations. These neighborhoods in particular could be considered slums in the sense that Davis writes about in *Planet of Slums* (2006). Davis describes a phenomenon of urban poor that is specific to geographic location: people who, in his words, have been 'deterritorialized', to then be placed in a new urban slum (Davis 2006).

The 'base location' to or of organizing is key to what the movements are creating, precisely because it is the site of protest. Protests occur on bridges or in major intersections; the intention of the *piquete*, for example, is to shut down that major artery but also to open up a new space on the other side of the blockade. Many began to refer to this space as new free *teritorio* (territory). Raul Zibechi's book, *Territorios en resistencia: Cartografía de las periferias urbanas latinoamericanos* (*Territories in Resistance: Cartography of the Latin American Urban Peripheries*), published in 2008, deals precisely with this issue. He speaks of the importance of territory and particularly about spaces on the periphery such as shanty towns and slums in post-industrial areas: these places are rapidly becoming sites not only of struggle, but of organization in ways that involve *autogestión* and often *horizontalidad*. Zibechi's book has been receiving a lot of attention within the movements in Argentina, as it brings more insight into the theory being developed in practice in the neighborhoods.[11] As Zibechi describes:

> The real divergence from previous time periods is the creation of territories: the long process of conformation of a social sector that can only be built while constructing spaces to house the differences. Viewed from the popular sectors, from the bottom of our societies, these territories are the product of the roots of different social relations. Life is spread out in its social, cultural, economic, and political totality through initiatives of production, health, education, celebration, and power in these physical spaces.
>
> (Zibechi 2008b)

As the book continues, Zibechi argues against the concept and framework of social movements as a way of understanding the new relationships developing in these new territories:

> I propose that in Latin America one differentiating feature of 1968 is the opening toward the territorialization of those involved: Indians, farm-workers, and popular urban sectors. However, the logic of territory is very different from that of the social movement. While one acts in accordance with the demands of the state, the other is 'living space' characterized by the capacity to integrally produce and reproduce the daily lives of its members in a totality that is not unified but rather diverse and heterogeneous. Territory has a self-centered logic: although it formulates demands from the state it is not organized with this in mind.
>
> (Zibechi 2008b)

This distinguishing of social movements from the creation of new relationships and forms of self organization in territory lends itself well to an additional change in relationships that has been taking place within these territories: that is, of the creation of alternative ways of producing value – forms that, while not outside capitalism, do not fit into traditional modes of capitalist production either. Sometimes this is because those producing alternative values have chosen to break from capitalism, and sometimes, as with many in the unemployed neighborhoods, they are not in the same framework because they are excluded from traditional forms of relating and thus have begun to create something new.

New values

The recuperated workplaces (comprising tens of thousands of workers and hundreds of thousands affected by the workplaces), the unemployed workers' movements, also numbering in the tens of thousands, and the many hundreds of thousands who participated in horizontal assemblies and barter networks, have all been contributing in various ways and to various degrees in the production of alternative value, and values, in Argentina. They are using *horizontalidad* and *autogestión* to create alternative ways of relating. They are creating new social relationships and

subjectivities based on the politics of affection and new subjectivities, and are doing so in ways that break with the rules of
capitalist production, creating less exploited and alienated lived
experiences. While these new relations break with the rules of
capitalist production, they are simultaneously creating new
values, and a new value-based relationship to production. Their
rule, the rule of those in the movements, is not the accumulation
of capital or surplus, but of affect and networks of solidarity and
friendship. This new value is experienced on the subjective level,
in the change in people and their relationships to one another,
but also concretely, in new ways of living based in these relationships. As described by Ernesto Lalo Paret, of the recuperated
workplace Cooperativa Unidos por el Calado (the former Gatic,
which makes Adidas footwear):

> This process has all of the problems that you could imagine, but
> it has made the factories viable which for the previous owners
> were not viable. Also, what is viability in a society full of shit?
> An economist might tell me about what something is worth
> in cash flow, but it is the person who is recovering their self-
> esteem, recovering their self-worth and confidence in themselves
> that puts the factory back to work. How much does it cost that
> this guy to be an example to his kid? And what is it worth to
> recuperate a factory for the community, for a family, and for
> society?
> (Interview at MU, August 2011)

Choices are made every day in the recuperated workplaces,
and while of course some of the choices are about being able to
sell the product or service and how much of it to produce, there
are also an equal, if not larger, number of decisions being made
with regard to solidarity with others, and the relationship to the
community and neighborhood. The decisions about solidarity
and production are both separated and intimately linked. In
this connection and separation the rules of production, under
market terms, begin to change. Decisions on production are
no longer made solely on what may sell the most or how
much workplaces need to produce to be most profitable, but
rather are taken into consideration together with the need or

desire to support others: therefore, solidarity becomes a part of the equation, creating a new equation of production. For example, imagine a recuperated workplace assembly. There is a conversation about who they are planning on selling their ceramics to: a discussion follows about the local, regional, and national possibilities, the cost, challenges, and so forth. Then there is a discussion about a neighboring workplace that was recently occupied and needs support and defense. Then there is another question about the group of schoolchildren who plan a trip to visit the factory during the week. Then there is the question of the proposed new nightly class for a new series of *bachilleratos*. The assembly makes decisions about all of the above. Some workers will be released each day this week to support the occupation. Three workers will be released for the hours that the schoolchildren are there to give the tour and answer questions, and how much should they allot to raise the amount of the electric bill to cover the new nightly classes. They also discuss whether they should include heating, since it is getting cold. All of these questions and answers are decided collectively, and are decided based on what the community needs and how they can help. The questions and answers do not begin with how much will it cost, or how much will be lost in production by releasing workers everyday in solidarity. The beginning point is solidarity, not competition or the market. Of course, all decisions include working to cover the basic costs of the workplace and the salaries of each worker, but generally the question of profit is not at the top of the list of priorities. The values are different ones, thus having an effect on both exchange and use value in production, and changing the terms of that relationship.

Raul Zibechi describes what was the beginning of this process in *Genealogía de la Revuelta* (*Genealogy of a Rebellion*, 2003), an analysis of the activities and politics in Argentina in the months following the popular rebellion in 2001, writing: 'What really changes the world is to learn to live other ways, in a more communitarian way ... Fraternity is what is key in social change' (Zibechi 2003: 18).

In his book *The Beginning of History: Value Struggles and Global Capital* (2007), the economist Massimo De Angelis argues for new values being created in various social movements around the globe: 'On the one side, a social force called capital pursues endless growth and monetary value. On the other side, other social forces strive to rearrange the web of life on their own terms' (De Angelis 2007: 135). The book discusses both the capitalist mode of value, around which society is organized, and the movements that are challenging and changing these modes of relation. He goes on to explain:

> This implies that different value practices will reproduce different societies, where value practices are understood to be 'those actions and processes as well as correspondent webs of relations that are both predicated on a given value system, and in turn (re)produce it.
>
> (De Angelis 2007: 25)

Holloway puts forward a similar argument, although connecting the creation of other values with the need to be part of a movement that is organizing beyond capital relations and towards new ways of being and doing:

> Democracy, no matter how 'direct' its structures, will have relatively little impact unless it is part of a challenge to the capitalist organisation of doing as labour … The creation of cooperatives solves nothing unless the articulation between different groups of doers is tackled at the same time. The move towards self-determination cannot be seen simply in terms of particular activities but must inevitably embrace the articulation between those activities, the re-articulation of the social flow of doing (not just production, but production and circulation) … Factory occupations or the creation of cooperatives are insufficient unless they are part of a movement, that is, unless they simultaneously reach beyond to the creation of new articulations between people who are beyond the particular cooperative project.
>
> (Holloway 2003b)

Along the lines of what Holloway is describing here, beginning in late 2009 many in the movements, specifically those that are *autogestionando*, began to speak of living *sin patron* (without a boss). This has been used to refer to workplaces specifically, such as Ceramica Zanon being renamed *Fabrica Sin Patron* (FaSinPat) as we have seen above, but this is now being articulated as a way of referring quite similarly to this new value production. *Sin patron* is not merely working without bosses and hierarchy; it is creating a new way of living and producing. It refers to a more general way of life that is horizontal, which creates new social relationships while directly taking on the question of production. This production can be in a workplace, but also in new autonomous productive projects. For example, as explained by Sergio Ciancaglini, one of the co-authors of the book *Sin Patron* (Lavaca 2004), which chronicles and details the hundreds of workplaces recuperated as of 2004:

> [S]omething else is also happening – there are many children being born from the workplaces – that are horizontal in the way they relate, that are autonomous, meaning from political parties and the state, and they are creating a style that is not only bossless, but are creating these projects outside the factory. There are hundreds and hundreds of projects, with thousands of people, projects such as health care, education, clothing production and many other things. And they are all in a cooperative form and working in solidarity.
>
> (Democracy Now! Radio program, Daily Independent Global News Hour, 19 May 2009)

This rethinking and reforming of forms of production does not function independently from, nor outside, capital. People creating these modes live in the capitalist world and its global neoliberal economy, but crucially they are operating under different assumptions, pushing the boundaries of the rules and forms of capitalist social relations.

As emphasized previously, these new values and forms of value production are breaking with (and creating something different from) capitalist market relations, yet simultaneously they exist within the overall framework of capitalism and are pushing (and moving) the boundaries of the limits of capitalist production value – not merely residing within it. What is being created and put forward is not a small group dropping out of society so as to grow crops and build homes together on the land, as with a commune, but rather the autonomous MTDs are thinking beyond the traditional concept of work and creating new relationships together, sustaining themselves while under capitalism, but with the agenda of going against and beyond capitalism. The aim of recuperated workplaces is not to organize cooperatives of the traditional sort (that is, cooperatives that create a parallel to the capitalist market while functioning entirely within the logic of the market); instead, they are using solidarity to break with alienation and as a way of creating new forms of production. In doing so they are laying the groundwork for a new economy based on exchange and new values. Of course all this is a work in progress, still being determined and created, but what these movements are doing is building a foundation upon which a new society can emerge, and which I argue *is* emerging. There is a great deal of literature that critiques this possibility, arguing, for example:

> Autogestion must also confront and resolve the problems of the organization of the market. Neither in its theory, nor its practice, does it deny the law of value. One cannot claim in its name to 'transcend' the market, the profitability of business, the laws of exchange value. Only centralized statism has had this excessive ambition.
>
> (Brenner and Elden 2009[1966]: 148)

Sin patron or alternative value production is not resolving the organization of the capitalist market or proposing a reorganization of the state – at least not yet. However, it is not sufficient to dismiss the reality of what is taking place, as is being done in the above passage. These are not only sites within capital, they are more than that. People, by the many thousands, explain that they are *creating themselves anew*, and are finding ways to survive based on new principles of solidarity, horizontalism, affective politics, and new values. They are doing this with a vision that is regional, national, and international, as evidenced by the number of groups, networks, and gatherings that have been taking place on all of those levels, as cited in this book. They are creating a new generation of people, as Sergio Ciancaglini explained, who are choosing a different way to organize their lives, different social relationships and different forms of relating to production. So, to ask one of the questions underlying this book: how does one determine the level of success with regards to these movements? No one has claimed that we are witnessing the absolute reorganization of all social relations, not yet at least. However, they do argue their lives are better, they walk with more dignity, and hold new values. In my interpretation, these products lie outside the capitalist frame of analysis.

The role of the state (as will be addressed in future chapters) is an outstanding question, but it is not one with which the movements are not engaging. It would benefit everyone to listen to what is being created, how it is being created and, most importantly, what it means to the people who are living *sin patron*. As Neka, from MTD Solano explained:

> Our perspective is grounded in the need for a new construction ... the most important thing is affect, something that is born from human need, the need to recognize others, to feel recognized, and to recover our self-esteem – that is to say, to recover our dignity ... One of the things that capitalism robs us of is precisely this possibility. It converts us into objects, it 'thing-ifies' us. I think all systems of domination convert us into objects. So, to recover our dignity is to recover this capacity to feel like people.
>
> (Conversation in Solano, 2004)

It is from this base that the movements are creating the groundwork for a new system of relations that is social as well as political and economic. For now this is within capitalism, but it is against capitalism, pushing its boundaries, creating value systems that can go beyond it.

SEVEN

The state rises: incorporation, cooptation, and autonomy

This chapter deals specifically with the relationship between the new autonomous social movements and the state. It begins with an overview of the popular rebellion and its implications at the state level, from the position of the state and its representatives. It then looks at the question of cultural hegemony by tracing the newly-elected government's attempts to regain legitimacy through some sort of social consensus, via human rights advances and the discourse surrounding them, financial incentives, and the incorporation of past Left activists into the newly-formed government. In addition, hegemony is examined in terms of 'power over': that is, through the government's use of direct repression and creation of divisions within the movements. Last, and most importantly for this book, the chapter delves into how the movements have been relating to the state: sometimes rejecting the state, and sometimes relating to it while attempting to maintain their own agenda and tempo.

What is a state without legitimacy?

On the 19th and 20th of December everything exploded. The president was physically removed from office. One week later, another president was removed by unanimous consensus and popular struggle. After that, there was no authority ... The system had completely lost its legitimacy, and the main challenge it confronted was the need to reconstruct this legitimacy.

(Conversation with Pablo in Colegiales, Buenos Aires, 2003)

As discussed in Chapter 2, '*Que se vayan todos*' really meant *todos* (everyone): it meant a rejection of the government and the judiciary. Many people spoke of how government officials were afraid to go out in public for fear of ridicule or even violence. While I have neither heard nor read any reports of physical violence against government representatives, I did hear many accounts of people yelling and throwing things at government officials when they were seen in public. Without a doubt, the state and government of Argentina lost its legitimacy. Not only had the state lost its legitimacy in terms of people 'believing' in it but, as described in Chapters 5 and 6, people were no longer looking to the state to resolve their problems. They began to look to one another, form horizontal assemblies, and decide how to run their lives together and collectively. This was a moment of crisis for the state so, of course the state had to begin to consider solutions.

The election of Néstor Kirchner in 2003 provided a starting point for the process of re-legitimizing the state. Initially, the neighborhood assemblies had organized for a 'No' vote (which in Argentina is illegal, as voting is mandatory). However, Carlos Menem then announced his candidacy for the presidency, and the situation changed. Menem is rightly blamed for the continuation of the process of neoliberalism which had begun during the time of the dictatorship: he sold off most of the country though the privatization of almost all its resources, from the airlines and the post office, to water and the zoo. Menem was responsible for the accumulation of tremendous national debt, which grew from US$8 billion at the end of the dictatorship in 1983, to US$180 billion at the time of the rebellion in 2001 (Salbuchi 2006). Menem also publicly announced that he would use direct repression to prevent movements from mobilizing and growing (Dangl 2009). He was not a popular figure and the prospect of his election, which was a possibility, considering the movements' plan not to vote, shifted the decision of most movement participants who decided to vote tactically; while the voter turnout was still exceptionally low, it was higher than initially planned by the movements. Kirchner was elected despite only gaining 23 per cent of the vote; his victory was indebted to the anti-Menem voters and far from any sort of popular consensus. Nevertheless, it was an election in which people had participated and thus was a part, or at least the beginning, of what became the reconstitution of the state.

From the time of the election began the process of the state working to regain its legitimacy with whatever means possible. Following the election, government funding was passed to the movements, former leftists were brought into the government, which began implementing a human rights discourse long absent from the state's repertoire. These tactics proved quite effective, at least during the first few years; however, by 2009 the role of the state again was being called into question.

Hegemony and social consensus

As described previously, there had been no state prosecution of those involved in the military dictatorship prior to the election of the Kirchners[1] – quite the opposite, in fact. Those who participated in the atrocities were forgiven under the guise of creating peace in society.[2] This left open a huge collective wound, and meant that none of the governments were fully legitimate with respect to human rights laws. With the election of Néstor and then later Cristina Kirchner, laws began to change and a rhetoric based on a discourse of human rights was adopted by the state. At this point it became a top priority to find and punish those military and even nonmilitary personnel who had participated in the disappearance of 30,000 people.

One highly symbolic act was Néstor Kirchner's removal of the photographs of Jorge Rafael Vidale and Reynaldo Bignone, the leaders of the military dictatorship, from the walls of the Military College. At the time Kirchner stated, quite significantly: 'I come to ask for forgiveness on behalf of the state for the shame of having remained silent about these atrocities during twenty years of democracy' (Tobar 2004). Néstor Kirchner also replaced numerous members of the Supreme Court which, many argue, led to the overturning in 2003 of the Ley de Punto Final of 1986, meaning that amnesty would no longer be granted to those who participated in the military dictatorship. This step was, and continues to be, hugely significant in that it led to the prosecution of dozens of military leaders and collaborators. Moreover, it has raised many questions with regard to who is prosecuted and how. Whether consciously or not, the Kirchner governments' human rights project has led to profound divisions within human rights movements, including, not insignificantly, a split in the Madres de la Plaza de Mayo, the Abuelas and even HIJOS. Each of these splits has been based on how much to support – or even if they should join with – the government in the pursuit of human rights, and how much to continue to remain autonomous from the state.

Adopting the language of human rights has played a central role in the re-legitimization of the state, as have various economic policies. Here, Antonio Gramsci's concept of hegemony, as well as the notions of political legitimacy and domination, become useful analytic tools (Haugaard and Lentner 2006). In the case of late twentieth-century Argentina, the state had become so totally de-legitimized that it needed to regain itself in every way possible: economically, politically, and socially. The state requires at least some form of support or consensus from the population, and it is this part of Gramsci's (1971) concept of hegemony that is most applicable to the Argentine example. It is precisely through the implementation of human rights discourses from which this support is born. While economic and political hegemony are important (and will be addressed later), it was the state's tremendous sociopolitical shift in perspective with regard to the military dictatorship that permeated all levels of society. While many were, and continue to be, critical of how the government is carrying out state prosecutions – for example, many people criticize the lack of direct participation from and by human rights organizations – no one is overtly critical of these prosecutions. Following Gramsci's concept, for the state to rule, particularly in a context of '*que se vayan todos*', some semblance of consensus and support is necessary. To be clear, my argument is not that the state took up the human rights banner so as to maintain hegemony – I imagine there are very real human rights motivations in the new policies – however, cultural hegemony was made more possible, even achieved, due to the adoption of human rights discourse.

Direct repression

Another fact of hegemony is the use of direct 'power over' domination. In the case of Argentina, since the elections of the Kirchners, repression has played a complex and sometimes contradictory role. Protest has been criminalized and movement members are evicted on a regular basis, sometimes even killed.[3] The Kirchner governments have been able to use physical repression in an insidious way. There is not a great deal of direct repression, relative to past governments or even many other governments in Latin America today. That said, there has been consistent, direct police repression of the movements, and a high level of criminalization of dissent and protest. For example, more often than not there is at least one attempted eviction a month somewhere in Argentina (lavaca.org). As discussed in Chapter 6, recuperated workplaces are not popular with the institutions of power, despite what would appear to be actions to the contrary, such as being granted legal cooperative status, thus being 'protected' by the recuperation process, so long as everything is done exactly as stated by law. However, there are many loopholes in this 'protection', meaning that often the state mobilizes or permits the police to evict workers, often in the process of recuperation, if one letter of the law is out of place. Additionally, they will also just look the other way when the police move in on a recuperation, 'legally' grounded or not. As stated previously, this is rarely successful thanks to the mobilization of the community and other recuperated movements.

International legitimacy

Internationally the Kirchner governments have been applauded for their role in progressing Argentina. It is understandable how someone from within the movements might be dismissive of this perspective, but there is an argument for the role that the government has played in global politics, in particular with regard to human rights and furthering global human rights discourse.

On an evening in March 2011, I was fortunate to participate in an event at the Venezuelan Consulate in the USA, where I met with the consul general. A part of our conversation related to Argentina, and the consul general stated how important Argentina is to Venezuela, as well as to processes of change in Latin America more generally. She explicitly mentioned the relevance of the new government having managed to renegotiate foreign debt with the International Monetary Fund (IMF). While the movements argue that the debt has been paid many times over and therefore does not need to be repaid, from the perspective of other countries trying to resist the neoliberal and international bank agenda, a country renegotiation on their own terms is a very big deal, and helps to pave the way for further, more independent relationships from the banks and from US or foreign control. In addition, she made very compelling arguments about the prosecution of participants from the military dictatorship, suggesting that this had helped to pave the way for the election of former leftists in Latin America. I am not sure that my own analysis would go that far, but hearing a representative of an important

Latin American nation, struggling for independence from international banks and US domination, argue the importance of the human rights discourse of the Kirchners for the rest of the Americas, convinced me that it is something that cannot be left out of this book in examining the role of the state.

Argentina was not alone in not prosecuting former military dictatorship participants and collaborators: most of Latin America has been guilty of this. That the Kirchners are prosecuting the lead organizers of the dictatorship and opening up a space within the government for former leftists, and even people who were part of the armed opposition, sets an example for other countries in Latin America. It is much easier for a nation to be one among many – particularly with regard to policies that do not please the USA – such as former leftist guerillas in government, than to do it alone. In this regard the Kirchner governments have opened up some space for other countries in Latin America to do the same.

Divisions deepening hegemony

As mentioned previously, the concept of hegemony requires at least some consensus and tacit support from the population (Gramsci 1971). However, hegemony is not just about creating consensus in a population; it is also about political domination of the more direct sort, which is often done through the creation of discord in oppositional movements – a simple form of divide and conquer. This is what the Kirchner government did quite brilliantly. It is unclear how much of the discord was intentionally created, and how much was a result of certain policies that the government instituted, but it does not matter since either way tremendous divisions were created, and these divisions benefited the state and its political hegemony. The two most important areas of division were with human rights organizations and the *piqueteros*. The divisions within these strong movements and organizations relied on the demobilization of the middle class.

Human rights

As mentioned previously, there tends to be considerable support for the Kirchner governments when it speaks out against the military dictatorship and prosecuting some of those who were involved. However, within this support tremendous disagreement has emerged regarding the question of whether to support the Kirchner governments absolutely or the human rights policies while remaining an outside force and not joining the government or any of its agencies. Unfortunately this has resulted in a more profound split. The Madres de la Plaza de Mayo now not only has two offices, one located in the large, well-known school and bookstore, and the other in a very small upstairs location a few blocks away, but they hold two separate marches in front of the Pink House every Tuesday and Thursday. The Association of the Madres, the one in the larger location, is the one led by Hebe Bonafini which decided to support the Kirchners absolutely: so much so that groups and movements that are organizing in opposition to the government cannot use the Madres' school or bookstore for events. Bonafini is now one of the most visible supporters of the Kirchner governments, regularly saying things such as, 'Néstor gave us our country back' and 'I am so proud of Cristina' (de Bonafini, 2011).

This is quite different to the message from the Madres de la Plaza de Mayo Linea Fundadora, who wrote in a letter in 2006 to the president:

> We support the positive steps you have taken to move the
> country forward, a country that you received in ruins and
> with tremendous suffering of the people. Still today there is so
> much more that needs to happen so as to advance, and that
> the Argentine people can live in dignity, justice, equality and
> solidarity, as our children dreamt and for which they gave their
> lives. Unfortunately there are still unacceptable violations of
> human rights … and the situation of extreme poverty persists,
> which makes it necessary to change the unfair distribution of
> wealth.
> (Madres de la Plaza de Mayo Linea Fundadora 2006)

Similarly based divisions have taken place in the Abuelas and HIJOS, although within HIJOS neither division absolutely and uncritically supports the Kirchner governments.

The middle class

I use the term 'middle class' again here, and as in Chapter 3, actually mean a broader understanding of the term: one that comprises working-class people who have had some sort of regular work for a majority, if not all, of their lives. As soon as the Kirchner government was elected in 2003, it began all sorts of economic reforms and, as will be discussed in the following section on the *piqueteros*, this economic reform was dependent on the class to whom it was geared. For example, with the middle class and those identifying as middle class, real jobs were created so as to make for a longer lasting and less dependent relationship on the state. 'Under the Kirchner administration, the government used liberal economic policies to create employment and stability, but also to effectively win the support of the middle class' (Dangl 2009: 71).

For segments of the middle class, the at least partial economic recovery was not the only factor leading to a decline in activism after the elections. The active incorporation of middle-class activists into the new government led to disorientation within many of the neighborhood assemblies. For example, the assemblies all had the position of not working from within the state, even if there were decisions to use the state and its resources. However, when the new government invited former radicals and even Montenero or Ejercito Revolucionario del Pueblo (ERP) participants to join its ranks, some saw this as an opportunity to create change. Previously some of these individuals had played important roles in their neighborhood assemblies, so leaving them and joining the government created tension and discord within the assemblies, resulting in less of a unified and clear path with regard to how to engage or not. Additionally, the new government offered many of the neighborhood assemblies food and shelter, as it did with the *piqueteros*. During the assemblies in which I participated, when the government presented an offer, hours of discussion and debate ensued. Generally offers from the state were rejected, but such lengthy debates frustrated many participants by derailing the movement's agenda. Often people would stop taking part because of this.

Taken together, the economic recovery, the incorporation of community leaders into the government, and the division of neighborhood assemblies led to a steady decline in their organization. Thus, with fewer neighborhood assemblies there were fewer structured relationships between and among the unemployed and recuperated workplaces and the middle class. Some critiques have argued that the middle class no longer supported the struggles of the unemployed or recuperated movements, but this is less true than there were fewer structures facilitating these relationships. This is borne out when looking at the past few years of political activity, and the fact that again the middle class is involved in projects such as the *bachilleratos* (as described in Chapter 6). The framework of the *bachilleratos* has helped to facilitate direct relationships with the unemployed and recuperated workplaces, together with the middle class.

Piqueteros

Numerous social scientists and analysts have focused a great deal of attention on the divisions that emerged within the *piquetero* movement after the election of Néstor Kirchner. Many of the *piquetero* groups came out in support of him for reasons similar to the Madres, but also because he promised to increase the number of unemployment subsidies to be distributed to the movements. Of all of these groups, few of them have been part of autonomous or *autogestiva* projects. There were, and are, dozens of *piquetero* groups who organized all along for the unemployment subsidy, and distributed this money to individuals in the movement. This is quite distinct from the movements which had a different conceptualization of power, as for example MTD Solano or Cipolletti. However, more complicated were the number of unemployed workers' movements that were once more autonomous and are now less so, but remain separate from Piqueteros K. This third grouping resembles a more traditional leftist group or party, in that it has a contentious relationship to the state, a political program (which includes an explicitly anti-capitalist and anti-imperialist stance), and recruits members in a similar way to political parties. Some of the unemployed workers' movements that are a part of the Frente began in ways similar to MTD Solano, and in fact some were in the same initial networks, such as MTD Anibal Veron. These groups made a political decision to form a new Frente, together with students and other political groups, so as to build what they call 'popular power and social change'. The main distinction between these groups and the autonomous unemployed workers' movements is that they are not attempting to create a base in the neighborhoods grounded in productive projects, neither do they focus as much on *horizontalidad* and the creation of new subjectivities. The Frente puts forward its political perspective as being grounded in many movements which have sought to take power, and sees the radical aspects of Peronism as a part of its political heritage. I am not suggesting here that there is no autonomous politics whatsoever in the Frente, but for the sake of the discussion at hand, I am focusing on the movements that have a clearer demarcation regarding their relationship or desired relationship to the state, and their autonomous construction in geographic areas.

Over the past eight years there have been both mobilizations of *piqueteros* opposed to the state, and those in favor of it. Those in favor are called the Piqueteros K (for Kirchner). As mentioned previously, they organize and mobilize in support of the president. Mobilizing in support of the state is new, but these groups were all along the ones that continued to organize with clientalistic relationships. As described earlier, there are those unemployed workers' movements that are creating autonomy and new social relationships, and those that organize along traditional hierarchical models, attempting to get as much from the state as possible. As explained and differentiated by the Argentine sociologist, Maristella Svampa:

> What happened on the side of the *piquetero* organizations? In other words, how did they interpret the new Peronist government? The change in political opportunities and in their analyses of them updated and brought to light the movement's different ideological matrices. Accordingly, today we can more clearly distinguish the three primary configurations: the populist groups, those linked to leftist parties, and lastly, what we can call the space occupied by the new left. From the beginning, the groups belonging to the populist strain developed a strong expectation for (re)integration. They hoped for the reconstruction of the national state under a new leadership, embodied by President N. Kirchner.
>
> (Svampa and Pereyra 2003b: 18)

Money and services as control

> To build a Latin American welfare state and bring about conciliation between social classes, centralizing power in the distributional state.
>
> (quoted in Lievesley and Ludlam 2009: 211)

This is what the Kirchner governments put forward as one of

their goals. While Argentina is no welfare state, the new governments have raised the quantity of people receiving benefits. These numbers rose under former president Eduardo Duhalde, between 2002 and 2003, from 700,000 to 2 million, and then again under Néstor Kirchner to 2.6 million (Svampa 2008). While the quantity did not increase, and considering that inflation arguably decreased, the numbers of people receiving benefits increased so much that more illusions were created that the government was going to solve people's economic needs. So while these illusions increased, material conditions for the vast majority of the poor, the unemployed, and the more precarious working class, changed very little (Svampa 2008). The situation of the most poor is not as desperate as it was at the time of the popular rebellion, where children were actually starving and the numbers of malnourished skyrocketed, but this is due only in part to the policies of the state in response to the mobilization of the population. It is these 'gifts', even if temporary and small, that together with an anti-neoliberal rhetoric adopted by Kirchner, helped to shift some of the consciousness in favor of the government (Svampa 2008). As a MTD Solano participant, who did not wish to be identified, explained in 2005:

> Right now, there are about five hundred to six hundred people involved in weekly movement activity in our neighborhood. At first there were around three hundred, but we kept growing until we were a bit over one thousand. Then when the electoral political campaigns began, there was a decrease because the political party apparatuses put up a lot of money to buy people into their campaigns. In the last electoral campaign in the neighborhood, they tried to buy *compañeros*. A sister said that someone who works for the government told her that political parties offer more money if a party broker can get someone who's involved in the movements, rather than someone who's not, and even more if they are a leader. It's more cost efficient to them to get a *compañera* because she is fighting.

The movements dance with dynamite[4]

Piqueteros, MTDs and movements for dignity

As a *compañera* from the MTD La Matanza commented in 2004:

For there to be autonomy, there must be a rupture with the state. It isn't easy, and our being relatively isolated makes the path less easy, but it is possible. We've continued as a movement for all of these years, and never accepted the *planes de trabajo* [state unemployment subsidies] ... You must reject the seduction that allows a dominant class to decide our values and principles, and in that construction you must build other principles, other values, and a different ethic. Maybe we don't know how to do this systematically, but we do know it's possible.

(quoted in Sitrin 2006: 169)

The policy towards accepting money from the state varies among the different movements, with a few, such as MTD La Matanza, not receiving subsidies, and others such as MTD Solano, Guernica, Allen and Cipolletti changing their position. Svampa describes here the diversity of the other political tendencies within the social movements, clarifying their positions not to join the state or the populism that it represents, and at the same time their attempt to create other social relationships:

[T]here is a third tendency under which we can also place the independent organizations. This tendency is less visible in the media, more innovative in terms of political practices, and associated with the spaces occupied by the new left. This heterogeneous frame, which contains organizations with long histories such as the MTR [Movement Teresa Rodriguez], the UTD from Mosconi, and the MTDs from A. Verón, includes an ideological spectrum ranging from 'guevarism', the radical left and its variants, all the way to the current forms of 'autonomism'. Beyond the differences that separate them, all of these groups managed to resist falling prey to the simplifying position in which, once again, Justicialism's historical strength threatened to place them. Therefore, they gave priority to more manageable neighborhood issues, without renouncing mobilization or the production of new strategies for action. Rather than dedicating resources to an unequal political struggle against a government backed by public opinion, these organizations chose to concern themselves with developing political awareness and training and producing new social relationships ('new power', 'popular power' or 'counterpower', depending on the various formulations). In sum, the most notable events and tendencies of the current period are, on the one hand, the recent emergence of a *piquetero* current, made up of groups supporting populism, which is linked to the government in power and, on the other hand, the separation of the block from La Matanza and the search for new strategies for action. Within an increasingly polarized political scenario, these strategies aim to coordinate with other social actors, diversify organizational forms, patterns and discourses.

(Svampa and Pereyra 2003b: 19)

The struggle to remain autonomous is common to all the movements; however, since 2009 even the more autonomous movements have begun to shift their positions and decided to relate to the state, but on their own terms. For example, El Vasco from the Movement for Social Dignity of Cipolletti explained:

I believe that relations with the state have always been complicated. To put forward autonomy necessarily implies not to get caught up in the state agenda, but to look for ways to meet your concrete necessities that you have and take them from the state – and to do it in a way that does not harm our sovereign space most of all.

Continuing a little later on the same point:

It is a difficult relationship, but there are issues that we are clear about in this regard: from the state we will take what we can get, and will not let the state condition our own practices or constructions. If it seems like that is happening, we have a sort of red light or alarm that goes off, and we all run fast the other way. But we start from the premise that everything the state has is ours, so then what we are doing is taking back what is ours, and always serving in the construction of an autonomous area … This does not mean that the state does not have crucifixions or is not constantly attempting to co-opt what we are trying to do. But we don't take it. We won't accept it.

(Conversation in Cipolletti, Patagonia, late 2009)

This relationship plays out in many ways in the movement,

from the very material of the building in which the community center of the movement is located, to the food that most participants eat and the walls of their homes on squatted land. Each of the above items are taken or received from the state, and then the movement together, in various working groups, use these raw supplies to do things such as build homes and cook food. This is all done collectively and there is no formal checking system. That said, there is an informal dynamic that many talk about, which includes forms of pressure on those who are not seen as carrying their weight. This can take the form of teasing someone, asking where they were, or sometimes a more formal conversation between a longer-standing participant of the movement and a newer one, describing the culture and what the group's ethics are about.

MTD Solano began a process with a very similar approach to that of Cipolletti in late 2009 and early 2010. First, it attempted to break from all formal economic relationships with the state between 2005 and 2006, generally not going out into the street in *piquetes* to demand the small monthly subsidy. Its collective opinion was that a constant *piquete* created a dynamic of perpetually asking for or demanding from the state, and that it detracted from autonomous creation in the neighborhood. Also, in later reflections on why it stopped taking subsidies, one of the things it pointed to was the effect on the internal relationships in the movement. As Neka commented in a conversation in late 2009:

> These experiences were sometimes of control, of centralization, and at a certain moment we noticed that within the movement we were reproducing the relationships of the state, and groups were administering collective things, and groups were deciding sometimes who would get more benefits than others.
>
> (Conversation in Solano, late 2009)

She goes on to describe the role that capitalism plays in all people's lives and relationships, and the deep desire to break with that relationship in Solano. One of the ways to do this, at that particular moment in Solano, was to stop demanding monthly money from the state. The demanding and accepting of money from the state, as she describes, did not end with the money magically arriving, but the movement had to decide how and when to distribute it, which in turn created the need for some form of administration. In other movements, the non-autonomous ones, this is simply enough: there is a *puntero* or someone similar to a *puntero*, and they decide who gets what and when.

In the few years since the movement broke all economic ties with the state, there have been a number of different projects and forms of organization that the movement has experimented with, including taking over dozens of hectares of land upon which they have built homes and farmed. However, these projects were not enough for the movements to become self-sufficient, and this contributed to the movement seeing a sharp decline in active participants.

By 2009, MTD Solano began to rethink its relationship to the state, recognizing that the point of concern had become what this relationship might look like. In the meantime there had been a shift in some of the incentives offered by the state to movements, including a new policy that resembled the cooperative law for recuperated workplaces. This new law grants money to collectives for specific projects, and in order to receive it a collective needs to register all of its participants with the state and create some sort of structure that demonstrates the active participation of all members, at which point they can request funds. This law is not dissimilar from the Communal Councils in Venezuela under president Hugo Chavez (Ness and Azzellini 2011): it is a very new process, and only began taking effect in 2010, so a full analysis has yet to be conducted.

What MTD Solano did decide was to reorganize as a movement into a movement that is a collective of collectives: a formal new name has yet to be decided upon. During the time that I was in Argentina in late 2009 and early 2010, the movement had begun to register people from the neighborhood into this new movement, and had more than 4,000 people at the last count. Many of these new participants are actually older participants who drifted away from the movement when there was no concrete financial assistance. Now, with this new proposal and formation there is still no monthly cash, as with unemployment, but there is a possibility of resource support. MTD Solano speaks, as does Cipolletti, of the relationship to the state being one of 'permanent tension', and that it will continue the relationship as long as it can maintain its own agenda and continue to do so autonomously.

Recuperated workplaces

The recuperated workplaces' relationship to the state is more straightforward; however, this is true as long as the state's intentions are clear – which is not always the case. As mentioned previously, the state allows recuperated workplaces to function legally for a certain period of time, as well as to apply for certain federal loans, but there are regular eviction attempts, with the state attempting to control all interactions related to commerce or any wider regional and international global networks.

Take the example of Chilavert, a printing press in Buenos Aires, as Placido explained in late 2009:

> The state is encouraging all workers to come together and form cooperatives [like MTD Solano is doing], though without any initial capital, and then the state proposes that it will support this project with initial capital. This is a good program to help alleviate unemployment, but for us this does not help since we need someone to sell to on the market. We are trying to continue to exchange things with other recuperated workplaces, and when this begins to go well, they [the state] then are there, always putting obstacles in our way, like inspections, permits, and right when you are going to get back to work, there is another bureaucratic obstacle that takes all your time and you end up doing nothing.
>
> (Conversation in Pompeya, Buenos Aires, 2009)

Then, giving another example, this time with regard to international relationships between movements and Left governments and recuperated workplaces, Placido explains what happened with Chilavert, which is also true for many of the workplaces. The government used laws to attempt to block solidarity:

> The idea here was to strengthen the recuperated factories with the help of Venezuela through economic credit or financial aid, but the state would not let it happen. The state does not want to let this, what they call public policy, out of their hands. Because

when people are in this desperate situation of not being able to decide their own destiny, which is what we are, we look for help on the outside, and that is where there is a block, where we get stuck, because the state is making policies that prevent this from happening.

(Conversation in Pompeya, Buenos Aires, late 2009)

The above example is specific to one particular international gathering that took place in Caracas, Venezuela. Dozens of agreements were made among and between recuperated workplaces throughout the Americas, as well as with the Government of Venezuela; however, the Kirchner government would not permit these exchanges as they were outside the formal relationships of exchange between states. Rather, it would allow the recuperated workplaces to create an international network of sustenance and survival based not on the market, but on the solidarity economy. The example of Chilavert above is only one of many, and indicative of the state's relationships with the various recuperated workplaces and international relations. Some have slightly different opinions of the state, but as a whole there is no policy of 'autonomy' or working within the state. Workplaces tend to use the state when necessary and in whatever way they can, and when it is an obstacle they look for other ways or defend themselves from attack.

FaSinPat (Ceramica Zanon) is a different scenario. Its workers have been calling for worker control through state expropriation of the factory for a number of years, as the comment by Alejandro below reflects:

We propose the expropriation of the factory, which is worker-controlled nationalization. The funds are then managed by workers, and the state provides the raw materials, energy and gas for the workers to produce and generate resources, renew technologies, and allocate those resources into a public works schemes ... Four hundred and fifty workers here can manage the factory and it can progress.

(Conversation in Nuequén, Patagonia, 2009)

Final expropriation has now been won, although the question of time will help in analyzing the difference in the *autogestiva* process of the workplace, as well as financial stability with regard to state dependency. FaSinPat is the only workplace in Argentina now to function under this new legal relationship. One thing is clear with FaSinPat, and I believe with most other workplaces, from the countless conversations I have had over the years: at their core they do not believe the state is on their side, but rather on the owner's side. This has always been their experience, and while contradictory today, it still remains:

> And governments govern for the employers – that is why these [recuperated] factories are here in Argentina. All policies that were carried out in the context of the international economic crisis were in order to guarantee profits to the employer.
> (Conversation in Neuquén, Patagonia, 2009)

Other movements for autonomy relate to the state

HIJOS does not act against the state – nor with it. As with other movements in contemporary Latin America (the Mexican EZLN [Ejercito de los Zapatistas de Liberacion Nacional] or the Brazilian MST), its interventions are rather independent from it. They are not anti-state in the sense of attacking it; they are anti-state because they build autonomy. Their radicalism and strength reside in the fact that they do not need the state. Even though, in turn, this produces a delegitimizing of the state, it is not the central point of the action. The *escrache* does not negate the power of the state to judge, it only points to its lack of action and its complicity with state terrorism.

(Benegas forthcoming)

Social movements can struggle for autonomy in the sense of escaping state control, while still very much engaging in political action.

(Stahler-Sholk 2004: 1)

The discussions about the structure of the organization, horizontality for example, got to the fore as H.I.J.O.S. was discussing more its proposals not only for political action but also for a new democratic country. As the state was showing fissures, the main task was no longer just opposing the state but rather imagining, practicing, and building new forms of social organizing. Away from the state forms of social intervention that rely on autonomy and imagination were emerging. Practicing new socialities and creating new institutions were ways to enact, to put in practice, concrete proposals for social change.

(Benegas forthcoming)

The most serious challenge to HIJOS's autonomy and horizontal decision making structures occurred in 2003 when the Ley de Punto Final of 1986 was revoked and the trials of the former military began. For HIJOS the challenge was how (and if) to participate in the trials without giving up on its deep questioning of institutional justice; how to get what it could from the system without compromising the bigger long-term goals of social transformation and the creation of new social relationships. For example, practising *escraches* is quite different from joining the state in trials of individuals, which shift the attention somewhat away from society as a whole and on to a number of bad people held responsible by a handful of good people.

On a number of occasions HIJOS has been asked to participate formally in the trials, as in collaboration with government agencies, and this has raised serious debates as to what the best role and place for HIJOS are; it is along these kind of debates that have split HIJOS into two groups. The more autonomous part of HIJOS believes that direct and regular engagement with the state by HIJOS representatives will break up the horizontal nature and spirit of the group. In another area, similar to a number of the MTDs discussed above, the state has offered some HIJOS groups money for projects, and for example HIJOS Cordoba accepted government funding and bought a printing press for the distribution of its material.

Like the unemployed workers' movements, HIJOS is struggling with the question of how to maintain its own autonomy and agenda, but at the same time to get what it believes to be theirs anyway from the state. The dance is a very dangerous and tricky one, but now that the discussion is taking place, there are more possibilities for autonomous creation.

Two more examples, similar to HIJOS and the unemployed workers' movements, are the media collective Lavaca and the photo collective, Coop Foto . Both groups have become official under the state but maintain their own agendas and do whatever work the collective decides. One of the ways that Lavaca has found to struggle in its relationship to the state is to make sure that it always happens with at least a few participants at a time, and that these roles rotate. As with the recuperated workplaces, at both collectives whatever monies are made from projects are divided equally among all participants.

Conclusion: it's a war, not a dance

The relationship with the state will always be contentious, it will always be a sordid war, always.
(El Vasco, MTD Cipolletti in Patagonia, in late 2009)

This chapter began a discussion of the 'dance with the state'. For the movements, the relationship to the state is more aptly described as a war, as El Vasco describes it above. The incredible strategy, foresight, and planning needed to have a relationship at all with an institution that wants to eradiate you is profound and constant. On the positive side, the movements also want to eliminate the state, and by creating autonomously in the cities, towns, and countryside throughout the country, they are creating bases from which the war is being waged. A war that is creating new value and values, new subjectivities, based in love and affect, and new people, on the one hand, and a war for the destruction or cooptation of these new social subjects, on the other hand. The future, as has been said, is yet unwritten, but for now the dance/war is gaining ground on behalf of the movements. Time has allowed for a much more sophisticated analysis of how to wage this war, and the participants are cautiously optimistic.

EIGHT

Measuring success: affective or contentious politics?

> Too often our standards for evaluating social movements pivot around whether or not they 'succeeded' in realizing their visions rather than on the merits or power of the visions themselves. By such a measure, virtually every radical movement failed because the basic power relations it sought to change remain pretty much intact. And yet it is precisely those alternative visions and dreams that inspire new generations to continue to struggle for change.
>
> (Kelley 2003b: ix)

> There have only been two world revolutions. One took place in 1848, the second took place in 1968. Both were historic failures. Both transformed the world. The fact that both were unplanned, and therefore in a profound sense spontaneous, explains both facts – the fact that they failed, and the fact that they transformed the world.
>
> (Arrighi 2008: 97)

Dreams, dignity, and a yardstick

Social movements are made up of people. People with ideas and dreams, dreams for themselves, dreams for the collective, and dreams for the movements and the world. On occasion these dreams and goals are comparable with those of social scientists who study social movements, who claim to know what constitutes a successful movement. Under a certain interpretation this might suggest that they claim to know the hopes and aspirations of the movement participants. James Petras argues, for example, that a movement must seize state and institutional power in order to be successful. MTD Solano participant Neka says that for her and for the movement, dignity and freedom in and of their relationships is a huge part of what they desire and dream. Who is right? Is Petras really stating that Neka is not successful because

Photo 7 Movement for Social Dignity – Chipolletti, Patagonia (youth group assembly)

she did not take over the state? Does his argument mean that she cannot know what success is for herself or for her movement, that she cannot know her very own dreams and desires?

This is an important point too often overlooked by social movement theorists. Who decides what constitutes success? Success can be determined only by those people in struggle, those who are fighting or organizing for something. Frances Fox Piven and Richard Cloward argue this at the very beginning of *Poor People's Movements* (1979). In fact, they added it to the book's introduction as a result of many people's first reaction to the manuscript that they had distributed. Many readers spent much effort arguing what the people in the movements 'ought' to have wanted.

> What clearly was lacking was a unified political organization (party, movement or combination of both) with roots in the popular neighborhoods, which was capable of creating representative organs to promote class-consciousness and point toward taking state power. As massive and sustained as was the

initial rebellious period (December 2001–July 2002) no such
political party or movement emerged – instead a multiplicity of
localized groups with different agendas soon fell to quarreling
over an elusive 'hegemony' – driving millions of possible
supporters toward local face-to-face groups devoid of any
political perspective.

(Petras 2004: 29)

The success of a movement, movement goals, and people's
desires come from those people, those social actors, not those
studying them or politically desiring to lead them. In fact, it is
against this way of thinking and organizing (be it on the Left or
Right) that the movements in Argentina were born. The rupture
was with the state or other forms of authority dictating what they
should be doing and how they should be doing it. This includes
not only governments and politicians, but also Left political
parties and scholars. As mentioned previously, '*Que se vayan
todos*' really does mean *todos*.

What does it mean for people in the movements in Argentina
to have been successful? What do other social scientists argue?
Is there any place of overlap? What can we learn from this for
future interpretation of movements, and is the gap between
theory and practice 'phantasmagorical', as Boaventura de Sousa
Santos argues?

The distance between the practices of the Latin American left
and the classic theories of the left is greater today than ever …
From the point of view of theory, a theoretical hodge-podge
is never theory. And from the point of view of practice, *a
posteriori* theorising is parasitic.

(de Sousa Santos 2009: 275)

So then, what is a scholar of the movements, who works
together with the movements, to do both in terms of methodology and analysis? Many of my friends and *compañeros* in the
movements in Argentina think that this question is waste of time
because they have been harmed by theorists, social scientists, and
leftist groups theorizing their ways of being and publishing the
results of these 'studies' so often conducted without their participation. I recall a late-night conversation in the home of Neka and

Alberto in the poor peripheral (now politically central) neighbor-hood of Solano. We were sitting in their recently built kitchen, in a home constructed on taken land, as were their neighbors' homes, all built collectively. We had just finished a late dinner with many from the community, who also were living in homes collectively constructed from random pieces of wood and cement. We were drinking wine and *mate* and many people were smoking, as is still the norm in Argentina. It was a nice moment of calm after a filling meal. I decided to use this opportunity, with some people around, to ask their feelings about academics, specifically people who have been writing that they, the *piqueteros*, and more gener-ally of the movements in Argentina, are at best totally unrealistic, and at worst, dead. Neka responded first. She smiled so openly at me, but also a little condescendingly, and said, 'So? Marina, don't worry about them. Who cares what they think? We know what we are doing, and we are doing it well.' For Neka, Alberto, Claudia, Maba, Claudio, Vladimir, and Ramon, my question was irrelevant. They continue, day in, day out, creating new lives, new social actors, and more dignity. They are succeeding with or without the opinions of outsiders, whether these scholars confirm what the participants already know or not. However, in my opinion, with the wrong framework or researchers asking the wrong questions, the movements can be detrimentally affected.

To clarify, I am not implying that all academics fail to understand or do not even try to understand. In fact, Susan Buck-Morss gave a talk in late 2011 in which she reflected:

> As the Egyptian Feminist Nawal Sadaawi, responded last spring: Make your own revolution. The ways forward will be as varied as the people of this world. Feminists globally have taught us the need for such variety. All of these ways forward deserve our solidarity and support. We, the 99 per cent, must refuse to become invisible to each other. The experiments that are going on now in thousands of locations need space, the space that Walter Benjamin called a *Spielraum* (space of play) to try out doing things differently. And they need time, the slowing of time, the pulling of the emergency brake, so that something new can emerge. This is time that state power wants to cut short, and space that old-style political parties want to foreclose. There is no rush. The slowing of time is itself the new beginning.

Every day that this event continues, it performs the possibility that the world can be otherwise. Against the hegemony of the present world order that passes itself off as natural and necessary, global actors are tearing a hole in knowledge. New forms emerge. They nourish our imagination, the most radical power that we as humans have.[1]

(Personal email communication, 26 January 2011)

This passage comes from her engagement with the new movements in the USA, which in turn are inspired by those movements around the globe in 2011. Her use of Benjamin's concepts of time and the notion of 'now-time', as discussed in earlier chapters (where movement participants speak of not waiting for a future time or event to change things), are more than comparable.

The talk that Buck-Morss gave initially was going to be titled 'A Communist Ethic', but she changed the word 'Communist' to 'Commonist' so as to reflect the changing politics that she sees and in which she is engaged. This is a fine example and one that other scholars and academics could follow: to be willing to change one's perspective and thus the terms and framing of one's understanding based on the world around us.

The movements in Argentina are a success and they continue to breathe, live and succeed. Within the movements new subjects are forming and are doing so in tandem with dignity. Often they struggle sometimes just to eat a balanced meal, sometimes a filling meal, but they do continue.

This question of success reminds me of a famous poem by the Cuban poet Nicolas Guillen, 'Tengo' ('I Have'). The poem describes in detail what he, the narrator, now has because of the Cuban Revolution. The poem is not about food, housing, or education, or any of the material things that were won from the revolution – things that poor blacks in Cuba did not have beforehand. What he writes is that he now has dignity. He writes of what it feels like to walk down the street. To hold his head high, and know his children will hold their heads high. He writes of how he feels and how he sees himself, and how others see him. What he does say is that now he has education, he can learn to read and write, and he follows those lines with, 'and to laugh, and to smile'. This kind of success is not as measurable as taking over of the state and making education free and food a right – but it is part of success. In Argentina, the measuring stick, as Neka taught me, is dignity. It is not just about winning a struggle, but about the process which, no matter how or where it takes place, forever transforms people's ways of seeing themselves and their relationships to others. Paula, an activist in Argentina, reflected on the experiences of the assemblies in this way:

> The experiences have produced profound transformations in people, in the subjectivity of people, in people feeling themselves as actors for the first time in their lives. In the assemblies people from all different backgrounds, of different ages and social situations, have come together to discuss and listen to each other, each person's opinion and voice not being valued more or less than any others. This is extremely important, especially considering how the political parties work, which is the opposite. What is being constructed is a new way to do politics. People are the protagonists, the subjects. If the assemblies disappeared tomorrow, it would not be something so serious because something fundamental has changed in people. People will never again be passive in their lives.
>
> (Conversation in Paternal, Buenos Aires, 2003)

This new way of being is imbued in most everything. It is seen in almost all the new political formations that have come about since the rebellion, groups that assume *horizontalidad* and a form of prefigurative politics:

> In terms of the process of changes in subjectivity, the interesting thing is that this is a social education. Imagine if the assemblies disappeared – we have had the social training of the assembly. The non-hierarchical structure and self-organization is something that you can use in the future and in other political experiences. In this sense, I'm not a pessimist. I can be more pessimistic in the short term, in the sense that I would like it if the assemblies were stronger. But in the long run, what I know now is that the crisis in the 1990s brought about lots of social education. We will learn from all these experiences of self-organization, and the next time we need an assembly we will

have had all the experiences from the assemblies of the 19th
and 20th.

(Conversation in Paternal, Buenos Aires, 2003)

Claudia goes on to describe why she thinks some academics
have a hard time understanding what the movements are doing.
She explains this by way of example:

In Chilavert, the neighbors were all there in the intense cold,
and they applauded and applauded with such pleasure in seeing
what they had accomplished – this is more than the feeling
that you are the owner of your experience. It is not a question
of property, it is more of a feeling of having given birth. What
you see there is that the people are so proud, and their children
are walking by themselves [upright] – this is *autogestión*. ... I
think that this is something that the academy cannot interpret
because it is something you have to see with a deep level of
sensibility.

(Conversation in Buenos Aires, late 2009)

This interview, with both Claudia and Sergio from Lavaca,
went on for a number of hours, and the question of both academic
or intellectual interpretation of the movements came up numerous
times. (I also spent most of my time in Buenos Aires during 2009
staying in their home, so the number of informal conversations
on this topic is exponential.) The movements are not unequivo-
cally against attempts to theorize their successes and failures;
however, they believe that traditional intellectuals have yet to do
so accurately. This is in part due to the 'nature' of the academy
and formal training within education, but it is also very much a
consequence of the changing and intuitive nature of the movements, which above all require full and active participation from
those interacting with them. As Claudia explains a little later:

I find that there are those who say, it's all co-opted, all useless,
and then when you get directly involved, it is the opposite, and
you say, this is full of life. In other words, between the discourse
and practice there is a great divorce. I think it will take many
years of thinking to figure out how to conceptualize or theorize
about what is happening now, it is quite challenging ... So,

the intellectual, logically, what he does is defends his position and holds his ground, because otherwise this process undermines him.

(Conversation in Buenos Aires, late 2009)

This does not mean that people cannot understand the movements, or help to lend their analysis and meanings. One such person, regularly referred to in this book, is Raul Zibechi, who has spent a great deal of time in Argentina with the movements. In late 2009 he spoke with Lavaca, and regarding questions of whether and how the movements have continued, and how to understand the current situation, he responded:

How to understand what happened on the 19th and 20th? Was it a slogan that then burst with the slogan, 'They all must go', that was never concretized? A problem only of the savers? Or is it a point of inflection in history, in the political culture of the country, and with crucial scope for all of what has happened in this decade that is now ending, and in so much of what is continuing to occur?

(Zibechi 2010)

We are the HIJOS of the 19th and 20th

An interesting phenomenon has arisen with regard to the question of success and longevity of the movements. Young people, those in their thirties, who were teenagers or in their twenties during the rebellion have begun to refer to themselves as 'HIJOS of the 19th and 20th'. What they mean is not that they became political during the rebellion, although many of them did; they mean that the way that they organize today using *horizontalidad* is what constitutes them as children of the rebellion. New forms of social relationships and interaction, seeing the means as a part of the end, is what it means to be a child of the 19th and 20th. It is important to note here that this term is being used all over Argentina and even recently in Greece, where a group of neighborhood assemblies collectively translated *Horizontalism*, the oral history I compiled. They also see themselves as children of the 19th and 20th, and most specifically a part of the history of horizontalism. This is taking place to a growing extent with the spread of the Real Democracy and Occupy movements around the globe, but it is especially present in the conversations in Argentina:

> I think that yes, we are children of the 19th and 20th, and in many ways we feel like the heirs of this time. Some people say, well, 'But the Palermo assembly is no longer, or the Medrano assembly, or another one', but for us, since we are looking from the inside of this process, the discussion is generated from there, from within the process ... It is that we say that we are the children of 2001, because we were formed by everything we lived within the assemblies, the factories, and everything that happened in the streets – it is there that we learned these cooperative principles of *horizontalidad*.
>
> (Conversation with Nicolas and Gisela,
> Buenos Aires, late 2009)

What position are academics coming from when studying social movements in Argentina? The framework below is generally conceived of in the USA, within the field of sociology in particular. Most of the movements' harshest critics whom I have discussed, such as Petras and Robinson, come from this tradition. Additionally, students continue to be trained in this framework, as I was, and those who become teachers in the USA are expected to carry on with it too.

A sociological framework to understand the movements and their success

Social movement theory and contentious politics

The precise definition of a social movement is contested territory in sociological theory. Prior to the 1970s, almost all of the work in the field coming from the USA viewed social protest as a 'form of deviance or pathology' (Flacks 2003: 135). However, Charles Tilly and Sidney Tarrow contributed considerably to what became a shift of this vision to one of understanding social movements as 'politics by other means' (Flacks 2004: 135). Of course, this was along with other social movement pioneers such as Frances Fox Piven and Michael Schwartz. According to Richard Flacks, many of those who played a role in shifting social movement theory were active in the movements of the 1960s, and in order to 'provide movement activists with intellectual resources they might not readily obtain otherwise' (Flacks 2003: 136).

Flacks argues that somewhere along the line the motivation shifted and a good deal of the research, or at least published work, resulted in a more '"professional" and "disciplinary" definition of purpose' (2003: 136). As Flacks argues:

> A sure sign of it, however, is the proliferation of journal articles in which social movement experience is turned into grist for the testing of hypotheses or the illustration of concepts, as well as writings (including this volume) aimed at establishing critiquing, or refining. Increasingly, the work of younger scholars is driven by the effort to refine theory rather than to contribute to the public knowledge about movements.
>
> (Flacks 2003: 136)

Flacks' article continues to critique not only the motives behind more recent predominant understandings of social movement theory, but also the theory itself as being limited in both form and content. He sees the framework of 'resource mobilization' and 'political contention', put forward by Charles Tilly, Sidney Tarrow, and Doug McAdam, as the predominant understanding in mainstream social movement studies in the USA. Flacks sees this as lacking for two reasons: the analysis focuses on a model rather than the possible flexibility of ideas, and the model does not take into consideration the question of culture. This second critique will be addressed and distinguished from the one I am making later.

In 1998, Meyer and Tarrow defined contentious politics as 'collective challenges to existing arrangements of power and distribution by people with common purposes and solidarity, in sustained interaction with elites, opponents and authorities' (1998: 4). Further, Meyer and Tarrow view social movements functionally as a 'way of making claims in national politics', and congruent with this approach, use the word 'citizen' to name social movement actors. To highlight the extent to which Meyer and Tarrow's conceptualization of social movements is predicated on the nation-state, and to give a sense of the character of the theoretical language that they employ, it may be best to quote one of their concluding questions:

[M]ore fundamentally, precisely because of the increasing incentives to engage in socially controlled collective action in our societies today, can we still regard the social movement in its classical form as a major player in the political struggle? ... We have seen that the movement society provides incentives for the professionalization of movement organizations, for their ability to shift into other organizational forms, for their institutionalization, as well as making it profitable for ordinary interest groups to adopt the methods traditionally associated with the social movement. To what extent have these changes done away with the special role of the movement as a challenger to the polity?

(Meyer and Tarrow 1998: 26)

The 'incentives' and profitability referred to above derive their fullest force from the 'political structuring of social movements' as proposed by Tarrow (1996: 41), whereby movements are understood to be shaped by changes in the structural opportunities, resources, and constraints granted by the political relations and institutions of the nation-state. In this view, citizens mobilize in response to these changes while 'movement entrepreneurs' manipulate them systematically.

Charles Tilly (2004) has been the preeminent contemporary definer of social movement theory, specifically the politics of contention. He lays out three criteria:

1. a sustained, organized public effort making collective claims on target authorities;
2. employment of combinations from among the following forms of political action: creation of special purpose associations and coalitions, public meetings, solemn processions, vigils, rallies, demonstrations, petition drives, statements to and in public media, and pamphleteering; and
3. participants' concerted public representations of worthiness, unity, numbers, and commitment on the part of themselves, and/or their constituencies.

What is important for this discussion in particular is that this generally accepted framework, as laid out by Tilly and generally accepted, is that it is a framework for social movements where all movements are assumed to be subject to the same social pressures that occur in the field, and addressing different claims is always done in the form of addressing from one body to another, excluding the possibility of self-organization and autonomy, as an anti-capitalist alternative.

There is a significant component of sociological social movement theory that puts forward the politics of contention as a framework for understanding movements and their relationship to various forms of domination and power. A contentious relationship to the state and authoritative powers is always an explicit or implicit part of the theory. A crucial aspect of this argument is that all social movements are in a contentious relationship to the state, or another form or institution with formal 'power over', whether demanding reforms from the state or institution or desiring another state or institution. The politics of contention is and continues to be useful in understanding social movements, but the framework does not work for all contemporary movements, specifically the autonomous anti-capitalist movements. These contemporary autonomous movements are attempting to organize themselves outside of the state and traditional forms of hierarchical and institutional power. These are movements that are against capitalism, hierarchy, and concepts of power as a dominating force. Their energy is placed in creating new societies and communities, rather than demanding the state change or asking for things from the state. As the data show, people in these movements are clear in not desiring a contentious relationship to power, but rather in their desire for (and creation of) alternative powers. Either space needs to be made within theories of contention to allow for these new autonomous movements and experiences, or a parallel theory needs to emerge.

McAdam, Tilly, and Tarrow are three of the most important and widely read contemporary social movement theorists. In 2001 their book *Dynamics of Contention* was published, and it is from this that the following definition is taken:

> By contentious politics we mean: episodic, public, collective interactions among makers of claims and their objects when (a) at least one government is a claimant, an object of claims, or a

party to the claims and (b) the claims would, if realized, affect the interests of at least one of the claimants.

(McAdam et al. 2001: 5)

Within these contemporary social movements there is a significant network of movements that are consciously developing a politics and practice that cannot be understood within the framework of contention. By this I mean that they do not place their desire for change onto the state or seek to change the state itself. Implicit in their politics is to live in a substantially different society. One of the core differences is the relationship to concepts of power, and particularly the understanding of state power as a potentially positive or liberatory force. These contemporary autonomous movements explicitly state that they do not want to take state power, and that the change they desire cannot come from the state apparati (as described in Chapter 5).

The explanation below by Tilly makes it difficult to find a space to explain the current autonomous social movements, such as those in Argentina, outside the context of contentious politics. It simultaneously traps the movements into a concept of power relations that they seem to be rejecting:

Although I did not speak much of 'contenders' before the 1970s, did not explicitly define my subjects as 'contention' until the 1980s, and did not start theorizing about 'contentious politics' until the 1990s, for half a century a major stream of my work has concerned how, when, where, and why ordinary people make collective claims on public authorities, other holders of power, competitors, enemies, and objects of popular disapproval. For many years I generally avoided the term 'social movement' because it sponged up so many different meanings and therefore obscured more than it clarified. Preparing detailed catalogues of contentious events for periods from the seventeenth to twentieth centuries in Western Europe and North America changed my mind.

(Tilly 2004: ix)

Tarrow defines contentious politics as a relationship to those in power, or who possess some dominating power. This again does not allow for those movements which, often after various forms of confrontation and contention, decide no longer to place demands upon the state or other formal institutions of power:

> Contentious politics occurs when ordinary people, often in league with more influential citizens, join forces in confrontation with elites, authorities, and opponents. Such confrontations go down to the dawn of history.
>
> (Meyer and Tarrow 1998: 4)

Cultural challenges to contention

There is a growing body of literature in the USA that purports to challenge the contentious framework, grounding the criticism in what it claims is a lack of attention paid to movements, such as identity-based movements, which examines changes in moral codes and the identities of people within those movements. This literature deals with movements that place demands on formal institutions of power, such as the state and state agencies, and as yet does not examine movements that are *reconceptualizing* power – movements that I term autonomous. They address movements such as the feminist movement which, while focusing on the issues of consciousness-raising and so forth, have placed demands on institutions as the main focus of organization, from equal rights to abortion rights.

Flacks addresses this perceived challenge to contention, and while he agrees that there needs to be more space in the understanding of these movements and their attention to internal changes, he also argues that this is not a new framework being put forward:

> This 'culturalist' perspective suffered a bit from being labeled 'new social movement theory'. For one thing, there was hardly a 'theory' being articulated, but rather a different set of emphases and questions.
>
> (Flacks 2003: 137)

He continues to argue that there is nothing new in this, and I would add that not only is it not historically new, but that all of the movements addressed are those with a contentious relationship to formal institutions of power. This grouping of cultural challenges within the contentious framework is something with which the framers of contention also agree (McAdam et al. 1996; Klandermans 1997; Tarrow 1998; Zald 2000).

My argument is not a cultural challenge, and while many of the autonomous movements place much importance on the internal changes of the movement itself, shifting identities, creating new relationships, and so forth, they are not focused on formal power, but rather on the creation of new and alternative powers. As emphasized previously, this does not mean that they are not engaging with the state (and forms of institutional power), but that the state is not the point of reference; the movement is – as is the creation of new values and new relationships. The movements are not contentious.

Conclusions, implications, and practical applications

Twentieth century history is full of births of worlds that embody 'old' social relations. This tumultuous reality has brought disastrous consequences: in general revolutions have not given birth to new worlds, though revolutionaries have tried to build them with the state apparatus. Although a good many revolutions have improved people's living conditions, which is certainly an important achievement, they have not been able to create new worlds. Despite the unimpeachable goodwill of so many revolutionaries, the fact remains that the state is not the appropriate tool for the creating emancipatory social relations … From this perspective, the most revolutionary thing we can do is strive to create new social relationships within our own territories – relationships that are born of the struggle, and are maintained and expanded by it.

(Zibechi 2010)

Despite the massive challenges that movements face in Argentina, revolutions continue in people's day-to-day relationships. This is the point from which my summary and conclusion begin. The subtleties of this point are examined throughout the book, but the ultimate conclusion is simply that the movements have been, and continue to be, successful. In accepting this conclusion, a number of other questions and suppositions must be considered. These are:

- the centrality of horizontal decision making;
- new conceptualizations of power;

- the importance of affect and emotion;
- the creation of new value production;
- the non-contentious political framework nature of the new movements; and
- rethinking the meaning of revolution.

I will address each of these separately, and then discuss the implications of these conclusions for the study of social movements, and an understanding of social change. Linked to these conclusions is the question of how to approach and study these points, that is the need for reexamining traditional methodologies of research.

Centrality of horizontal decision making

Horizontalidad is a point of reference in Argentina, and over the years has become one around the globe. Activists use it as a sort of vernacular to signify that they do not use hierarchy or will not work with political parties. Most recently in Egypt some of the younger activists were describing how they were organizing as horizontalism. A UK *Guardian* article in February 2011, entitled 'From Paris to Cairo, these protests are expanding the power of the individual', Paul Mason (2011) wrote, 'But the sociology of the movements is only part of the story. Probably the key factor is "horizontalism" which has become the default method of organising.' At the time of writing people throughout the USA, beginning in New York with Occupy Wall Street, have been organizing in assembly forms, using variations of direct democracy, assuming some sort of horizontal relationships and using the language of horizontalism. In Spain the Democracia Real Ya! movements are organizing horizontally and using assemblies for decision making. In Greece, the movements use direct horizontal democracy. Increasingly, it is becoming an assumption that organizing will be horizontal.

Horizontalism has come to mean a great deal more than only participation in the process of making a decision, but the beginning point and heart of the new relationship is still a person having an active role in what happens around them, and in deciding their fate, or possible future. The examples in this book, of *horizontalidad* in the various movements in Argentina, from the unemployed and working class to the middle class and indigenous, show the centrality of direct participatory decision making in the larger process and project of social transformation. Without horizontalism the autonomous and *autogestiva* projects would not be successful. This already seems a given conclusion for many, especially the people involved in social movements, but only ten years ago this was not the case. Political parties as a vehicle for change, and voting as the only way that a group would make a decision, was taken as the rule, not the exception. Argentina has played a tremendous role in shifting the global conversation among activists on how to bring about change in the most empowering way. That change is not only made by what one does, but how one does it, is of equal importance. By sharing the experiences and arguments in this book, I hope to add to the global conversation about how change is created and why there has been such a massive global break with vertical and hierarchical forms of organization.

Power as a noun or a verb?

The contemporary autonomous movements in Argentina, as with the Zapatistas in Chiapas, Mexico, contribute a tremendous amount to the understanding of power and social change, particularly in the social sciences. When John Holloway published his book, *Change the World Without Taking Power: The Meaning of Revolution Today* in 2002, the Argentine rebellion was in its first months. The argument that Holloway puts forth was met at the time with applause from certain sectors and severe criticism from others. Generally, it was the social movement participants applauding, and the university scholars frowning, and taking power as a means to change remains a deeply contentious issue. However, in the nine years since the book was first published, discussions on power have changed and the movements in Argentina have played a large role in that shift.

This debate on power is not only a discussion on the taking of power, but more generally the concept of power: power as a thing, as something to use, wield, and hold over another, or as a verb, that is active, interactive, and can be dynamic when used together, as a 'power with' rather than a 'power-over'.

There are still many social scientists who continue to see power within the Weberian frame. It is against this rigidity, seeing power as only one thing, that Frances Fox Piven talked about in

her address to the American Sociological Association conference
in 2007, 'Can Power from Below Change the World':

> I propose that there is another kind of power based not on
> resources, things, or attributes, but rooted in the social and
> cooperative relations in which people are enmeshed by virtue
> of group life ... This kind of interdependent power is not
> concentrated at the top but is potentially widespread.
>
> (Fox Piven 2008: 5)

It is the above sort of power that is being created in the
autonomous movements in Argentina and about which I write
(particularly in Chapter 5). The movements' experiences in
Argentina contribute a great deal to this conversation on power
and rethinking it in the process of social transformation. It is not
presented as the only concept of power, but is meant to be a part
of a conversation, to expand the ways in which social scientists
in particular see change and how it can be created.

Challenging the contentious politics frame

> The potential for the exercise of power from below must, I
> believe, command the attention of sociologists. But are our
> intellectual traditions and institutional locations suited to
> conduct such inquiries?
>
> (Fox Piven 2008: 3)

These newer conceptions of social movements and social change
in Argentina can contribute to questioning the preconceived
frameworks used for the study of movements. Chapter 8 of
this book takes issue with the contentious politics framework
for understanding social movements in Argentina, but it is not
only the specific framework that is the issue. Conducting a study
beginning with a framework rather than trying to understand
first what a group or movement is doing (and then searching for
the various theories and tools that exist to help understand the
phenomenon), is the issue. What this book has tried to do is to
expand concepts of power and social movements but also, even
more importantly, to challenge the ways in which studies are
conducted.

Affective politics and new subjectivities

The seriousness in which participants in the movements in Argentina take emotion, the politics of affect and personal transformation, and the way that it is communicated in this book is, I hope, the beginning of a much larger conversation on the central role of emotion in revolutionary change. Affect and subjectivity have been considered unimportant for too long, relegated to 'cultural' interpretation, only peripherally related to 'real' politics, or discussed within the context of identity politics such as gender, sexual orientation, or 'race'.

As the participants in the movements in Argentina show, and as has been demonstrated in this book, without acknowledging a shift in their own subjectivity, their own understanding, and without their movements being based on trust and affection, they would not be as militant. These aspects of affective politics and emotion are notions that do not fit neatly into preconceived frameworks. Hopefully, coupled with a rethinking of methodology, they will become their own area of study.

Value production

Raul Zibechi, along with many other organic intellectuals in Latin America and around the world, has been reconceptualizing value production (de Sousa Santos 1998; Davis 2006; De Angelis 2007; Zibechi 2008a; Holloway 2010; Harvey 2012). Their studies have taken into consideration many of the autonomous movements around the world, as well as more generally the growing urban peripheries where the poor are forced to function outside the system, as the system no longer permits them on the inside:

> Production of livelihood in the territories signals a second
> radical break from the industrial past. The popular sectors
> have erected for the first time in an urban space a set of
> independently controlled forms of production. Although these
> remain connected to and dependent on the market, vast sectors
> now control their forms and rhythms of production, and are no
> longer dominated by the rhythms of capital and its division of
> labor.
>
> (Zibechi 2010)

Through examination of recuperated workplaces and unemployed workers' movements, this book hopes to have demonstrated how what is being produced is being done outside the frame of capitalist market production. I do not argue that it is outside capitalism as a whole, but that what determines how much people work, when they work, and what to do with their final product is decided upon by themselves, both together and autonomously. *Horizontalidad* is the way in which the vast majority of the workplaces function, as it is also the base from which the MTDs organize. What this means is that the movement decides together questions related to production. This then raises incredibly important questions on value production.

What is produced by the autonomous movements and the relationship of that production to the state and capitalist market – or outside of it – is central to the construction of alternative ways of being. The movements in Argentina are not only creating horizontal relationships in which the participants feel better and happier, but in many areas they are finding new ways of surviving, whether by taking over workplaces and running them together, or creating micro-enterprises. In and of themselves these are not answers to the capitalist market, but within the experience, within the creation of alternative ways of producing value, one can begin to see the seeds of an alternative economy that is central to the total transformation of society.

The meaning of revolution

The above arguments and contributions to the discussion on social change, power, production, and social relationships brings the book to one of its most central arguments, which is that of a rethinking of the meaning of revolution.

In the same way that the meaning of revolution for those in the autonomous movements is not that of taking over from the state, the ways in which revolutions are perceived also should be different, subtler, and perhaps quieter. These quieter, everyday revolutions can be seen all over Argentina, if one chooses to see them in the same way as the movements. We can see them in the little girl from MTD Solano who requests an assembly of adults because she does not think that her mother should be allowed to yell at her. We see it in the assembly in the occupied building in Lomas de Zamora, where there is a serious discussion of what to do about a case of sexual harassment of a *compañera*, and the matter is resolved in a way that all feel to be acceptable. We see it in the discussion of what to do in the occupied grocery store, how to pay the electric bill, or order new supplies. We see it in the exchange of healthcare in a recuperated clinic, with the printing of clinic brochures in a recuperated print shop. These are daily occurrences of which there are thousands in Argentina. Each of these discussions is using *horizontalidad* and struggling to create autonomously from institutional power – struggling to maintain their own agendas.

Determining success

The first and last question of this book is what it means to be successful; and now, at the end, I add the question of who is to determine this answer. If the perspective is that of the movements, those people creating transformations within themselves and their communities, then the answer is that they now feel more dignity and power – they are social subjects and agents in their lives, finding new ways to survive, together and with affect. They are successful.

Methodology and studying by listening

The methodology used for any study has direct implications on that study and, of course, on the results. It is one thing to read about a movement, and quite another to spend time with it. It is not the same to pay someone to do fieldwork, then to do one's own – and not all fieldwork is the same. The same is true for one's intellectual, political, and theoretical frameworks. One's starting point greatly affects the conclusions, sometimes distorting them so much that the conclusions reached – as with the example of James Petras in Chapter 5 on power – miss the point completely.

To cite Frances Fox Piven, but this time as a question: 'The potential for the exercise of power from below must, I believe, command the attention of sociologists. But are our intellectual traditions and institutional locations suited to conduct such inquiries[?]' Are we able to situate ourselves to study these new movements, whether in Argentina, or now Egypt, or another movement that will undoubtedly arise and be outside the traditional framework of analysis?

Fox Piven's question is one of the things that this book hopes to ask, answer, and then continue to ask. I hope with these pages to push the boundaries of research, by placing research 'from below' (Lynd 1993; Brecher 1995) at the heart of it, as well as giving more space to the field of the sociology of narrative (Berger and Quinney 2005; Selbin 2010). Together the intention is to bring forward the voices of those in the movements around the world. Not uncritically, but first methodologically, listening to what people are saying and seeing what they are doing, then finding tools of theory and experience to add to what is being heard and done, and to find ways of working together with the movements. This is an area that many contemporary social movement activists who are also in the academy have come to call 'co-research' or 'militant research' – or social science for another world. This does not mean uncritically reflecting on the experiences of the movements, but building relationships with those people making history, so as to help to write better the history – their history – with them.

Notes

Introduction

1. One of the motivations behind the *cacerolazo* was the government declaring that all bank accounts were frozen indefinitely. This was a product of growing financial crisis for more than a decade, linked to privatization policies related to structural adjustment agreements with international financial institutions.

2. To my knowledge the first person to write extensively on the use of this the term was Wini Breines in her writing on the politics of the 1960s, and what she saw as a different way of thinking and organizing in part as a rejection of the centrism and vanguardism of the Communist Party:

> The term *prefigurative politics* ... may be recognized in counter institutions, demonstrations and the attempt to embody personal and anti-hierarchical values in politics. Participatory democracy was central to prefigurative politics ... The crux of prefigurative politics imposed substantial tasks, the central one being to create and sustain within the live practice of the movement, relationships and political forms that 'prefigured' and embodied the desired society.
>
> (Breines 1989: 6)

That Breines used the term to reflect on a practice that was specific does not mean that she discovered a historical practice. People have created movements that desire their means to be their ends throughout all of history, from the Industrial Workers of the World (IWW) in the USA organizing a 'New society in the shell of the old', to Gandhi in India speaking of 'Being the change you want to see in the world', to the articulation of beloved community by Ella Baker and others in SNCC in the Black Freedom Struggles in the USA.

3. There is no exact translation of the word *compañero* as it is used within the movements in Argentina. Many have translated it as 'comrade' or 'friend', and it is often either or both, but not always. Many do not like the term comrade as it harkens back to political parties, and 'friend' alone does not reflect the political relationship implied. It also can refer to someone with whom one collaborates on a common political project. However, most often it is used with an

intentional affect, reflecting care and trust in the relationship being described.

Chapter 1

1. In October 2011 in Argentina, along with sixteen former military officers, Astiz was sentenced to life in prison for crimes against humanity (Amnesty International 2011)
2. There is a long history of debate within the human rights field as to the 'proper use' of genocide. While the Universal Declaration of Human Rights of 1948 does not include political groups in the definition of genocide, this has been contested in the years since, particularly by some countries in Latin America. There is documented evidence that Argentina's military dictatorship wanted to eliminate all political opposition, thus fitting into the definition now used by some human rights courts.
3. Actions can take many forms; this above described is only one of many possible variations. Another *escrache* similar to this is described in the book *Winning Small Battles, Losing the War* (2008) by Marieke Denissen.
4. This is a link to a video of part of the 2006 *escrache* at San Fachon discussed here: www.youtube. com/watch?v=I-AtL_2iHPI&feature=related.
5. This is addressed more in Chapter 2 on rupture as well as in Chapter 7 on the challenges to autonomy.
6. The use of dignity is addressed further in Chapters 4 and 8. Dignity is also the way in which the Zapatistas talk about what they are creating.

Chapter 2

1. The Zapatistas of Chiapas first coined the term, 'One No, Many Yesses', and since then it has become a kind of slogan for the global justice movements throughout the world.
2. *Potencia* is the word used for power, both in Spanish, meaning power as a verb, versus *poder*, power as a noun, but also in English to indicate the relational use of power and not as a thing. This is explored in Chapter 5 on power and autonomy.
3. The *caracazo* was a popular rebellion in Venezuela which took place on 27 February 1989. It began in the urban peripheries of Caracas and rapidly spread to other cities throughout the country, encompassing more than a million people. The rebellion was in response to growing poverty and austerity programs implemented by the government of Carlos Andres Pérez. The *caracazo* was met with severe repression, with untold thousands being killed. It is a moment in Venezuelan history that many link to the beginning of the radical movements that followed and continue today under President Hugo Chávez.

4. This is explored more in Chapter 6 on *autogestión*.
5. The conversation with Liliana took place in the street outside Brukman while workers were camping outside and fighting to get back into their factory.
6. '*El otro soy yo*' means 'The other is me' – the idea of seeing oneself in the other. This phrase was first used in Argentina by the Madres de la Plaza de Mayo, and similarly, before them by the Zapatistas with the concept of *Todos Somos*, meaning that we are all the other.
7. The neighborhood assembles comprised those people identifying as middle class. There is a long debate as to what the meaning of middle class is, particularly in Argentina, where it is generally defined based on the clothes that one wears, the coffee shops that one hangs out in, and where one shops, and less on a person's relationship to production or decision making at work. For the sake of this book I am going to use the term 'middle class' quite loosely, as do most Argentines. Whether people are actually middle class or choose to identify that way is not the point as much as the social label and the meaning behind it. Historically the middle class was something that people saw as snobbish, standoffish, and proud. It was also a class that, aside from the revolutionary youth movements that often came from it, were politically moderate, if not on the Right.
8. There is a website that contains some of the notes from the *interbarrial*, although the accuracy of this site has yet to be substantiated. It is real, but many people who were at some of the assemblies claim that there were more people in attendance, or that many of the topics were left out.
9. It is not easy to translate the use of cursing at protests in Argentina. What literally sounds negative or even crass and gross in context can sound powerful and full of dignity. I have never experienced demonstrations and direct confrontation so filled with graphic cursing and imagery; it is something to behold in context to understand it. Writing that little children hold *palos*, the sticks used to fight back against the police, and stand near the tires on fire blocking the road, then to skip to 'I am a fucking *piquetero*' can sound odd, but in reality, one wants to join in – the feeling is overwhelmingly powerful. All words and categories are up for retaking and reinterpreting.
10. In the later 2000s those neighborhood assemblies that still exist now use Facebook as a means of communicating and sharing information. A search in March 2011 reflected more than twenty-four Facebook pages for such assemblies.

Chapter 3

1. This is a reference to the Zapatistas and how they positioned themselves in the last elections with the Other Campaign, stating that they did not want to go from the bottom up, but rather from below and to the left. The way that they described where they were going was within and without, so from the heart out and then back again.

2. Since the book *Horizontalism* came out in 2006, the word in English has become more popularized, generally relating closely to the intended meaning, coming from the movements in Argentina but sometimes not. It is important to note how a word from one experience can be translated and reinterpreted very differently. For example, I found a website that took verbatim paragraphs from the introduction to my book, without citations, describing *Horizontalism*. This website was for accountants in the San Diego area. The one change they made to my writing was to put in the word 'management' in place of 'power'. Then again in 2011, in a very positive way, 'horizontalism' was used as a way to refer to the movements in Egypt by the BBC.

3. Galeano is referring to the Argentine filmmaker Fernando Birri and the film *El Siglo de la Tormenta*.

4. There are countless versions of this story. The one included here is the one most widespread in English, due mainly to Subcomandante Marcos retelling it and having it translated first on the internet and then in the book, *Questions and Swords: Folktales of the Zapatista Revolution* (2001).

5. Interview with Claudia Acuña, Buenos Aires, Argentina, 2007.

6. The creation of new people, new subjectivities, is discussed in Chapter 4. I also have a forthcoming book on the question of direct democracy and the various forms of horizontal democracy in the contemporary Occupy and assembly movements.

7. *Mate* is a part of almost all gatherings. An infusion leaf-based tea, it is a drink that is shared with whoever is around. The person holding the *mate* gourd fills it with water and passes it to the left. Each person drinks, emptying the gourd through a metal straw, and then passes it back to the person with the thermos of water. It is customary to drink and pass it on – one does not say no as it is part of being social. It is also customary to hand round the gourd to everyone.

8. Throughout the interviews people refer to specific *encuentros*. Generally speaking, an *encuentro* is a gathering, and it is intentionally different from a meeting. The two specific *encuentros* referred to in the conversations are the bi-weekly ones that were held in the first two years after the rebellion, and the yearly international one. Maba here is referring to the former. For two years participants from the various autonomous movements would gather together for an entire Saturday to discuss the topics and issue areas that affected them. So, for example, there was a Saturday dedicated to the practice of autonomy, another to the idea of power, etc. People from the neighborhood assemblies and MTDs tended to form the majority at these gatherings, sometimes but there were also participants from the recuperated factories and indigenous movements.

9. There are numerous websites of those organizing against the mining companies. One such site is http://www.noalamina.org/mineria-esquel/mineria-noticias-esquel/esquel-olor-a-mina. Lavaca.org also has regular updates directly from the assemblies on its site.

Chapter 4

1. It is worth mentioning that this is also true for many in the Communal Councils and other formations in Venezuela as well as El Alto and Cochabamba, Bolivia and even most recently in Egypt, Greece, and Spain.

2. Hanisch, in a new introduction to her piece 'The Personal is Political' posted on her website (www.carolhanisch.org/CHwritings/PIP.html), not only explains the intention behind her writing – the article being that of addressing the politics of consciousness-raising – but also informs that the title to the article was not her invention, but rather of the people who printed the piece.

Chapter 5

1. In both 2005 and again in 2009, participants from MTD Solano, MTD Allen and the Lavaca collective all shared with me the fact that as movements they decided collectively no longer to meet with James Petras when he requested it. This was based on their reading an article of his published in 2002 in *Monthly Review* where, among other things, he claims that the movements are dead. I have had numerous discussions with these movements and they do not find it important to meet with scholars whom they perceived as spreading misinformation.

2. 'The most radical ideas often grow out a concrete intellectual engagement with the problems of aggrieved populations confronting systems of oppression' (Kelley 2003a). By way of example, John Holloway's book discussing not taking state power refers to the Zapatistas in Mexico, as Raul Zibechi refers to Bolivia and the Colectivo Situaciones in Argentina. First the movements acted against the idea of hierarchical power, and then the theorists helped to develop the concepts.

3. Most of the young people participating in MTD Cipolletti come from an upbringing in incredibly violent neighborhoods, so while it might sound outrageous for them to suggest defending young women with guns or bats, it is something that they have learned, and in the movement are unlearning. Also interesting in this unlearning process is that one of the adults in the movement was a Montenero, having used violence as a means to try to create a new society. It is the adult who was in a guerilla group which argues the most passionately against violence, and it is his voice that the young men listened to the most.

Chapter 6

1. As is explored later in this chapter, the argument here is not that the new relationships are beyond capital, but that the relationship to production specifically is changing and not based on capitalist value – i.e. to profit and money alone.

2. The first two such events took place in Buenos Aires, and the third in Mexico City, involving an even broader array of people.

3. This study was conducted by eighty-five students at the University of Buenos Aires who conducted in-depth interviews consisting of 121 detailed questions. The result was that 73 per cent of the workers went with occupation of the plant, and 50 per cent confronted some type of repression or threat coming from judicial orders (from 2002–2004).

4. In every conversation I had with participants in recuperated workplaces and those supporting them, I never once heard of a situation where a workplace was taken over and recuperated without support from the community in one way or another: 35 per cent of the workplaces hold regular cultural and educational events, and more than 30 per cent give donations to, and collaborate with, neighborhood organizations (Ruggeri 2010a).

5. A note here on an Argentine lunch: this is not a light sandwich or salad. Lunch is a heavy meal, often with meat and potatoes or some version of stew or soup. Lunch is something that would have to be planned and cooked in advance and with care. In the first few years, until sometime in 2004 or 2005, this was often done by the neighborhood assemblies. Later, as the neighbors organized less within this formation, it was former assembly participants with other neighbors and networks of political friendships that continued cooking the lunches.

6. This was even better than my previous visits, where the press office has an 'official' tour and usually workers are not to be interrupted for interviews while they are working. On this visit I was able to spend hours on the shop floor interviewing many workers.

7. This is totally distinct from the global historical and contemporary cooperative movement. The International Cooperative Alliance has been facilitating the development and growth of cooperatives globally since 1895 (see: www.ica.coop).

8. See Chapter 2 for a full discussion of the *carteneros* and the question of recycling in society.

9. Not only would the workers from the former Medrano clinic not speak to me on the record, but there are a number of other researchers and writers who have attempted to follow up with them, and they too have been refused. As of 2010 there were no recorded interviews with the Medrano workers since the state took over the workplace. It is unclear whether this is because the workers are sad and feel regret, or due to a gagging order from the government.

10. 'A world in which many worlds fit' is an expression coined by the Zapatistas in Chiapas, and is now used widely around the globe in the more autonomous social movements.

11. The role of Zibechi's work on territories to the movements today is similar to the role that John Holloway's book, *Change the World Without Taking Power* (2002), played in the months after the popular rebellion in 2001.

Chapter 7

1. I refer throughout this chapter to the Kirchners, and while Néstor and Cristina governed Argentina at different times, their politics and relationship to the movements as well as human rights have been fairly consistent, and so not worth separating out each time that their politics or perspectives are described.
2. This is discussed specifically with regard to the Ley de Punto Final of 1986 in Chapter 1.
3. It is difficult to differentiate between centrally controlled repression, i.e. the central state, or repression that takes place in the regions around Buenos Aires and throughout the country that the government might know about, but there is not always hard evidence that they do. For example, when police worked with locally hired goons to kidnap and attack workers from Ceramica Zanon, in Neuquén, or when *piqueteros* were killed in the north in Mosconi, with the oversight of local police, it is unclear how much the Kirchner governments knew, although many argue that they should have known and it is still their responsibility, even if not their active doing.
4. This phrase is taken from the title to Ben Dangl's book, *Dancing with Dynamite* (2009), discussing the relationship of social movements to the state in Latin America.

Chapter 8

1. Susan Buck-Morss's first footnote is as follows: 'This paper grows out of a presentation for the conference, "Communism: A New Beginning", convened by Slavoj Žižek and Alain Badiou at Cooper Union, NYC, October 2011. The author felt increasingly uncomfortable with the word communist. The "u" had to go. Commonist describes more accurately the ethical argument being made. I want to thank my colleagues in the Committee on Globalization and Social Change at the CUNY Graduate Center, who will recognize here the influence of our discussions.' The discussions to which she refers often were about the new social movements of 2011, as well as the Argentine autonomous movements, as I am a participant in this City University of New York seminar as well.

Bibliography

Adamovsky, Ezequiel, 2006. 'Autonomous politics and its problems: Thinking the passage from social to political'. *Reimagining Society Project.* Retrieved 12 June 2012 from http://www.zcommunications.org/autonomous-politics-and-its-problems-by-ezequiel-adamovsky

Alcorta, Juan. 2007. 'Solidarity economies in Argentina and Japan'. *Studies of Modern Society* 40(12) (in Japanese). Retrieved 6 June 2012 from http://dspace.lib.niigata-u.ac.jp:8080/dspace/bitstream/10191/8691/1/40_263-296.pdf

Altaf Mian, Ali, 2011. 'The turn to affect'. *John Hope Franklin Humanities Institute, Duke University.* Retrieved 12 February 2011 from http://www.fhi.duke.edu/blog/turn-to-affect

Amnesty International, 2011. 'Argentina convicts former military officials for "Dirty War" crimes', 27 October. Retrieved 7 June 2012 from http://www.amnesty.org/en/news/argentina-convicts-former-military-officials-'dirty-war'-crimes-2011-10-27

Antón, Gustavo, Jorge Cresto, Julián Rebón and Rodrigo Salgado, 2010. 'Una década en disputa. Apuntes sobre las luchas sociales en Argentina'. *Observatorio Social de América Latina* 28: 95–116.

Arrighi, Giovanni, Terence Hopkins and Immanuel Wallerstein, 1989. *Antisystemic Movements.* London: Verso.

Atzeni, Maurizio and Pablo Ghigliani, 2007. 'Labour process and decision-making in factories under workers' self-management: Empirical evidence from Argentina'. *Work, Employment and Society* 21(4): 653–671.

Aufheben, 2003. 'Picket and pot-banger together: Class recomposition in Argentina?' Retrieved 22 December 2006 from http://libcom.org/library/argentina-aufheben-11

Auyero, Javier, 1999. 'Remembering Peronism: An ethnographic account of the relational character of political memory'. *Qualitative Sociology* 22(4): 331–351.

Auyero, Javier, 2000a. 'Political clientalism in Argentina: An ethnographic account'. Paper presented to the Sociology Department of State University of New York Stony Brook, Stony Brook, NY, 14 March.

Auyero, Javier, 2000b. 'The logic of clientelism in Argentina: An ethnographic account'. *Latin American Research Review* 35(3): 55–81.

Auyero, Javier, 2003. *Contentious Lives: Two Argentine Women, Two Protests, and the Quest for Recognition*. Durham, NC: Duke University Press.

Auyero, Javier and Timothy Moran, 2005. 'The dynamics of collective violence: Dissecting food riots in contemporary Argentina'. *Social Forces* 85(3): 1341–1367.

Auyero Javier, Pablo Lapegna and Fernanda Page PomaPatronage, 2009. 'Politics and contentious collective action: A recursive relationship'. *Latin American Politics and Society* 51(3): 1–31.

Ballve, Teo and Vijay Prashad (eds) *Dispatches from Latin America: On the Frontlines Against Neoliberalism*. Cambridge, MA: South End Press.

Bayer, Osvaldo, 2002. *Patagonia Rebelde*. Buenos Aires: Planeta Editorial.

Bedggood, D. 2002. 'Lost in the crowd? Hardt and Negri's empire and the multitude in Argentina'. Retrieved 12 June 2012 from http://www. reocities.com/davebedggood/ negrionargentina.html

Benegas, Diego Loyo, forthcoming. *Against Terror: Trauma and Political Action in Post Dictatorship Argentina*. Río Cuarto: Ediciones Universidad Nacional de Río Cuarto.

Benjamin, Walter, 1973. 'Tesis de la filosofía de la historia'. In *Discursos interrumpidos I*. Madrid: Taurus, pp. 178–192.

Berger, Ronald and Richard Quinney, 2005. *Storytelling Sociology: Narrative as Social Inquiry*. Boulder, CO: Lynne Rienner Publishers.

Berho, Debbie, 2000. 'Working politics: Juan Domingo Perón's creation of positive social identity'. *Rocky Mountain Review of Language and Literature* 54(2): 65–76.

Boggs, Carl, 2010[1977]. 'Marxism, prefigurative communism, and the problem of workers' control'. Libcom.org, 23 September. Retrieved 12 June 2012 from http://libcom.org/ library/marxism-prefigurative- communism-problem-workers- control-carl-boggs

Böhm, Steffen, Ana Cecilia Dinerstein and André Spicer, 2010. '(Im)possibilities of autonomy: Social movements in and beyond capital, the state and development'. *Social Movement Studies* 9(1). Retrieved 12 June 2012 from: http://opus.bath.ac.uk/18413/

Boletín de Estadísticas Laborales Historico, 2005. 'Población urbana total y población económicamente activa, 1991– 2003'. *Ministerio de Trabajo, Empleo y Seguridad Social de la República Argentina*, document 1.1.1.1. Retrieved 23 December 2005 from http://www. trabajo.gov.ar/left/estadisticas/ belOnline/pdfroot/11001.pdf

Boltanski, Luc and Eve Chiapello, 2007. *The New Spirit of Capitalism*. London: Verso.

Boron, Atilio and Mabel Thwaites-Rey, 2004. 'La expropiación en la Argentina: Genesis, desarollo, y los impactos estructurales'. In James Petras and Henry Veltmeyer (eds) *Las privatizaciones y la desnacionalización de América Latina*. Buenos Aires: Promoteo Libros, pp. 113–182.

Bourdieu, Pierre, 1977. *Outline of a Theory of Practice* (trans. Richard Nice). Cambridge: Cambridge University Press.

Bourdieu, Pierre, 1990. *The Logic of Practice* (trans. Richard Nice). Stanford, CA: Stanford University Press.

Bourdieu, Pierre, 2000. *Pascalian Meditations* (trans. Richard Nice). Cambridge: Polity Press.

Branford, Becky, 2002. 'Hunger follows crisis in Argentina'. *BBC News*. Retrieved 11 March 2007 from http://news.bbc.co.uk/2/hi/business/2307491.stm

Brecher, Jeremy, 1995. *History from Below: How to Uncover and Tell the Story of Your Community, Association, or Union*. Connecticut: Commonwork/Advocate Press.

Breines, Winnie, 1989. *Community and Organization in the New Left, 1962–1968: The Great Refusal*. Piscataway, NJ: Rutgers University Press.

Brenner, Neil and Stuart Elden, 2009[1966]. 'Theoretical problems with autogestion'. In Henri Lefebvre, Neil Brenner and Stuart Elden (eds) *State, Space, World: Selected Essays*. Minneapolis, MN: University of Minnesota Press, pp. 138–153.

'Brukman riots escalate', 2002. *Buenos Aires Herald*. Retrieved 22 December 2006 from http://www.buenosairesherald.com/argentina/note.jsp?idContent=1095296

Byrnes, Brian, 2009. 'Barter clubs expose Argentina's weakness'. CNN.com, 21 June. Retrieved 5 June 2012 from: http://edition.cnn.com/2009/WORLD/americas/05/20/argentina.barter/

Cáffaro, Cora, 2006. 'Look social'. *Clarín*. Retrieved 18 March 2007 from http://www.clarin.com/diario/2006/01/11/conexiones/t-01122542.htm

Cahill, Caitlin, 2006. 'The personal is political: Developing new subjectivities through participatory action research'. *Gender Place and Culture* 14(3): 1–38.

Central de Trabajadores de la Argentina, 2006. 'Informe sobre conflictividad laboral y negociación colectiva en el 2006'. In *Boletín Electrónico Periódico*. Buenos Aires: Central de Trabajadores de la Argentina. Retrieved 15 March 2007 from http://obderechosocial.org.ar/docs/anual_conflictos_2006.pdf

Cerioli, Gabriela, 2009. 'Bartering – here to stay?' *PS-Inter Press Service Latin America*, 9 April. Retrieved 9 April 2009 from http://ipsnews.net/news.asp?idnews=46452

Chatterton, Paul and Jenny Pickerill, 2010. 'Everyday activism and transitions towards post-capitalist worlds'. *Transactions of the Institute of British Geographers* 35(4): 475–490.

Clegg, Ian, 1972. *Workers' Self-management in Algeria*. New York: Monthly Review Press.

Colectivo Situaciones, 2001. *ContraPoder: Una Introduccion*. Buenos Aires: De Mano en Mano.

Colectivo Situaciones, 2002. 10 y 20: *Apuntes para el nuevo protagonismo social*. Buenos Aires: De Mano en Mano.

Colectivo Situaciones and MTD Solano, 2002. *Hipótesis 891. Más allá de los piquetes [Hypobook 891: Beyond the Pickets]*. Buenos Aires: De Mano en Mano.

Colectivo Situaciones, Rafael Leona and Mesa de Escrache Popular (eds), 2009. *GAC Pensamientos Practicas Acciones*. Buenos Aires, Argentina: Tinta Limon.

Cooley, Mike, 1980. *Architect or Bee: The Human/Technology Relationship*. Boston, MA: South End Press.

Corradi, Juan, Patricia Weiss Fagen, Manuel Antonio and Garretón Merino, 1992. *Fear at the Edge: State Terrorism and Resistance in Latin America*. Berkeley, CA, University of California Press.

Damill, Mario, 2005. 'La economía y la pólitica económica: Del viejo al nuevo endeudamiento'. In Juan Suriano (ed.) *Nueva historia argentina: Dictadura y democracia (1976–2001)*. Buenos Aires: Editorial Sudamericana, pp. 155–224.

Dangl, Benjamin, 2009. *Dancing with Dynamite: Social Movements and States in Latin America*. Oakland, CA: AK Press.

Davis, Heather and Paige Sarlin, 2011. 'No one is sovereign in love: A conversation between Lauren Berlant and Michael Hardt'. *Coalition 'Sexual and Health Rights of Marginalized Communities*, 5 December. Retrieved 6 June 2012 from http://coalition.org.mk/2011/12/heder-dejvis-sto-e-toa-sto-ja-pravi-ljubovta-predizvikuvacki-odnosno-politicki-interesen-koncept/?lang=en

Davis, Mike, 2006. *Planet of Slums*. New York: Verso.

Day, Richard, 2005. *Gramsci Is Dead: Anarchist Currents in the Newest Social Movements*. London: Pluto Press.

de Bonafini, Hebe, 2011. 'Hebe de Bonafini's letter to Cristina Kirchner'. *M24Digital.com*, 2 January. Retrieved 7 June 2012 from http://m24digital.com/en/2011/01/02/hebe-de-bonafinis-letter-to-cristina-kirchner/

de Sousa Santos, Boaventura, 1998. *Reinventar a Democracia*. Lisbon: Gradiva.

de Sousa Santos, Boaventura, 2008. 'Depolarised pluralities: A Left with a future – the phantasmagorical relation between theory and practice'. In Patrick Barrett, Daniel Chavez and Cesar Rodriguez-Garavito (eds) *In The New Latin American Left: Utopia Reborn*. London: Pluto Press, pp. 255–271.

De Angelis, Massimo, 2007. *The Beginning of History: Value Struggles and Global Capital*. London: Pluto Press.

Deleuze, Gilles and Felix Guattari, 1986. *One Thousand Plateaus*. New York: Semiotext(e).

Denissen, Marieke 2008. *Winning Small Battles, Losing the War*. West Lafayette, IN: Purdue University Press.

Dinerstein, Ana, 2003. '¡Que se vayan todos! Popular insurrection and the *asambleas barriales* in Argentina'. *Bulletin of Latin American Research* 22(2): 187–200.

'Dirty War generals' portraits removed/Argentine leader angers officers, honors victims, apologizes for his own silence', 2004. *Los Angeles Times*, 25 March. Retrieved 2 February 2011 from http://www.sfgate.com/cgi-bin/article.cgi?f=/c/a/2004/03/25/MNGIV5QTOO1.DTL

Earle, Duncan and Jeanne Simonelli, 2005. *Uprising of Hope: Sharing the Zapatista Journey to Alternative Development.* Lanham, MD: Altamira Press.

Esteva, Gustavo, 1999. 'The Zapatistas and People's Power'. *Capital and Class* 23(2): 153–182.

Esteva, Gustavo, 2001. 'The meaning and scope of the struggle for autonomy'. *Latin American Perspectives* 28(2): 120–148.

Esteva, Gustavo, 2008. *The Oaxaca Commune and Mexico's Autonomous Movements.* Oaxaca, Mexico: Basta! Press.

Fajn, Gabriel, 2003. *Fábricas y empresas recuperadas: Protesta social, autogestión, y rupturas en la subjectividad.* Buenos Aires: Centro Cultural de la Cooperación, Institutio Movilizador de Fondos Cooperativos.

Fajn, Gabriel and Julián Rebón, 2005. 'El taller ¿sin cronómetro? Apuntes acerca de las empresas recuperadas'. *Revista Herramienta* 28. Retrieved 15 January 2006 from http://www.herramienta.com.ar/print.php?sid=300

Farmer, Paul, 1979. 'Enjoying language: An adventure with words'. *The English Journal* 68(5): 58–61.

Fernández, A. 2006. 'La utopía de un mundo sin patrones'. *Hoy La Universidad* 18. Retrieved 21 March 2007 from http://www.prensa.unc.edu.ar/hoylauniversidadpapel/18/numero%2018%2014–05–06.pdf

Ferrara, Francisco, 2003. *Mas Alla Del Corte de Rutas: La Lucha por Una Nueva Subjectividad.* Buenos Aires: La Rosa Blindada.

Finquelievich, Susana, 2002. 'Social organization through the internet: Citizen assemblies in Argentina'. In Stewart Marshall, Wal Taylor and Xinghuo Yu (eds) *Using Community Informatics to Transform Regions.* Hershey, PA: IGI Global Publishers, pp. 66–177.

Flacks, Richard, 1988. *Making History.* New York: Columbia University Press.

Flacks, Richard, 2003. 'Knowledge for What'. In Jeff Goodwin and James M. Jasper (eds) *Rethinking Social Movements: Structure, Meaning, and Emotion (People, Passions, and Power).* Lanham, MD: Rowman & Littlefield, pp. 135–154.

Fourier, Charles, 1971. *Design for Utopia: Selected Writings (Studies in the Libertarian and Utopian Tradition).* New York: Schocken.

Foweraker, Joe, 1995. *Theorizing Social Movements.* London: Pluto Press.

Fox, Jonathan, 1994. 'The difficult transition from clientalism to citizenship'. *World Politics* 46(2): 151–184.

Fox Piven, Frances, 2008. 'Can power from below change the world?' *American Sociological Review* 73(1): 1–14.

Fox Piven, Frances and Richard Cloward, 1979. *Poor People's Movements: Why They Succeed, How They Fail.* New York: Vintage.

Freeman, Jo, 1972. 'The Tyranny of Structurelessness'. *The Second Wave* 2(1): 20.

Fundación Pro Tejer, 2006. 'Cadena productiva textil justa y solidaria en Argentina'. *Actividades: Sección Solidaria.* Retrieved 11 December 2006 from http://www. fundacionprotejer.com/ actividades-accion.php

Galeano, Eduardo, 1993. *Walking Words.* New York: W.W. Norton & Company.

Gaudín, Andrés, 2003. 'Argentina: Bursting the barter bubble'. Retrieved 28 April 2010 from http://www.lapress.org/Article. asp?IssCode=&IanCode=1&art Code=3245

Gaudín, Andrés, 2005. 'The Kirchner factor'. *NACLA Report on the Americas* 38(4): 16–18.

Gobierno de la Ciudad de Buenos Aires, 2007. 'Una clase en la fábrica recuperada'. *Cooperativa de Trabajo Artes.* Retrieved 21 March 2007 from *Página 12* http://www.pagina12. com.ar/diario/sociedad/3– 76412–2006–11–19.html.

Goldstone, Jack and Charles Tilly, 2001. 'Threat (and opportunity): Popular action and state response in the dynamics of contentious action'. In Ronald R. Aminzade, Jack A. Goldstone, Doug McAdam, Elizabeth J. Perry, William H. Sewell, Sidney Tarrow and Charles Tilly (eds) *Silence and Voice in the Study of Contentious Politics.* Cambridge: Cambridge University Press, pp. 179–194.

Gónzalez, Cándido, 2005. 'Interview en la quadrille'. La Tribu 88.7 FM, Buenos Aires, 2 August.

Goodwin, Jeff and James M. Jasper, 2003. *Rethinking Social Movements: Structure, Meaning, and Emotion (People, Passions, and Power).* Lanham, MD: Rowman & Littlefield.

Gráfica Campichuelo Limitada, 2007. Lista de empresas, Buenos Aires Ciudad. Retrieved 19 March 2007 from http:// www.buenosaires.gov.ar/ areas/com_social/emp_recup/ lista_empresas/detalles. php?id=8&menu_id=8531

Gráficas El Sol Limitada, 2007. Lista de empresas, Buenos Aires Ciudad. Retrieved 18 March 2007 from http://www. buenosaires.gov.ar/areas/ com_social/emp_recup/lista_ empresas/historia.php?id=3

Gramsci, Antonio, 1971. *Selection from Prison Notebooks* (trans. Quintin Hoare and Geoffrey Nowell-Smith). London: Lawrence & Wishart.

Gramsci, Antonio, 2000. *The Antonio Gramsci Reader: Selected Writings 1916–1935.* New York: New York University Press.

Gramsci, Antonio, 2003. *Selections*

from the Prison Notebooks. New York: International Publishers.

Grupo de Arte Callejero, 2006. 'Situating rights/e- misférica'. *Hemispheric Institute for Performance and Politics* 3(1). Retrieved 2 March 2010 from http://criticalspatialpractice. blogspot.com/2006/09/grupo-de-arte-callejero.html

Halevi, Joseph, 2002. 'The Argentine crisis'. *Monthly Review* 53(11): 15–33.

Hanish, Carol, 1969. 'The Personal Is Political'. Retrieved 14 October 2011 from http://www.carolhanisch.org/CHwritings/PIP.html

Hardt, Michael, 2007. 'Foreword'. In Patricia Ticineto-Clough and Jean Halley (eds) *The Affective Turn*. Durham, NC: Duke University Press, pp. xi–xiii.

Hardt, Michael and Antonio Negri, 2004. *Multitude: War and Democracy in the Age of Empire*. London: Penguin.

Harvey, David, 2012. *Rebel Cities: From the Right to the City to the Urban Revolution*. New York: Verso.

Haugaard, Mark and Howard Lentner, 2006. *Hegemony and Power: Consensus and Coercion in Contemporary Politics*. Lanham, MD: Rowman & Littlefield.

'Hebe Bonafini dio su apoyo a cualquier posible fórmula de los Kirchner' ['Hebe Bonafini gives her support to any possible Kirchner formula]', 2010. M24 *Digital*. Retrieved 7 April 2010 from http://m24digital.com/2010/07/29/hebe-bonafini-dio-su-apoyo-a-cualquier-posible-formula-de-los-kirchner/

Hodson, Randy and Teresa Sullivan, 2008. *The Social Organization of Work*. Wadsworth, OH: Wadsworth Publishing.

Holloway, John, 2002. *Change the World Without Taking Power: The Meaning of Revolution Today*. London: Pluto Press.

Holloway, John, 2003a. 'Is the Zapatista Struggle an Anti-Capitalist Struggle?' *The Commoner*. Retrieved 5 May 2009 from http://www.commoner.org.uk/holloway06.pdf

Holloway, John, 2003b. 'Moving against-and-beyond or interstitial revolution'. Talk given at the World Social Forum, Porto Alegre, Brazil. Retrieved 6 June 2012 from http://ccs.ukzn.ac.za/files/Porto%20Alegre%20–%20Inst.%20Freire.pdf

Holloway, John, 2010. *Crack Capitalism*. London. Pluto Press.

Holloway, John and Eloina Pelaez (eds), 1998. *Zapatistas! Reinventing the Revolution in Mexico*. London: Pluto Press.

Holloway, John and Marina Sitrin, 2007. 'Conversation with John Holloway and Marina Sitrin: Against and beyond the state'. *Znet online*. Retrieved 12 June 2012 from http://www.zcommunications.org/against-and-beyond-the-state-by-john-holloway

Horvat, Branko, 1982. *The Political Economy of Socialism: A Marxist Social Theory*. Armonk, NY: M.E. Sharpe, Inc.

James, Daniel, 1981. 'Rationalisation and working class response: The context and limits of factory floor activity in Argentina'. *Journal of Latin American Studies* 13(2): 374–402.

James, Daniel, 1988. *Resistance and Integration: Peronism and the Argentine Working Class, 1946–1979*. New York: Cambridge University Press.

James, Daniel, 1994. *Resistance and Integration: Peronism and the Argentine Working Class, 1946–1979*. New York: Cambridge University Press.

Jardim, Claudia and Jonah Gindin, 2004. 'Venezuela: Changing the world by taking power'. Venezuelanalysis.com, 22 July. Retrieved 6 June 6 2012 from http://venezuelanalysis.com/analysis/598

Jay, Martin, 1973. *The Dialectical Imagination: A History of the Frankfurt School and the Institute of Social Research, 1923–1950*. Boston, MA: Little, Brown & Co.

Jordan, John, 2003. 'Diary of a revolution', *Guardian*, 25 January. Retrieved 6 June 2012 from http://www.guardian.co.uk/world/2003/jan/25/argentina.weekend71

Jossa, Bruno, 2005. 'Marx, Marxism, and the cooperative movement'. *Cambridge Journal of Economics* 29(1): 3–18.

Kelley, Robin, 2003a. 'History and hope: An Interview with Robin D.G. Kelley'. *Minnesota Review* 58–60. Retrieved 12 June 2012 from http://www.theminnesotareview.org/journal/ns58/kelley.htm

Kelley, Robin, 2003b. *Freedom Dreams: The Black Radical Imagination*. Boston, MA: Beacon Press.

Kingsnorth, Paul, 2004. *One No, Many Yesses*. London: Simon & Schuster.

Klandermans, Bert, 1997. *The Social Psychology of Protest*. Boston, MA: Blackwell.

Klein, Naomi, 2003a. 'Argentina's luddite rulers: Workers in the occupied factories have a different vision – smash the logic, not the machines'. *Dissident Voice*, 25 April, p. 1.

Klein, Naomi, 2003b. 'How Argentina's new president deals with the occupied factories will be hugely significant'. Guardian, 28 April. Retrieved 12 June 2012 from http://www.guardian.co.uk/world/2003/apr/28/usa.globalisation

Korol, Claudia, 2004. 'Diálogo con Ana Esther Ceceña: Los 20 y 10 del zapatismo. La revuelta de la dignidad'. *Rebellion Internacional* 24 January. Retrieved 12 June 2012: http://www.rebelion.org/hemeroteca/internacional/040124korol.htm

Kropotkin, Peter, 1989. *Mutual Aid: A Factor of Evolution*. Montreal: Black Rose Books.

Krueger, Anne, 2002. 'Crisis prevention and resolution: Lessons from Argentina'. Paper presented to the International Monetary Fund National Bureau of Economic Research Conference on 'the Argentina Crisis', Cambridge, MA, 17 July. Retrieved 25 January 2007 from http://www.imf.org/external/np/speeches/2002/071702.htm

Lavaca, 2004. *Sin Patrón: Fábricas y empresas recuperadas por sus trabajadores*. Buenos Aires: Lavaca Editora.

Lavaca, 2005. *Concluyó en Venezuela el 1º Encuentro Latino Americano de Empresas Recuperadas* [*The 1st Meeting of Latin American Recuperated Businesses Concluded in Venezuela*]. Buenos Aires: Lavaca Editora.

Lavaca, 2009a. *Sin Patrón*. Retrieved 6 June 2012 from http://lavaca. org/libros/sin-patron/

Lavaca, 2009b. 'Que es Lavaca'. Retrieved 11 June 2011 from http://lavaca.org/que-es-lavaca/

Lavaca, 2010. '19 y 20: los días que parieron una década', 20 December. Retrieved 11 June 2012 from http://lavaca.org/notas/19–y-20–los-dia-que-parieron-una-decada

Lavaca, 2011. 'Lacar: Los Trabajadores hacen justicia', 14 October. Retrieved 12 June 2012 from http:// lavaca. org/notas/lacar-los-trabajadores-hacen-justicia/

Lazzarato, Maurizio, 2004. 'Struggle, event, media' (trans. Aileen Derieg). *Republicart.net*, May. Retrieved 7 January 2006 from http://www.republicart. net/disc/representations/lazzarato01_en.htm

Lee Boggs, Grace, 2004. 'The beloved community of Martin Luther King'. *Yes Magazine*, 20 May. Retrieved 8 September 2010 from http://www. yesmagazine.org/issues/a-conspiracy-of-hope/the-beloved-community-of-martin-luther-king

Lievesley, Geraldine and Steve Ludlam, 2009. *Reclaiming Latin America: Experiments In Radical Democracy*. London: Zed Books.

Lindenfeld, Frank, 1982. 'Workers' cooperatives: Remedy for plant closings?' In Frank Lindenfeld and Joyce Rothchild-Whitt, *Workplace Democracy and Social Change*. Boston, MA: Porter Sargent Publishers, pp. 337–352.

Littek, Wolfgang and Tony Charles (eds), 1996. *The New Division of Labor: Emerging Forms of Work Organization in International Perspective*. Berlin: Walter de Gruyter.

Little, Adrian, 1996. *The Political Thought of André Gorz*. London: Routledge.

Logue, John, 1998. 'Rustbelt buyouts: Why Ohio leads in worker ownership'. *Dollars & Sense*, September–October. Retrieved 10 November 2006 from http://www. dollarsandsense.org/archives/1998/0998logue.html

Lukes, Steven, 1974. *Power: A Radical View*. New York: Palgrave Macmillan.

Lynd, Staughton, 1993. 'Oral history from below'. *Oral History Review* 21(1) 1–8.

McAdam, Doug, John D. McCarthy and Mayer N. Zald (eds), 1996. *Conceptual Origins, Current Problems, Future Directions: Comparative Perspectives on Social Movements. Political Opportunities, Mobilizing Structures, and Cultural Framing*. Cambridge: Cambridge University Press.

McAdam, Doug, Sidney Tarrow and Charles Tilly, 2001. *Dynamics of Contention.* Cambridge: Cambridge University Press.

McChesney, Robert, 1997. 'The global media giants: We are the world'. *Fairness and Accuracy in Reporting*, November/December. Retrieved 6 June 2012 from http://www.fair.org/index.php?page=1406

Madres de la Plaza de Mayo Linea Fundadora, 2006. 'Carta abierta al presidente de la nación', 26 May. Retrieved 7 June 2012, from http://www.madresfundadoras.org.ar/pagina/cartaabiertaalpresidentedelanacin/63

Magnani, Esteban, 2003. *El cambio silencioso: Empresas y fábricas recuperadas por los trabajadores en la Argentina.* Buenos Aires: Promoteo Libros.

Magnani, Esteban, 2005. 'On the road to somewhere: The story of recovered factories in Argentina'. *Briarpatch Magazine*, 1 February. Retrieved 23 September 2010 from http://briarpatchmagazine.com/2005/02/01/on-the-road-to-somewhere-the-story-of-recovered-factories-in-argentina/

Magnani, Esteban, 2010. 'Autogestión'. *Pagina 12*, 24 October. Retrieved 12 June 2012 from http://www.pagina12.com.ar/diario/suplementos/cash/17-4708-2010-10-24.html

Marcase, Herbert, 1964. *One-dimensional Man: Studies in the Ideology of Advanced Industrial Societies.* Boston, MA: Beacon Press.

Marcos, Subcomandante, 2001, *Questions and Swords: Folktales of the Zapatista Revolution.* El Paso, TX: CincoPuntos Press.

Marshall, Peter, 2008. *Demanding the Impossible: A History of Anarchism.* Oakland, CA: PM Press.

Marx, Karl, 1967[1867]. *Capital: A Critique of Political Economy, Volume 1. A Critical Analysis of Capitalist Production.* New York: International Publishers.

Mason, Paul, 2011. 'From Paris to Cairo, these protests are expanding the power of the individual', *Guardian*, 7 February. Retrieved 22 April 2011 from http://www.guardian.co.uk/commentisfree/2011/feb/07/paul-mason-protest-twitter-revolution-egypt

Massetti, Astor, 2004. *Piqueteros: Protesta Social y Identidad Colectiva.* Buenos Aires: Editorial de las Ciencias.

Massey, Doreen, 2009. 'Concepts of space and power in theory and in political practice', *Documents d'Anàlisi Geogràfica* 55: 15–26.

Mazzeo, Miguel, 2007. *El sueño de una cosa (Introducción al Poder Popular).* Caracas: Monte Ávila.

Merleau-Ponty, Maurice, 1962. *Phenomenology of Perception* (trans. Colin Smith). London: Routledge and Kegan Paul.

Merril, Derek, 2004. 'The case of Argentina: Recuperated factories and the multitude'. *Variant* 21(3). Retrieved 16 March 2006 from http://www.variant.randomstate.org/pdfs/issue21/argentina.pdf

Meyer, David S. and Sidney Tarrow (eds), 1998. *The Social Movement Society: Contentious Politics for a New Century.* Lanham, MD: Rowman & Littlefield.

Montes, Verónica Lilian and Alicia Beatriz Ressel, 2003. 'Presencia del cooperativismo en Argentina'. *UniRcoop Magazine* 1. Retrieved 12 November 2006 from http://www.unircoop. org/documents/revue/Release/Vol1No2.02.Unircoop. Argentine(1).pdf

Montoneros, 1970. 'Communiqué No. 5' (trans. Mitchell Abidor). *Marxists.org.* Retrieved 12 November 2008 from http://www.marxists.org/history/argentina/montoneros/1970/communique-05.htm

Moulaert, Frank and Oana Ailenei, 2005. 'Social economy, third sector and solidarity relations: A conceptual synbook from history to present'. *Urban Studies* 42(11): 2037–2054.

Movimiento de Trabajadores Desocupados de Solano y Colectivo Situaciones, 2002. *Más allá de los piquetes [Beyond the Pickets]*. Buenos Aires: De Mano en Mano.

Munck, Ronaldo, Ricardo Falcon and Bernardo Galitelli, 1987. *Argentina from Anarchism to Peronism: Workers, Unions and Politics, 1855–1985.* London: Zed Books.

Munck, Ronaldo, Ricardo Falcon and Bernardo Galitelli, 1998. 'Mutual benefit societies in Argentina: Workers, nationality, social security and trade unionism'. *Journal of*

Latin American Studies 30(3): 573–590.

Negri, Antonio and Jim Flemming (eds), 1996. *Marx Beyond Marx: Lessons on the Grundrisse* (trans. Michael Ryan, Mauricio Viano and Harry Cleaver). Oakland, CA: A.K. Press.

Ness, Immanuel and Dario Azzellini (eds), 2011. *Ours to Master and to Own: Workers' Control from the Commune to the Present.* Chicago, IL: Haymarket Books.

Noble, David, 1984. *Forces of Production: A Social History of Industrial Automation.* Oxford: Oxford University Press.

Olesen, Thomas, 2005. *International Zapatismo: The Construction of Solidarity in the Age of Globalization.* London: Zed Books.

Palomino, Hector, 2003. 'The workers' movement in occupied enterprises: A survey'. *Canadian Journal of Latin American and Caribbean Studies* 28(55): 71–96.

Pearson, Ruth, 2003. 'Argentina's barter network: New currency for new times?' *Bulletin of Latin American Research* 22(2): 214–230.

Petras, James F., 1981. *Class, State, and Power in the Third World.* Montclair, NJ: Allanheld, Osmun & Co.

Petras, James, 2002. 'The unemployed workers movement in Argentina'. *Monthly Review* 53(8). Retrieved 12 June 2012 from http://monthlyreview.org/2002/01/01/the-unemployed-workers-movement-in-argentina

Petras, James, 2003. 'Argentina: 18 months of popular struggle – a balance'. *The James Petras Website*, Retrieved 18 February 2011 from http://lahaine.org/petras/articulo.php?p=1669&more=1&c=1.

Petras, James, 2004. 'Argentina: From popular rebellion to "normal capitalism"'. *The James Petras Website*, Retrieved 19 February 2011 from http://lahaine.org/petras/articulo.php?p=1675&more=1&c=1

Petras, James F. and Henry Veltmeyer, 2002. 'Worker self-management in historical perspective'. *Rebelión.org*. Retrieved 12 June 2012 from http://www.rebelion.org/hemeroteca/petras/english/worker021002.htm

Petras, James F. and Henry Veltmeyer, 2005. *Social Movements and State Power: Argentina, Brazil, Bolivia, Ecuador*. London: Pluto Press.

Piñeiro Harnecker, Camila, 2005. 'The new cooperative movement in Venezuela's Bolivarian process'. *Venezuelanalysis.com*, 17 December. Retrieved 30 March 2007 from: http://venezuelanalysis.com/analysis/1531

Polletta, Francesca, 2002. *Freedom Is an Endless Meeting: Democracy in American Social Movements*. Chicago, IL: University of Chicago Press.

Poletta, Francesca, 2006. 'How participatory democracy became white: Culture and organizational choice'. *Mobilization: An International Journal* 10(2): 271–288.

Portes, Alejandro, 1998. 'Social capital: Its origins and applications in modern sociology'. *Annual Review of Sociology* 24: 1–24.

Proudhon, Pierre-Joseph, 1970. *Selected Writings of Pierre-Joseph Proudhon* (ed. Stewart Edwards, trans. Elizabeth Fraser). London: Macmillan.

Ranis, Peter, 2005. 'Argentine worker-occupied factories and enterprises'. *Socialism and Democracy* 13(3): 93–115.

Ranis, Peter, 2006. 'Learning from the Argentine worker: To occupy, to resist, to produce'. *Situations: Project of the Radical Imagination* 1(2): 57–72.

Rebón, Julián, 2004. *Desobedeciendo al desempleo: La experiencia de las empresas recuperadas*. Buenos Aires: La Rosa Blindada.

Rebón, Julián, 2006. *Empresas recuperadas. La autogestión de los trabajadores*. Buenos Aires: Capital Intelectual.

Ressler, Oliver, 2004. '*Change the World Without Taking Power*: John Holloway'. Video transcription recorded in Vienna, Austria (23 mins). Retrieved 27 January 2011 from http://www.ressler.at/change_the_world_without_taking_power/

Robinson, William, 2008a. *Latin America and Global Capitalism: A Critical Global Perspective*. Baltimore, MD: Johns Hopkins University Press.

Robinson, William, 2008b. 'What's new for the Left in Latin America?' *North American Congress on Latin America*, 6

February. Retrieved 6 June 2012 from http://nacla.org/news/ what's-next-left-latin-america

Rock, David, 2002. 'Racking Argentina'. *New Left Review* 2(17): 54–86.

Rohter, Larry, 2006. 'A widening gap erodes Argentina's egalitarian image'. *New York Times*. Retrieved 26 December 2006 from http://www.nytimes. com/2006/12/25/world/ americas/25argentina.html?_r=1

Romero, Alberto Luis, 2002[1994]. *A History of Argentina in the Twentieth Century*. University Park, PA: Pennsylvania State University Press.

Ruggeri, Andrés, 2006. 'The worker-recovered enterprises in Argentina: The political and socioeconomic challenges of self-management' (trans. Marcelo Vieta). Paper presented at the Another World is Necessary: Center for Global Justice Annual Workshop. Retrieved 16 December 2006 from http:// www.globaljusticecenter.org/ papers2006/ruggeriENG.htm

Ruggeri, Andrés, 2010a. 'Autogestión obrera y empresas recuperadas, límites y potenciales en elcapitalismo neoliberal globalizado'. Manuscript for Facultad Abierta, Facultad de Filosofia y Letras, University of Buenos Aires.

Ruggeri, Andrés, 2010b. ' Las empresas recuperadas en la Argentina. 2010: Informe del tercer relevamiento de empresas recuperadas por los trabajadores'. Retrieved 6 June 2012 from http://www.

recuperadasdoc.com.ar/ Informes%20relevamientos/ informe_ultima_correccion.pdf

Ruggeri, Andrés, Carlos Martinez and Hugo Trinchero, 2004. 'Las empresas recuperadas en la Argentina'. Manuscript for Facultad Abierta, Facultad de Filosofía y Letras, Universidad de Buenos Aires.

Ruggeri, Andrés, Carlos Martinez and Hugo Trinchero, 2005. 'Las empresas recuperadas en la Argentina: Informe del Segundo Relevamiento del Programa. Buenos Aires: Programa de Transferencia Científico-Técnica con Empresas Recuperadas por sus Trabajadores (UBACyT de Urgencia Social F-701)'. Manuscript for Facultad Abierta, Facultad de Filosofía y Letras, Universidad de Buenos Aires.

Sábato, Ernesto, 1984. *Nunca más: Informe de la Comisión Nacional Sobre la Desaparición de Personas*. Buenos Aires: Editorial Universitaria de Buenos Aires.

Sad, Elizabeth L., 2005. 'Argentina: Barter clubs' (trans. David Epstein). *Toward Freedom*, 27 May. Retrieved 10 March 2010 from http:// www.towardfreedom.com/ americas/147--argentina-barter-clubs-0304

Said, Edward, 1992. 'Lost paradises: A review of *Culture and Imperialism* by Nancy Scheper Hughes'. *New York Review of Books*, 3 March, p. 44.

Said, Edward, 1994. *Culture and Imperialism*. New York: Vintage Books.

Salas, Ernesto José, 1999. 'Barricadas de carne en Mataderos'. *Clarín*, 10 January. Retrieved 22 January 2007 from http://www.clarin.com/ suplementos/zona/1999/01/10/i-01201d.htm

Salbuchi, Adrian, 2006. 'How to solve Argentina's recurrent foreign debt crises: Proposal for a long-term solution'. *Center for Research on Globalization*, 7 November. Retrieved 12 March 2009 from http://www. globalresearch.ca/index. php?context=va&aid=3750

Schwartz, Michael, 1976. *Radical Protest and Social Structure: The Southern Farmers' Alliance and Cotton Tenancy, 1880–1890.* Chicago, IL: University of Chicago Press.

Selbin, Eric, 2010. *Revolution, Rebellion, Resistance: The Power of Story.* London: Zed Books.

Sitrin, Marina (ed.), 2006. *Horizontalism: Voices of Popular Power in Argentina.* Oakland, CA: A.K. Press.

Sitrin, Marina and Trip McCrossin, 2004. 'Imagine autonomy – Enero autonomo Argentina'. Indymedia UK, 13 January. Retrieved 12 June 2012 from http://www.indymedia.org. uk/en/2004/01/283833.html

Solnit, Rebecca, 2005. 'The uses of disaster: Notes on bad weather and good government'. *Harpers Magazine*, October, p. 31.

Solnit, Rebecca, 2009. *A Paradise Built in Hell: The Extraordinary Communities that Arise in Disasters.* New York: Viking.

Solnit, Rebecca, 2011. 'The butterfly and the boiling point: Charting the wild winds of change in 2011'. *Tomdispatch. com*, 20 March. Retrieved 20 March 2011 from http://www. tomdispatch.com/blog/175369

Stahler-Stolk, Richard, 2004. 'Carving out space from below: The Zapatista autonomy movement in Chiapas, Mexico'. Paper presented to the Meeting of the Latin American Studies Association, Las Vegas, NV, 7–9 October.

Svampa, Maristella, 2002a. 'Las dimensiones de las nuevas movilizaciones sociales: las asambleas barriales'. *El Ojo Mocho* 17. Retrieved 12 June 2012 from http://www. maristellasvampa.net/archivos/ ensayo13.pdf

Svampa, Maristella, 2002b. 'Movimientos sociales en la Argentina de hoy: Piquetes y Asambleas', Centro de Estudios de Estado y Sociedad. Retrieved 5 June 2012 from http://www. maristellasvampa.net/archivos/ ensayo07.pdf

Svampa, Maristella, 2008. 'Argentina after Kirchner'. *New Left Review* 53: 79–96.

Svampa, Maristella and Sebastian Pereyra, 2003a. *Entre la Ruta y El Barrio: La Organizaciones Piqueteros.* Buenos Aires: Editorial Biblos.

Svampa, Maristella and Sebastian Pereyra, 2003b. 'Dimensions of the *Piquetero* experience: Organizations of the unemployed in Argentina'. *Maristella Svampa.net*. Retrieved 9 August 2010 from http://www. maristellasvampa.net/archivos/ ensayo18.pdf

Tarrow, Sidney, 1996. 'States and

opportunities: The political structuring of social movements. In Doug McAdam, John D. McCarthy and Mayer Zald (eds) *Comparative Perspectives on Social Movements*. Cambridge: Cambridge University Press, pp. 41–62.

Tarrow, Sidney and Charles Tilly, 2001. 'Silence and voice in the study of contentious politics: An introduction'. In Ronald R. Aminzade, Jack A. Goldstone, Doug McAdam, Elizabeth J. Perry, William H. Sewell, Sidney Tarrow, and Charles Tilly (eds) *Silence and Voice in the Study of Contentious Politics*. Cambridge: Cambridge University Press, pp. 1–14.

Tilly, Charles, 1999. *Durable Inequality*. Boulder, CO: Paradigm Publishers.

Tilly, Charles, 2003. *Stories, Identities, and Political Change*. Cambridge: Cambridge University Press.

Tilly, Charles, 2004. *Social Movements, 1768–2004*. Boulder, CO: Paradigm Publishers.

Tobar, Hector, 2004. 'Argentine ceremonies cast light on "Dirty War"'. *Los Angeles Times*, 25 March. Retrieved 7 June 2012 from http://articles.latimes.com/2004/mar/25/world/fg-argen25

Trigona, Marie, 2003. 'Brukman workers continue to fight for factory'. *Znet online*, 9 June. Retrieved 22 December 2008 from http://www.zcommunications.org/brukman-workers-continue-to-fight-for-factory-by-marie-trigona-1

Trigona, Marie, 2006a. 'Workers in control: Venezuela's occupied factories'. *Venezuelanalysis.com*, 9 November. Retrieved 21 December 2008 from http://www.venezuelanalysis.com/articles.php?artno=1872

Trigona, Marie, 2006b. 'Argentina 30 years after the coup'. *IRC Americas*, 29 March, p. 3. Retrieved April 2011 from www.Americas.irc-online.org

Trigona, Marie, 2009. 'Argentine factory in the hands of the workers: FASINPAT a Step Closer to Permanent Worker Control'. *Upsidedownworld*.org, 26 May. Retrieved June 7 2012 from http://upsidedownworld.org/main/argentina-archives-32/1875–argentine-factory-in-the-hands-of-the-workers-fasinpat-a-step-closer-to-permanent-worker-control-

Trigona, Marie, 2010. 'Landmark human rights case in Argentina puts torture on trial'. *Upside Down World*, 5 January 2010. Retrieved 12 March 2010 from http://upsidedownworld.org/main/news-briefs-archives-68/2293–landmark-human-rights-case-in-argentina-puts-torture-on-trial

Valente, Marcela, 2006. 'Activist artists subvert the message'. *Inter Press Service News Agency*, 13 February. Retrieved 4 May 2010 from http://www.ipsnews.net/news.asp?idnews=32140

Vieta, Marcelo, 2005. 'Witnessing the political on the street in Buenos Aires: Flaneuring from 9 de Julio to Plaza de May'. *Thoughts on Argentina's Conjunctures*, 29 July. Retrieved 8 August 2008 from http://

www.vieta.ca/thoughts/2005/07/witnessing-political-on-street-in.html

Vieta, Marcelo, 2006. 'The worker-recovered enterprises movement in Argentina: Self-management as a potential path to recovering work, recomposing production, and recuperating life'. *Thoughts on Argentina's Conjunctures*, 19 February. Retrieved 8 August 2008 from http://www.vieta.ca/thoughts/2006/06/worker-recovered-enterprises-movement.html

Vieta, Marcelo, 2008. '*Autogestión* and the worker-recuperated enterprises in Argentina: The potential for reconstituting work and recomposing life'. Toronto: Programme in Social and Political Thought, York University. Retrieved May 2009 from http://lsj.sagepub.com/content/35/3/295.abstract

Vieta, Marcelo and Andrés Ruggeri, 2009. 'The worker-recovered enterprises as workers' co-operatives: The conjunctures, challenges, and innovations of self-management in Argentina and Latin America'. In Darryl Reed and J.J. McMurtry (eds) *International Co-operation and the Global Economy*. Cambridge: Cambridge Scholars Press, pp. 178–226.

Weber, Maximilian, 1990[1962]. *Basic Concepts in Sociology* (trans. H. Secher). New York: Citadel Press.

Wilkinson, Eleanor, 2009. 'The emotions least relevant to politics? Queering autonomous activism'. *Emotion, Space and Society* 2: 36–43.

Retrieved 5 June 2012 from http://leeds.academia.edu/EleanorWilkinson/Papers/664408/The_emotions_least_relevant_to_politics_Queering_autonomous_activism

Winn, Peter, 2006. *Americas: The Changing Face of Latin America and the Caribbean*. Berkeley, CA: University of California Press.

'Workers' economy conference, Buenos Aires', 2007. *Interactivist Info Exchange*. Retrieved 25 March 2007 from http://info.interactivist.net/article.pl?sid=07/03/15/2329242

Yerrill, P. and L. Rosser, 1987. 'Revolutionary unionism in Latin America: The FORA in Argentina' (pamphlet). London: AsP.

Zald, Mayer, 2000. 'Ideologically structured action: An enlarged agenda for social movement research'. *Mobilization* 5(1): 1–16.

Zibechi, Raul, 2003. *Genealogía de la Revuelta: Argentina. La Sociedad en Movimiento*. Buenos Aires: Letra Libre.

Zibechi, Raul, 2006a. 'Another world is possible: The Ceramics of Zanon'. In Teo Ballve with Vijay Prashad (eds) *Dispatches From Latin America: On the Frontlines Against Neoliberalism*. Cambridge, MA: South End Press, pp. 350–358.

Zibechi, Raul, 2006b. 'Worker-run factories: From survival to economic solidarity'. In Teo Ballve with Vijay Prashad (eds) *Dispatches From Latin America: On the Frontlines against Neoliberalism*.

Cambridge, MA: South End Press, pp. 339–349.

Zibechi, Raul, 2006c. 'Movimientos sociales: nuevos escenarios y desafíos inéditos', *Observatorio Social de América Latina* 7(21): 221–230.

Zibechi, Raul, 2008a. *Territorios en Resistencia: Cartografía política de las periferias urbanas latinoamericanas*. Buenos Aires: Lavaca.

Zibechi, Raul, 2008b. 'The revolution of 1968: When those from below said "Enough!"'. *Americas Program*. Retrieved 5 June 2012 from http://www.cipamericas. org/archives/662

Zibechi, Raul, 2010. 'The rising of slum democracy'. *New Internationalist*, October, p. 26. Retrieved 29 January 2011 from http://www. exacteditions.com/exact/ browse/386/422/7632/2/26

Index

Note: page numbers in italic denote illustrations